Corruption and Human Rights

Corruption and Human Rights

Editor

V.N. Viswanathan

ALLIED PUBLISHERS PVT. LTD.

New Delhi • Mumbai • Kolkata • Lucknow • Chennai
Nagpur • Bangalore • Hyderabad • Ahmedabad

ALLIED PUBLISHERS PRIVATE LIMITED

1/13-14 Asaf Ali Road, **New Delhi**–110002
Ph.: 011-23239001 • E-mail: delhi.books@alliedpublishers.com

47/9 Prag Narain Road, Near Kalyan Bhawan, **Lucknow**–226001
Ph.: 0522-2209942 • E-mail: lko.books@alliedpublishers.com

17 Chittaranjan Avenue, **Kolkata**–700072
Ph.: 033-22129618 • E-mail: cal.books@alliedpublishers.com

15 J.N. Heredia Marg, Ballard Estate, **Mumbai**–400001
Ph.: 022-42126969 • E-mail: mumbai.books@alliedpublishers.com

60 Shiv Sunder Apartments (Ground Floor), Central Bazar Road,
Bajaj Nagar, **Nagpur**–440010
Ph.: 0712-2234210 • E-mail: ngp.books@alliedpublishers.com

F-1 Sun House (First Floor), C.G. Road, Navrangpura,
Ellisbridge P.O., **Ahmedabad**–380006
Ph.: 079-26465916 • E-mail: ahmbd.books@alliedpublishers.com

751 Anna Salai, **Chennai**–600002
Ph.: 044-28523938 • E-mail: chennai.books@alliedpublishers.com

5th Main Road, Gandhinagar, **Bangalore**–560009
Ph.: 080-22262081 • E-mail: bngl.books@alliedpublishers.com

3-2-844/6 & 7 Kachiguda Station Road, **Hyderabad**–500027
Ph.: 040-24619079 • E-mail: hyd.books@alliedpublishers.com

Website: www.alliedpublishers.com

ISBN: 978-81-8424-751-0

Published by Sunil Sachdev and printed by Ravi Sachdev at Allied Publishers Pvt. Ltd. (Printing Division), A-104 Mayapuri Phase II, New Delhi-110064

Preface

The failures of governance at various levels are largely due to the rampant corruption practised by those who are at the helm of affairs and as a result the citizens got frustrated and lost faith in the governing systems. It is unfortunate that many of the anti-corruption measures which were originally initiated by World Bank for developing nations focused on financial aspects of corruption which led to checking of financial impropriety, embezzlement, etc. But there are other new forms of corruption evolved which are out of bound from anti-corruption measures. Understanding these aspects, the UN agencies involved in preparing UN Convention Against Corruption (UNCAC) and many nations became a signatory of such historic Convention, including India.

It is interesting to note that when politicians and bureaucrats failed to check these large corruptions, the civil society organizations has taken altogether a different role. The future governance in India lies also on the effective functioning of civil societies. It is on such proposition, this seminar preparations are evolved in association with civil societies such as Anti-Corruption Movement, We the People of India and the Fifth Pillar (Chennai-based civil societies). To upgrade our knowledge on anti-corruption strategies we also associated with Indian Association for Criminology and Transparency International. The major focus of this seminar is to adopt human rights approaches to check corrupt practices in India. Institutional mechanisms, though effective, much depends on the persons occupying it and it lacks mass backing. Through human rights approaches, different sections of population affected by corruption may also join with anti-corruption movements started by civil societies. Besides, this seminar is also intended to impart the much needed values of corruption-free mind among the young minds.

The main objective of the UGC-sponsored national seminar is to identify concrete ways in which governments' efforts to fight corruption are assisted by and contribute to human rights protection. The seminar built on the increasing awareness within the community about the detrimental impact of widespread corruption on human rights both through the weakening of institutions and the erosion of public trust in government as well as through impairing the ability of governments to fulfil human rights, particularly the economic and social rights of the most vulnerable and marginalized. The paper presenters will also address the abuses and derogations to human rights made in the name of the fight against corruption, limiting, interalia, the rights to privacy, due process and freedom of expression.

Accordingly, the seminar focuses on six themes in six different panels:

Panel   I : Corruption and Human Rights Linkage
Panel II : Corruption and Political Rights
Panel III : Police Corruption and Right to Life and Liberty
Panel IV : Securing and Protecting Different Kinds of Rights
Panel V : Corruption and Economic Rights
Panel VI : Corruption and Specific Rights Issues.

The following problems were drawn from the other paper presentations:

1. Violations of human rights are both a cause and an effect of corruption
2. There is a wide range of human rights that are affected by corruption
3. Civil service appointment system is especially important. Although there is no perfect system—each has advantages and disadvantages—basic elements include: transparent procedure and criteria, competitive and non-political appointments, etc.
4. Corruption is universal but it appears to be better controlled in countries that have adequate procedures, mechanisms and active public accountability
5. Access to information is fundamental to the elimination of corruption.

I certainly hope that at the end of the seminar, a report will be prepared on the strategies to combat corruption from human rights approach and thereby making anti-corruption movement as a mass movement.

I extend my sincere thanks to Dr. R. Thilagaraj, Prof and Head, Department of Criminology for his valuable guidance, Principal of Presidency College Prof. P.S. Raghuraman and civil society organizations such as Transparency International, Anti-Corruption Movement, We the people of India, Institute of Human Rights, Indian Institute of Public Administration (Puducherry local branch) and the Fifth Pillar. Of course, it goes without saying that the success of seminar much depends on quality of papers presented and I am individually thanking all the contributors hailing from different parts of the nation. Lastly, I extend my thanks for the UGC for the financial assistance to conduct the seminar under Ethics and Human value Education Scheme under XIth Plan. Thanking you all for the cooperation.

Sincerely

Date: 15.06.2011   **V.N. Viswanathan**
Station: Chennai   *Seminar Director*

Acknowledgement

This useful publication is indeed an effort of many scholars and members of NGOs such as Anti-Corruption Movement, Fifth Pillar, We the People of India, India against Corruption and Institute of Human Rights. Let us first express my gratitude to the University Grants Commission (UGC), New Delhi for their generous support under the 'Promotion of Ethics and Human Values' of Human Rights Education Scheme (XIth Plan). The Indian Society of Criminology provided the much needed support in terms of inviting resource persons for several sessions of the national seminar on "Corruption and Human Rights". The Department of Political Science, Presidency College (Autonomous) has done a commendable job of hosting 32 delegates from all over India. The seminar is in fact a joint effort of academicians, officials, members of non-governmental organizations and the research scholars from different disciplines.

I am indebted to all the research scholars for their tireless search into the various corruption reports, journals and web pages, for preparing the seminar concept note, doing typing and proofreading, finding out the follow up decisions that needed continuity and were indeed time consuming. In this regard I must also mention the names of Shri T. Arumugam, Dr. D.S. Makalanban, R. Elangovan, N. Thirumalai and Ms. Veda who assisted me greatly in doing the proofreading of abstracts and the full papers presented in the seminar.

I shall consider my effort a success if this book assists the members of NGOs, officials, academicians and activists in their efforts and helps others in their search for precedents to advance the cause of eradicating corruption in India by adopting human rights strategies.

Chennai
08.08.2011

V.N. Viswanathan

Contents

Introduction

V.N. Viswanathan

Department of Political Science, Presidency College (Autonomous), Chennai

Corruption erodes public confidence on government and other agencies of the State. A multi-disciplinary approach to study the impact of corruption on human rights is not made so far by academicians at national level. Since last three decades, there has been considerable concerns expressed by different stake-holders who aspire for a corrupt-free government. In every nation, there is a movement started to fight the ever growing nature of corrupt practices. Corruption is the worst form of elements against democracy and the working of Parliamentary system. Based on these basic premises, the authors from the disciplines of political science, law, public administration, economics, history and sociology have contributed articles for this book. Besides, the book also some of the papers presented by members of non-governmental organizations. These authors analysed the impact of corruption on various human rights enlisted by UNO and the national basic law, the constitution.

Generally, it is viewed that the quantum corruption in developing world has increased into manifold times after the introduction of open economy and it is very much true with India. Multi-national Corporation found that the developing countries economy and environment is highly suitable for getting undue advantages by extending corruption to greedy politicians and civil servants. The nexus among bureaucrates, politicians and criminals further accelerated the tendency for corruption. In Indian Parliament at present, there are, 152 members with a criminal background. Many tainted civil servants were awarded with lucrative central posts for their support for politician's corrupt practices. Land mafia joined with politicians to grab land belonging to vulnerable groups in the urban areas. All such development in the post-liberalization period shows the failure of governance at all levels. The space created by the failure of governance now legitimately occupied by non-governmental organizations. The failure of governance also resulted in the rising frustration of young citizens and they formed collectivities such as Maoist movement and many insurgency movements in the north-eastern part of India.

The linkage between corruption and human rights is less understood and only very recently after the initiation of UN agencies the link between corruption and human rights are well researched. This UGC sponsored national seminar primarily aimed to contribute to the existing relationship between these two. This national seminar addresses a conceptual linkage between corruption and human rights. It is viewed that corruption and the violation of human rights from a power-relation perspective, as it reflects an asymmetric relationship between the subject and object of power. Corruption and the violation of human rights comprise a social phenomenon which concerns the distribution of benefits among different groups of people and individuals. It affects the social, political and economic rights of the people who are not in a position to stand against the people with power, the politicians and the civil servants.

Corruption is an important contributing factor to the violation of human rights by facilitating, serving or creating an environment in which the violation can take place. The papers presented in the seminar demonstrate how corruption subverts human rights in different forms and degrees, from denying the basic rights of people to access services to threatening their lives. The abuse of human rights will be pervasive if corruption does not cease.

It is understood that the less understanding of the relations between corruption and human rights is largely due to the fact that the major impetus of the anti-corruption agenda evolved by World Bank in the context of its developmental policies in the early 1990s. Corruption became a main plank of discussion and debate in development discourse between developed and developing nations. Some developing nation elite circle thought and justified that corruption is needed to overcome the problems of bureaucratic red tapism. Corruption has become a source of political and economic powers and the entire society established a mindset that corruption is a way of life and developed a culture to support corruption. However, it was the emergence of the good governance agenda sponsored by the Bretton Woods institutions, and the World Bank in particular, from the end of the 1980's that brought corruption to the center stage of development policy. Since then corruption began to be seen as a major impediment to the success of economic reforms. Peter Eigen the founder of the leading global anti-corruption non-governmental organization, Transparency International, was a manager of World Bank Manager programs in Africa and Latin America. Based on his experiences at the World Bank, he founded Transparency International to promote accountability and transparency in international development. It was Transparency International which mooted the idea of linking corruption and human rights in drive against corruption in corporate sector and in many developing nations. It has been viewed, that large scale corruption in a nation will make State to refrain from fulfilling the mandatory obligations of the State and thus directly affecting the rights of the vulnerable people. Human Rights violations will be on higher rate in those nations where the corruption is at peak.

Corruption is an act of abuse of power. It distorts the power relationship between people, particularly against the interests of the weaker section of the society. Corruption could be found in many forms, such as bribery, extortion, negligence of duties, nepotism, cronyism, embezzlement and fraud.

Lord Acton, an English political philosopher said that "Power tends to corrupt, and absolute power corrupts absolutely". In the words of an economist Robert Klitgaard, who defined corruption in terms of the equation:

Corruption = Monopoly Power + Discretion – Accountability

The relationship between corruption and the violation of human rights is framed by unequal power relations. Both acts take place when there is abuse of power. Corruption benefits those who have access to power and abuse it, and victimizes those who do not have access to power. From this perspective, human rights are subjected to violation when power is abused by corrupt practices.

Political system when it becomes corrupt, it denies the right to political participation. In the same way, when judiciary becomes corrupt it violates the rule of law and equality before law. Corruption in public administration endangers the right to life when it allows the manufacture of hazardous products. When the state fails to curb the spread of corruption, it may be concluded that the government has failed to fulfill its obligation to protect human rights.

The seminar confirms the foregoing premises through an extensive and contextual discussion of civil and political rights, social and economic rights as well as minority rights in the Indian context. For example, Panel–It discusses the importance of freedom of expression in exposing corruption as well as the manner in which the Indian government and the administration have compromised the ability of a free press to report openly about corruption particularly when it involves senior governmental officials.

The socialist phase of Indian economy from 1950 to 1990 had created a system of License Raj in which the politicians and the civil servants thrived well by swindling money from the industrialist and other entrepreneurs. This led to slow economic growth and poverty. In the post-independent India, the national leaders with visionary zeal opened up a flood gate of infrastructure development in India which gave much scope for the politicians and the civil servant to involve in corrupt practices but certainly it was confined to a very few. Understanding the failure of socialistic economic development and because of the pressure exerted by the World Bank and IMF, the government of India shifted to open economy policy.

The open economy policy of India started in the year 1990–91 introduced what is popularly known as LPG—Liberalization, Privatization and Globalization. Many multi-national companies entered India to start their business and found that by greasing the palms of politicians and civil servants they can more concessions from the government. India is now ranked 84th in the Corruption Perceptions Index (CPI) calculated by Transparency International (TI). The Vohra Committee report (1993) suggested that criminalization of politics resulted in the establishments of parallel government and institutionalization of corruption. It also discussed criminal gangs who enjoyed the patronage of politicians of all political parties and the protection of government functionaries. It revealed that political leaders had become the leaders of gangs. They were connected to the military.

Political and bureaucratic corruption in India is a major concern. A 2005 study conducted by Transparency International in India found that more than 15% of Indians had first-hand experience of paying bribes or influence peddling to successfully complete jobs in public office. Taxes and bribes are a fact of daily life and common between state borders; Transparency International estimates that truckers pay US$5 billion in bribes annually. In 2010, India was ranked 87th out of 178th countries in Transparency International's Corruption Perceptions Index.

The former Central Vigilance Commissioner Shri N. Vittal in the **Chapter II** on "Corruption and Human Rights" traced the recent developments in fighting against corruption in India and the reforms he had brought while he served as the Central Vigilance Commissioner. He asserted that politics is the root cause of corruption in our country. The corrupt politician and bureaucrats corrupt on every aspect of governance and they are mostly corruptible various organizations of governance. They have two tools in suspension and transfer to make the bureaucracy dance to their tune. They can also give the attraction of cushy postings and what are called lucrative assignments to make a corrupt bureaucrat make lot of money. The judgment of the Supreme Court in the Thomas case has introduced a very healthy principle of integrity of the institution to be taken into account. Based on his personal experiences, he has also suggested a number of recommendations for cleaning the body politic from corrupt practices.

Dr. V. Vijayakumar, the Vice-Chancellor of the Tamil Nadu Dr. Ambedkar Law University, in **Chapter III**, had quoted many case laws to prove how the court took a stringent action against the corrupt civil servants and the politicians. In his view, there are two ways in which the corrupt practices lead to violation of human rights. In the first place, the preamble to the Indian Constitution seeks to protect the 'dignity' of every individual, more particularly, the dignity of the person who is forced to pay the bribe (the person who receives it does not bother about his dignity nor that of the others, including the person who is compelled to pay the bribe); and in the second place, when welfare measures fail to reach the designated people who suffer from human rights violations when those welfare measures do not reach them for sheer human existence, or reach them to a limited extent. His paper has laid the foundation for other papers of this book.

Joseph Benjamin in **Chapter IV** analyses the impact of corruption on human life and the negative impacts of corruption on different kinds of human rights. He opined that, corruption attacks the fundamental values of human dignity and political equality of the people and hence there is a pressing need to formulate a fundamental human right to corruption-free service. He adds that probity in governance is an outcome for an efficient system of governance and for socio-economic development. An important requirement for ensuring probity in governance is the absence of corruption. The other requirements may be effective laws, rules and regulations that govern every aspect of public life coupled with effective law enforcement and criminal justice systems. Identifying the specific links between corruption and human rights may persuade key actors—public officials, parliamentarians, judges, prosecutors, lawyers, business people, bankers, accountants, media and the public in general—to take a stronger stand against corruption. This may be so even in countries where reference to human rights is sensitive. He observes that the power relationship among people is a major concern. Considering the issues of corruption and human rights through the lens of power relations enables us to see them as relationship between different social groups or individuals who are able to access power differently.

In **Chapter V**, Anamika Ajay brings out the normative context of corruption and human rights linkage and in the end of the paper brought in the existing realities of the linkage. She asserts that most corrupt practices could lead to violations of human rights in the long run. However, it is important to distinguish between corrupt acts that directly violate rights which have an immediate effect on people's living conditions from the acts that may lead to denial of rights in future. Such differentiation of corrupt practices based on their impact on human rights could enable a better understanding of the extent of harm that corruption could have on the well-being of the individuals and the State at large. Human rights framework, therefore, lends itself for prevention, early intervention and punishment of corrupt acts. India, in the recent past, has been plagued with large scale corruption in the public and private sectors leading to public outcry for a rigid legislation against corruption. The paper here is aimed at identifying the specific human rights that are directly violated through corrupt practices prevalent in the public and private sectors in India using the human rights framework provided by the Constitution of India and the international human rights treaties. The paper discusses the above-stated phenomenon in the context of the recent developments related to corruption in India.

According to Professor P.S. Vivek, in **Chapter VI**, has discussed the phenomenon of corruption which affects many countries. He has highlighted the damages that it brings to economies and democracies. When corruption is wide-spread and especially when it contaminates the actions of the policymakers in democratic, market-oriented economies, it becomes more difficult to argue in favour of such economic and political arrangements. It should be remembered that many dictators or potential dictators make the fight against corruption as one of the reasons why they should be given the reigns of a country. The disillusion among the population of some economies in transition and some developing countries with both market economies and democratic processes is very much caused by the widespread corruption that prevails in these countries and is wrongly attributed to the market economy and the democratic process.

Dr. S. Saravana Kumar had said in **Chapter VII** that corruption affects the poor disproportionately, due to their powerlessness to change the status quo and inability to pay bribes, creating inequalities that violate their human rights. The Human Rights Based Approach (HRBA) with its main elements of Express Linkages to Rights, Accountability, Empowerment, Participation and Attention to Disadvantaged Groups, has been developed specifically to address these inequalities and to ensure that the poor and disadvantaged people are also equal partners in development. However, if corruption creates fundamental inequalities in the poor's access to justice and to development services, the results envisaged by the HRBA cannot be achieved. Therefore, anti-corruption should be added to the main elements of the HRBA that have now generally been agreed upon. When applying a HRBA to accessing justice, it is even more crucial that issues of corruption in the justice sector be addressed as a priority.

Janmejay Sahu in **Chapter VIII** examined corruption and human rights in Indian context. It is very essential to look into the nature and behavior of the people of India as well as the people working under the governance system of the country having lack of the accountability as well as responsibility that creates a space for the corruption and violence of human right. Now, it is unfortunate that while a section of civil society are taking up the corruption issues and bringing remedies such as a Draft "Jan Lok Pal Bill" by Anna Hazare and others, many political parties including the ruling party in the Government of India are neither directly opposing nor indirectly giving a clear path for its actual mean that is a big concern/threat in India. This paper critically examines scenario of corruption and its consequences that fingers towards the violation of human rights. It argues that the corruption has been affecting human rights of the people.

Dr. Syed Umarhathab in **Chapter IX** listed out various threats faced by Indian public because of rampant corruption. The first and foremost threat is the growing nature of corruption. The second biggest issue is that absence of autonomy and accountability of criminal justice official and their social responsibility. The third biggest issue being slow motion justice as approximately 20 million cases are pending in Indian courts. The fourth biggest issue is in connection with the third, is that disparities in verdict, judgments, and sentencing, one case and many verdicts is something unbearable for most of the Indians. The fifth biggest issue is that we suffer from lack of agency(s) to which the Ministers and High Dignitaries are accountable. The sixth biggest issue is that use of technology and scientific approach in fighting crime in order to dispose the cases which require technology support while delivering the justice. Using technology would speed up the process of justice in prompt and appropriate manner. The seventh biggest threat is lack of researches, awareness and transparency

In **Chapter X**, Prof. N.M. Nilofer Nisha has pleaded the need for corruption- free public services to people. The development of a fundamental human right to a corruption-free society will be observed initially from an international perspective so as to elevate the violation of this right to the status of an international crime. This would provide the comparative basis to elevate the right to corruption-free service to the status of a fundamental right within the framework of the Indian Constitution. Corruption not only perpetrates injustice, resulting in the breakdown of the governance machinery, but also violates the fundamental rights that are guaranteed to citizens. Conversely, it may be argued that the present proposal to include the right to corruption-free service as a part of the scheme of fundamental rights might strengthen the other rights, including the right to equality and the freedoms that are enshrined in other portions of Chapters III and IV of the Constitution.

Dr. Shan Eugene in **Chapter XI**, traces the history of police corruption in India. Police Corruption is also violation of human rights as it denies some very basic rights to the citizens. The fundamental right of being protected by a law enforcing agency, mainly constituted for this purpose is being denied by the prevailing corruption. The right to self-defense is under a threat with more and more cases of custodial crimes and wrongful persecution and prosecution being reported. With the present day situation worsening, the basic right to life granted under Article 21 of the Constitution is being denied. Cases of fake encounters, rising death toll in the prisons, and unnecessary delay in investigation makes one feel insecure and vulnerable.

In **Chapter XII**, Dr. M. Thamilarasan and G. Venkatesan provided a sociological perspective of Corruption and Human Rights and studied the impact of political corruption on political institutions. Corruption poses a serious development challenges. In the political realm, it undermines democracy and good governance flouting or even subverting formal processes. Corruption in elections and in legislative bodies reduces accountability and distorts representation in policymaking; corruption in the judicial system compromises the rule of law; and corruption in public administration results in the inefficient provision of services. It violates a basic principle of republicanism regarding the centrality of civic virtue. More generally, corruption erodes the institutional capacity of government as procedures are disregarded, resources are siphoned off, and public offices are bought and sold. At the same time, corruption undermines the legitimacy of government and such democratic values as trust and tolerance.

The research scholar Mr. T. Arumugam in **Chapter XIII**, demonstrated how political corruption will ruin parliamentary democracy and other political institutions. The paper focused on the prevailing role of corruption in various stages of electoral process in electing the peoples representative to the democratic institutions and thereafter in the exploring political corruption. The muscle and money power played an important unhealthy role which appeals to the narrow interest of the caste, community, religion and language. Candidates who are capable of winning by fair means are defeated and fouled are selected. Even criminals associated with murder, decoy and rape get elected only with the help of the black money.

Dr. R. Thilagaraj and Dr. S. Latha in **Chapter XIV**, enlisted various committees appointed by governments to probe into the various aspects of corruption since 1947 in India. Political corruption is the use of legislated powers by government officials for illegitimate private gain. Misuse of government power for other purposes, such as repression of political opponents and general police brutality, is not considered political corruption. Neither are illegal acts by private persons or corporations not directly involved with the government. An illegal act by an officer constitutes political corruption only if the act is directly related to their officer duties. The major cause of concern is that corruption is weakening the political body and damaging the supreme importance of the law governing the society. Elections in many parts of the country have become associated with a host of criminal activities.

Mr. M.D. Allen Selvakumar follows a case study method to prove his proposition in his paper in **Chapter XV**. He had presented five case studies of the personal experiences of those who had greased the palm of greedy officials to get their work done.

According to Prof. Joman Mathew in **Chapter XVI**, there is close link between corruption and poverty. The practice of corruption and the outflow of money from the domestic economy affect the economic growth in a variety of ways. It may be noted that corruption hinders economic progress in the following manner:

- It reduces domestic and foreign investment
- It reduces the volume of tax revenue of the government
- It reduces the quality of public infrastructure
- It takes away huge amount of income from the domestic economy
- It shrinks the volume of non tax revenue of the government
- It discourages the young entrepreneurs from undertaking new business.

In **Chapter XVII** P. Arunachalam has discussed about the state of unchecked political corruption. He has called it as kleptocacy (rule by thieves). At times, bribes are given to avoid punishment. For some people, being corrupt is a way to get what they desire. In societies which ignore corruption, it becomes a way of life. People getting very low wages feel they have to demand bribes in order to lead decent lives. But they do not realize that corruption causes suffering to others.

Dr. D.S. Makalanban in **Chapter XVIII** "Combating Economic Fraud in Global Sphere with Reference to Role of UNCAC" has highlighted one of the legal instruments of

IO that tries to combat corruption in Global sphere. The United Nations Convention Against Corruption (UNCAC) is the only legally binding universal anti-corruption instrument. The Convention's far-reaching approach and the mandatory character of many of its provisions makes it a unique tool for developing a comprehensive response to a global problem. The UNCAC covers five main areas: (i) prevention, (ii) criminalization and law enforcement measures, (iii) international cooperation, (iv) asset recovery, and (v) technical assistance and information exchange.

Shri S.M. Arasu represents the civil society organization which primarily focused on anti-corruption movement in Tamil Nadu. In **Chapter XIX**, S.M. Arasu sketches the role of civil societies in eradicating corruption. The role of civil society in reforming governance in India is well established when many laws were legislated under the initiation of civil society by prolonged demand and protest movements. According to the author, the absence of concerted efforts by the Government to eradicate corruption, number of organizations have been started to involve people in the fight against corruption. There are organizations that are more than 10 years old. The Fifth Pillar, Anti-corruption Movement, Lanjam Kodathor Eyakkam (Non-bribe givers, movement), are some of the more popular associations which have bases in the districts of Tamil Nadu and functioning effectively. Transparency International Chennai chapter, and Catalyst Trust are also lending a helping hand in the process. These organizations take action to conduct public awareness meetings against corruption and also address the students in educational institutions.

Shri L.S. Jeganathan representing civil society known as "Luncham Koodathoor Iyyakam" (a movement for non-payment of bribes) pointed out the alarming nature fall in ethics and values in politics in **Chapter XX**. He laments that people are fast losing faith in political parties and elections and thereby democratic governance due to continuous declining of their moral ethics and ever increasing electoral irregularities, but also it has paved way for the growth of extremism and terrorism for which state of affairs no political party feels sorry.

Dr. M. Sarumathy in **Chapter XXI**, highlighted the root cause of corruption in India. She felt that the colonial system of administration is one major reason for the practice of corruption in many levels of governance. Besides she also correlates that the education is the only way to develop a mindset of the younger generation towards a corrupt-free society. Morals and ethics can percolate only through proper education and thus education remains the strongest tool to prevent corruption. Education spreads awareness against corruption and thus helps in strengthening the moral or ethical values of society. Raising general levels of awareness in the population is essential as this establishes citizens' demands for accountability, and education creates a culture of accountability by emphasizing ethical practice and by creating the need for such practice.

Sunitha Kuppusamy in **Chapter XXII** has covered the news items carried on media on 2G corruption which shacked the entire nation. It is a research conducted by the author of two news papers—the Dinamalar and the Times of India. She has emphasized that qualitative, independent media reporting is the need of the hour which will pressurize the government to act in public interest. Being a watch dog, media should play a key role in processes of establishing and maintaining well functioning government institutions.

In **Chapter XXIII**, Andrew S. Philominraj , Juan A. Rock and Maria J. Valenzuela have viewed that there exists a close relationship between corruption and human rights. Accountability is a key element for both human rights and good governance. Applied to the context of human rights, accountability rests primarily on the duty of states to protect, enforce or promote the rights that have been internationally ratified. They have cited the examples from Latin American nations of how corrupt practices ruin the development of the nations.

The last **Chapter XXIV** is the observations and recommendations that were discussed in the seminar. Scholars have argued for recognition of a right to live in a corruption free world. They do so on the grounds that endemic corruption destroys the fundamental values of human dignity and political equality, making it impossible to guarantee the rights to life, personal dignity and equality, and many other rights.

REFERENCES

[1] International Council on Human Rights Policy (2009), *Corruption and Human Rights: Making the Connection.* Versoix, Switzerland, ICHRP.

[2] Klitgaard, Robert (1988), *Controlling Corruption,* Berkeley, University of California Press, Lukes, Steven (1986), *Power: A Radical View,* Hong Kong, Macmillan.

[3] Pilapitiya, Thusina (2004), *The Impacts of Corruption in the Human Rights Based Approach to Development,* UNDP Oslo Governance Center, September.

[4] Pope, Jeremy (2000), *Confronting Corruption: The Elements of a National Integrity System.* TI Source Book 2000, London, Transparency International.

[5] Rajkumar, C. (2002), *Corruption and Human Rights, Frontline,* Vol. 19, No. 19, September 14–27.

[6] Terracino, Julio Bacio (2008), Corruption and Human Rights, International Council on Human Rights Policy (ICHRP).

[7] Transparency International. *What is Corruption?* Retrieved December 5, 2008, from http:// www.transparency.org/ about_us

Corruption and Human Rights

N. Vittal

Former Commissioner of Central Vigilance Commission (CVC), New Delhi

Corruption has been dominating the headlines in the media practically from the middle of last year. We seem to be observing 2010–2011 as "years of corruption."

Simultaneously, we are also observing in a way, these years as "years of human rights". This was the first time when, thanks to the highlighting of the issue of corruption in the media, the occurrence of state elections in five major states and the activism on the part of judiciary civil society organizations and NGOs participated actively in expressing the revulsion of the common citizen against corruption in every sector of public life. This was catalysed by the initiative taken by two charismatic leaders Anna Hazare and Baba Ramdev.

It has been observed that the Indian political dialogue has been marked by three streams, the rational, the emotional and the saintly. The rational was symbolized by the actions of the judiciary. The media hyped the issues and built a high emotional pitch. The saintly stream was represented by Anna Hazare and Baba Ramdev. Anna Hazare represented the Gandhian tradition of ahimsa and his own inspiration as recorded by him was derived from Swami Vivekananda who has become an icon for Indian youth and renaissance. Baba Ramdev was in the more conventional tradition of a yoga guru. But using the modern technology of television, he had built a cult following of thousands all over the country cutting a swathe across the entire spectrum of the society. He had also built incidentally a flourishing commercial empire spanning ayurvedic drugs, cosmetic inputs and of course, widespread literature on yoga.

It was Anna Hazare who took the first step. When he went on a fast of 5th April, 2011 at Jantar Mantar in Delhi, he focused attention on the fact that in the root cause of widespread corruption in our country today is politics and for punishing the corrupt politicians and bring them to book there was no single agency. Lok pal was thought of as early as 1962, when the Santhanam committee report on corruption was published to be the agency to tackle the issue of political corruption. More than four decades have passed but there is zero action on this issue. Hazare's fast was focused on the single demand for establishing the Lokpala.

Incidentally he has also highlighted the fact that the billions of dollars of Indian money has been siphoned away by the well to do in to Swiss accounts and other tax heavens. The release of the report on this subject and the massive display of money in elections naturally focused attention on the black money problem in the country. Baba Ramdev seeing the public mood displayed in response to the Anna Hazare initiative, jumped in to the fray with the special focus on bringing the black money back to India. He also launched a fast on 4th of June 2011.

Anna Hazare was able to get a concession from the government which agreed for a joint drafting committee for Lokpal with equal number of representatives from the government and civil society, of five ministers and five from the civil society. Baba Ramdev on the other hand was viewed with probably greater awe by the government which sent four of its senior ministers to receive him at the airport when he landed in a private jet, but soon things went wrong and the entire exercise of Baba Ramdev's fast ended up as a farce. The attack on the peaceful women and children who were sleeping at midnight of 4th and 5th of June 2011 evoked universal revulsion against the government and the issue is still being vigorously debated.

The current focus on the government and the civil society organizations therefore makes the theme of this Conference, 'Corruption and human rights', very timely and relevant.

From a cynical point of view, there was another development during this period, which highlights in a ironic way, the link between corruption and human rights. A former Chief Justice of India, soon after his retirement, became the Chairman of National Human Rights Commission. Soon allegations surfaced about his integrity and allegations that he helped his relatives to amass wealth. Right now, the whole issue is being examined. He has been advised by some of his senior icons in the judiciary to resign from the post of chairman NHRC and so far he has not done so. So, corruption and human rights therefore, have an uncanny mutual resonance.

One of the sub-themes of this conference is, 'Is corruption, a violation of human rights?' No human right treaty refers explicitly to corruption. Will it be possible to qualify certain forms of corruption as human right violation itself? This could be a starting point of our exploration of our theme of 'Corruption and human rights'.

Corruption is the abuse of public office for private gain. The issue of human rights can arise only in a society which is well governed and respects the dignity of an individual. Good governance as I see it, should satisfy the following conditions:

1. There should be the rule of law
2. There should be minimum corruption
3. There should be an environment where every person has the opportunity to rise to his full human potential

4. There should be maximum total factor productivity so that there is no wastage of physical, financial or human resources.

Checking corruption is essential for good governance, because, no rule of law is possible if there is corruption. The fundamental principle of rule of law is that before law all are equal. Article 14 of the constitution spells out that all citizens are equal before law and are entitled to equal protection of law. When corruption intervenes, then there is no fairness and to that extent straightaway, the basic rule of law is violated. Therefore, you cannot have good governance if there is corruption.

As Central Vigilance Commissioner, I viewed corruption as a social evil. I highlighted the fact that the basic structure of our constitution is preserved in the fundamental rights chapter of our constitution. In that chapter, untouchability was recognized by our fathers of the constitution as a social evil. Under article 17 it was specifically abolished. If a social evil like untouchability can be taken note of and its abolition provided for in the chapter on fundamental rights should we not think in terms of corruption as a social evil and make a corruption free government, a fundamental rights of the citizen? I moved this point before the Justice Venkatachalaiah Commission on review of the constitution appointed by the NDA government in the year 2000. Unfortunately, the issue was not pursued. In fact, one member of parliament from Maharastra, belonging to Shiva Sena introduced a private members bill on the very subject for introducing a new Article 17A, under which every Indian citizen will be entitled to corruption free government. This was also not vigorously pursued.

Perhaps, now a time has come in our country where it will be worthwhile to at least initiate a debate starting with this conference on the need for incorporating corruption free government as one of the fundamental rights of every citizen.

Another sub-theme of the conference I find is 'Linking human rights with the natural environment in which people live'. This issue became prominent, following the government initiative to set up a series of special economic zones to encourage investment on a massive scale for exploitation of natural resources like coal and minerals. These resources generally occur in remote places, mostly under forests, where tribals live. Ultimately, the situation today is, for acquiring the land and implementing the projects, the tribals have to be shifted. To that extent, the fundamental rights of tribals to enjoy the forest produce and live in tune with nature has emerged as a major issue. The challenges which projects like Vedanta or Posco are facing in Orissa and elsewhere, highlight the dilemma faced by the government.It has to resolve the tension between the human rights of the tribals and the need for massive large scale economic development of the country.

We may now analyse at some depth the issue of corruption. If we are able to eliminate corruption, automatically, we will be creating an environment where citizens will be able to enjoy full human rights without any difficulty. The issue of corruption ultimately, depends on three factors. First is the value of integrity cherished by people at the individual level. The second is the set of values cherished at the social level and the importance given to integrity. Third, of course, is the system of governance, which takes into account the need for maintaining highest level of integrity.

Where do we begin? Naturally we should focus on individual to begin with. The significance of the individual is obvious from the fact that many a time we find in utterly corrupt organization, some honest people still surviving. It is these honest few who, to use the biblical expression, are the salt of the earth. It is because of these few honest and committed public servants, that the machinery of government at least is maintaining a certain degree of credibility and essentially moves. Otherwise, the entire system would come to a halt. The entire system of governance will become a vast keptocracy.

As I see it, two values are very vital, if we want to reduce corruption in our country. The first value is for each person to realize the importance of maintaining integrity and leading a clean life. We have got enough literature on morals. Our political leaders have zero credibility even if they mouth eloquently, about the need for integrity. One of the greatest leaders we have ever had in our life is Mahatma Gandhi. He was credible for the simple reason that he was absolutely transparent and he walked his talk. The problem we face today is, how to convince the younger generation, who have seen corruption everywhere that they should cherish integrity and lead a moral life. This is the challenge which each one of us faces.

I have been lucky in my life. I got in to IAS and had a very sheltered life. I was fortunate to have had parents who believed in god and cherished the best values of integrity and hard work. They never used to explicitly preach to us children, but we imbibed their values which they practised in times of great adversity. I did not realize the importance of leading a clean life till an incident occurred when I became CVC.

After becoming CVC, I initiated a process under which I put on the website of the CVC the names of corrupt IAS, IPS and other senior public servants in January 2000. This created a tremendous healthy impact on the public, but also landed me in some trouble. The wife of one of the officers was named but was no more threatened me with a defamation suit. Newsweek wrote story about me under the title "E-Shame". He came back and gave me a feedback which shocked me. He said, 'Sir, many of your colleagues and especially your seniors are so angry with you. I told them, if you have any muck against Mr. Vittal to throw, why don't you give it to me and I can publish that also? I was surprised to find that even your enemies do not have any muck to throw at you.' This made me to realize with a shock how having a clean life is one of sources of strength and authority because nobody can blackmail you. The weakness of our leaders in different walks of life today is because they cannot stand exposure. They are all vulnerable to blackmail. As we say in tamil, *madila ganam iruntha vazhila bhayam:* if you have something weighty and precious in your pocket, then only you have to be afraid after safety in the path.

When I am asked to convince the youngster about the need for integrity, I always mention this incident in my life. I tell them that for succeeding in life two things are vital. One, faith in God, so that you will never lose hope and two, keeping your life clean so that nobody can blackmail you and that leads to self confidence and success.

If we want to make our country free of corruption and ensure good governance we must nurture not only integrity at the individual level but also cultivate love for our country. It is on this second requirement of patriotism I find a difficulty when I address the youth of today. I find it very difficult to find a very convincing argument.

As cynics say, patriotism is nothing but an emotional attachment to a piece of real estate. But when we read the poetry of great poet like Bharatiar, every Indian will feel proud of the tradition we have. Patriotism basically is love. We automatically love our mothers because we know that they are the ones who brought us in this world. But somehow we have become so materialistic that patriotism is now old fashioned. People in these days of borderless world and globalization ask how can you identify with one piece of real estate called your mother country.

But the fact is that it is this attachment that helps us to plan at least for a larger society like our country and continue to progress. As of today, neither China nor the United States or any of the countries would let go their national interest. We only seem to be very lacking as a nation. Is it due to ignorance or lack of capability? The latest example is the report about how in Chengdu [China] a group of anti Indian interests have been hacking in to our computers in sensitive government organizations. The fact that nearly 70% of our equipments in telecom sector come from China shows that China is in a position today to exercise a strangle hold in critical points of our communications. The Chinese perhaps have a greater sense of patriotism than we have. These are the issues where every citizen of India will have to think.

How to convince our youngsters that they should nurture patriotism? In fact, it is our lack of patriotism that makes the army find it difficult to recruit officer cadre to fill the enormous vacancies in the defence services. For the youngsters today, defence services are the last option or not even considered at all.

The dynamics of corruption in our country depends on a vicious cycle of what I will call the neta, babu, lala, jhola and dada. Politics is the root of corruption in our country. The corrupt politician and corrupt on every aspect of governance and they are mostly corruptible various organizations of governance. They have two tools in suspension and transfer to make the bureaucracy dance to their tune. They can also give the attraction of cushy postings and what are called lucrative assignments to make a corrupt bureaucrat make lot of money.

This vicious cycle has to be broken. In this vicious cycle, apart from the politician and the bureaucrat, who provide perhaps the engine for nourishing of corruption in this country. There are other players. The corporate sector is equally an important player. Apart from every bribe taker, there is a bribe giver. In the height of that crisis, 14 eminent attached to the prime minister seeking about reducing the government area of discretion so that the corruption arising out of influence peddling can be checked. Prabhu Chawla wrote an article in The New Indian Express called "Outrage of Hypocrisy" making incisive comments on this development. He questioned whether any of the signitaries had failed to take advantage the very discretion which they were now condemning.

Instead of going into every aspect of corruption, taking into account the developments in the last two years 2010 and 2011 we can think of a pragmatic strategy to tackle corruption and through this ensure good governance safeguarding human rights.

The series of corruption scandals in different sectors like 2G, CWG, IPL, Adharsh scam etc show that we have a multiple organ failure of governance. When a person become sick and multiple organ failure occurs, a team of doctors will be in a position to take care and by god's grace, could help the patient to back to health. In fact, I had a personal experience of this type in 2007 when a team consisting of a cardiologist, a nephrologist, a pulmonoligist, a urologist and a diabetologist had to co-ordinate their efforts and helped me to recover my health after one month's treatment in the intensive care unit at the hospital.

For the nation, who will be the doctors? Let us not forget that the doctors themselves have to be not only healthy but also knowledgeable about their subject. The doctors who can cure our nation out of corruption are the three Constitutional bodies, the Judiciary, the Election Commission of India and the Comptroller and Auditor General of India and the statutory body, the Central Vigilance Commission.

But we must ensure that only the right people come to occupy the position. Justice Kapadia in his judgement on the P.J. Thomas case pointed out that we should not only look at the integrity of the individual but we should also look at the institutional integrity. The very fact that Thomas was accused in the Palmolien case was indicative of the fact there was a remote chance that he could be found guilty. If we are selecting a person to head an organization designed to be an instrument to fight corruption. Appointing a person who may be held guilty of a criminal charge amounts to risking the integrity of the institution of CVC. Therefore, he ruled that the consideration of Mr Thomas for the post was ab initio void and non-est.

The judgement of the Supreme Court in the Thomas case has introduced a very healthy principle of integrity of the institution to be taken in to account. As I see it, this principle virtually eliminates the loophole enjoyed by criminal politicians in our country so far.

Even framing a charge sheet or facing a case in the court of law by itself is not a proof of guilt. So, everybody is innocent till proved guilty. Taking advantage of that presumption, they used to get elected to parliament and make laws to protect themselves. In fact, the rules provide that candidates who have been convicted in the court of law but the punishment does not exceed two years could also contest. In other words, rules today provide that convicted criminals facing case in courts and get elected to the parliament!

This flies straight in the face of the integrity of the institution principle articulated by Justice Kapadia in the Thomas case. So I would suggest that the Chief Election Commissioner, one of the doctors identified for cleaning up the country, on his own authority issue an order to the effect that to maintain the integrity of the institution of parliament all candidates against whom criminal cases are pending in the courts, should be debarred from contesting election till their names are cleared in the court of law. This can be a good starting point.

With this starting point, I would suggest that we must adopt the 2Tprinciple to select the people for occupying any post in any institution, particularly, key institutions like the judiciary, CEC, CAG etc., The first T is that there should be transparency, so far as eligibility and selection process are concerned. The second T is that the selection process itself must be such that there is a TINA factor for selection, There Is No Alternative but to select the right person.

For example today, the 2T condition is eminently fulfilled so far as the post of CVC is concerned. Thanks to the judgement earlier by Justice Verma, only a candidate who has an excellent track record can be considered for the post of CVC and he has to be selected by a high power Committee consisting of the Prime Minister, Home Minister and the Leader of Opposition in Lok Sabha. The CVC will not only have excellent track record but also politically neutral. In the Kapadia judgement, the person should also be of impeccable integrity. Further, once a person is appointed as CVC, he is given a term of four years and after the term he is permanently debarred from occupying any office of profit under the central or state governments He can not be considered for even constitutional posts like Governor, Vice President of India, and President of India. Thus the conditions are so designed that a person selected as CVC will be competent, will have an unblemished record of integrity and will not be tempted for a post retirement sinecure. So the 2T condition is fulfilled and the government has no alternative but to select the right person to the post of CVC Thus we have Mr. Pradeep Kumar as a replacement to Mr. Thomas in spite of a gloomy prediction made by one great civil servant.

Similar conditions of service have to be created for the post of CEC and CAG. Today, their selection process depends on the Prime Minister and the President. In fact, a high power committee as in the case of appointment of CVC should be used for selection of CEC and CAG and they must also to be banned from post retirement temptation as in the case of CVC.

So far as the judiciary is concerned, respecting the independence of judiciary, the cleansing process must begin by the judiciary itself and similar 2T principles of selection must be introduced right through the judicial system. Today, the politician is able to dictate and control because of the twin bramhastra of suspension and transfer he wields. This is must be curbed by fixing a fixed tenure for key posts. Suspension cases should be referred to CVC, who must give their views within 48 hours. The political leadership will never introduce such reforms because it amounts to limiting their own power. Limitation on the power of the policians will come only as a result of judicial directives. The weapon of PIL and RTI act must be used by as a weapon by citizens and civil society pressure like Anna Hazare movement for Lok Pal.

The cleansing of the political criminalization could be done by the Chief Election Commissioner by changing the rules so that candidates facing criminal cases can not contest election till they are cleared by the courts.

Our legal procedures are very time consuming and that is why there no fear of law. There should also be time limit so far as corruption cases are concerned. There should be only one appeal in corruption cases and both the trial and appeal should be completed within 12 months, if necessary by adopting summary trial procedure and hearing the cases on a day to day basis. This will help in making our system much better.

If these three or four steps are taken we would have initiated a process of cleansing our system of governance and also ensure citizens enjoying better human rights.

Amartya Sen wrote a nice book called he Argumentative Indian. Arguments and counter arguments have been in our blood. Our culture and tradition have always believed in discussion and debate and that is probably why the country got independence in 1947 and remain a democracy unlike Pakistan and Bangladesh.

Ultimately, we will have to practice what the Traitiya Upanishad says, if we want to go ahead:

- Sahana vavatu Sahanau bhunaktu
- Saha Viryam kara va vahai
- Tejas vina maditha vastu
- Ma vidh visha vahai
- Om Shanti! Shanti! Shanti.

Let us come together. Let us enjoy together. Let our strengths come together. Let us move from darkness to light. Let us avoid the poison of misunderstanding and hatred. That way lies progress.

Corruption and Human Rights

V. Vijayakumar

Vice-Chancellor, Dr. Ambedkar Law University, Chennai, Tamil Nadu

The contemporary developments linking corruption with human rights became inevitable as the limits of tolerance to corruption in public life in India, like many other countries, were challenged and questioned from time to time. The response to those questions challenging corruption in public life was very 'knee-jerk' reaction rather than leading to any concrete development.

In the recent past many writers have been expressing their views to prove the links between corruption and human rights and concluded by saying that corruption violated human rights. Such conclusions have not been successful in explaining the kinds of rights that are violated by different corrupt practices.

Reasons for prevailing levels of corruption in India may be attributed to the following:

1. Lack of meaningful accountability in civil service;
2. Lack of political will among the power holders, the legislators at the centre and at the states;
3. Deadly combination of the executive power and legislative power in one, that is the legislature, both at the Centre and at the States;
4. Failure to internalize the values of 'parliamentary system of governance' of the British origin by the elected representatives in India;
5. Hero worship (Dr. Ambedkar spoke vehemently against the hero worship that will destroy democracy) in the working of Indian democracy;
6. Delayed and prolonged prosecutions resulting in wiping out even the very little evidence that is available;
7. Laws and legal institutions, including the judiciary, that are expected to punish the corrupt are used to protect the corrupt by advocacy, delay, retraction of witnesses, destruction of evidences and the like;
8. Creation of too many agencies and organizations to prevent corruption without any coordination (equal care resulting in total neglect);

9. Culture of the general public to be a silent party, knowingly or otherwise, to corruption;

10. Non implementation of applicable laws due to political compulsions including that of the Prevention of Corruption Act. Generally speaking, the compulsions arising out of coalition governments make the implementation against the violators or the accused non-realizable;

11. Lack of personal officer liability in public administration for the misdeeds committed or other omissions. The Right to Information Act, 2005 as well as the Disaster Management Act, 2005 have inserted legislative provisions for making the officers liable personally. This needs to be strengthened through various legislative amendments as such personal officer liability by and large remains as judicial pronouncements;

12. Sanction for prosecution from the appropriate authority. There are various statutes seeking sanction from appropriate authorities for prosecuting the government servants for corruption and related offences. On many occasions, the sanctions are not given within reasonable time thereby diluting the entire process. Because of this, a large number of government servants, both at the Centre and at the States continue to be employed ever after the prima facie case being proved against them. Although the importance of seeking sanction need not be overemphasized, the inordinate delay and denial of sanctions to prosecute the government servants could be addressed by inserting a proviso for deemed sanction. Accordingly, if the sanction by the appropriate authorities are not communicated within 30 days or so, it can be taken for granted as 'deemed sanction'. A brief review of the developments in this regard would indicate that the Prevention of Corruption Act, as well as the institutions responsible to implement that legislation by and large remained at the beck and call of the political power holders. The sanction to prosecute those individuals in bureaucracy and other 'public servants' made the legislation 'Prevention of Corruption Act' as one of the 'Protection of the Corrupt Act'. It is pertinent to cite the decision in M.P. Special Police Establishment v. State of M.P. In this case, the reports of the Madhya Pradesh Lokayukta made out prima facie case against the Ministers for their Prosecution for offences under Prevention of Corruption Act and also for offences of criminal conspiracy. The Council of Ministers refused to grant sanction. However, the Governor, based on the Reports of Lokayukta, granted sanction to prosecute the Ministers. When the matter went to the High Court of Madhya Pradesh challenging the sanction granted, a single judge as well as a Division Bench of the High Court set aside the sanction as they held that the Governor is bound by the advise of the Council of Ministers. However, on appeal to the Supreme Court, a Constitution Bench observed that 'in the facts and circumstances of the present case, we have no doubt in our mind that when there is to be a prosecution of the Chief Minister, the

Governor would, while determining whether sanction for such prosecution should be granted or not under Section 6 of the Prevention of Corruption Act, as a matter of propriety, necessarily act in his own discretion and not on the advice of the Council of Ministers'. Accordingly the decisions of the single Judge and Division Bench were set aside. The court went on to add that 'as the case is very old, we request the Court to dispose of the case as expeditiously as possible'.

In yet another case, the Supreme Court in Deputy Director of Collegiate Education (Administration), Madras V.S. Nagoor Meera, observed that a government servant need not be kept in service until his appeals against a conviction on charges of corruption are disposed of by the highest court. The Court observed that 'the more appropriate course in all such cases is to take action under clause (a) of the second proviso to Article 311 (2) once a government servant is convicted of a criminal charge and not to wait for the appeal or revision, as the case may be. If, however, the government servant-accused is acquitted on appeal or other proceeding, the order can always be revised and if the government servant is reinstated, he will be entitled to all the benefits to which he would have been entitled to had he continued in service. The other course suggested, viz., to wait till the appeal, revision and other remedies are over, would not be advisable since it would mean continuing in service a person who has been convicted of a serious offence by a criminal court (emphasis added); and

13. s. 293-A of the Companies Act, authorizing companies including government companies to contribute to political parties.

As the menace could not be prevented or controlled at the domestic level in many of the developing countries, the UN adopted a convention Against Corruption (GA Res. 58/4 of 31 Oct 2003) that entered into force on Dec 14, 2005 and India ratified the same on 12 May 2011. Kofi A. Annan, former Secretary General of the UN observed in this regard that 'corruption is a key element in economic underperformance and a major obstacle to poverty alleviation and development…The provisions of the convention—the first of their kind- introduce a new fundamental principle, as well as a framework for stronger cooperation between states to prevent and detect corruption and to return the proceeds.

After ratifying this Convention, a Bill titled 'The Prevention of Bribery of Foreign Public Officials of Public International Organizations Bill, 2011 was introduced in the Lok Sabha with the objective to prevent corruption relating to bribery of foreign public officials. Similarly, another Bill titled 'The Public Interest Disclosure and Protection to Persons Making the Disclosure Bill, 2010' was also introduced in the Parliament of India. The objectives of this Bill indicate that the Bill is introduced 'to establish a mechanism to receive complaints relating to disclosure on any allegation of corruption or willful misuse of power or willful misuse of discretion against any public servant and to inquire or cause an inquiry into such disclosure and to provide adequate safeguards against victimization of the person making such complaint and for matters connected therewith and incidental thereto'. This Bill refers to the UN Convention Against Corruption and observed in the preamble that 'the Convention expresses concern about the seriousness of problems and threats posed by corruption to the stability and security of societies, undermining the institutions and values of democracy, ethical values and justice and jeopardising sustainable development and the rule of law; and about cases of corruption that involve vast quantities of assets, which may constitute a substantial proportion of the resources of States, and that threaten the political stability and sustainable development of those States'.

In my view there are two ways in which the corrupt practices lead to violation of human rights. In the first place, the Preamble to the Indian Constitution seeks to protect the 'dignity' of every individual, more particularly, the dignity of the person who is forced to pay the bribe. (the person who receives it does not bother about his dignity nor that of the others, including the person who is compelled to pay the bribe); and in the second place, when welfare measures fail to reach the designated people who suffer human rights violations when those welfare measures do not reach them for sheer human existence, or reach them to a limited extent.

As there are well researched papers discussing various dimensions of the linkages between corruption and Human Rights, I do hope that the points mentioned above are also included. I wish the deliberations over the next two days will discuss many dimensions of the relations between corruption and Human Rights.

Corruption: Violation of Human Rights

Joseph Benjamin

Department of Political Science, St. Francis De Sales' College,
(RTM Nagpur University) Seminary Hills, Nagpur

INTRODUCTION

In common parlance *Corrupt* means 'willing to use power to do dishonest or illegal things in return for money or to get an advantage.' Oxford Dictionary defines 'Corruption' as dishonest or illegal behaviour, especially of people in authority. The purpose of being dishonest is to earn money illegally or influence the work done in ones favour. Gibbon, a well known British historian, termed corruption the most infallible symptom in constitutional liberty. Corruption in simple terms can be described as "an act of bribery". It has also been described as "the misuse of public power for private profits in a way that constitutes a breach of law".

Corruption is wide spread in the society in several forms. No doubt, the people who are having political power, use or misuse it to earn money illegally or influence to work done. Besides people in power, common man is also involved in corruption in different forms. Forms of corruption vary from people to people. To communicate the intended form of corruption, the corrupt and the corruptible, over the time, have developed a parlance to convey their intension. Thus, the expression like *ooper ki kamaee*, *baksheesh* to the peon in the office, *hafta* to the police constable, and *chaipani* to (*babus*) clerk in the office, convey specific meaning, causing no doubt or misgivings. There is no dearth of such expression and no end to the forms of corruption. It takes new forms time to time.

The present paper is an attempt to study the corruption in India. However, corruption is the violation of Human Rights. The present paper would try to study how corruption is a violation of human rights. The paper would be confined to corruption in India. Each and every citizen especially women, children have right to development, right to food, right to health etc. The paper would also study how corruption retards progress and development globally and affects the women, children and minority.

CORRUPTION: A GLOBAL SCENARIO

In Countries like India, Pakistan, Indonesia, Bangladesh, Philippines and other third world countries, corruption affects all walks of life. In entire developing regions of Asia, Singapore is the only government that is more or less free from corruption. China has curbed it with an iron hand.

Graph I

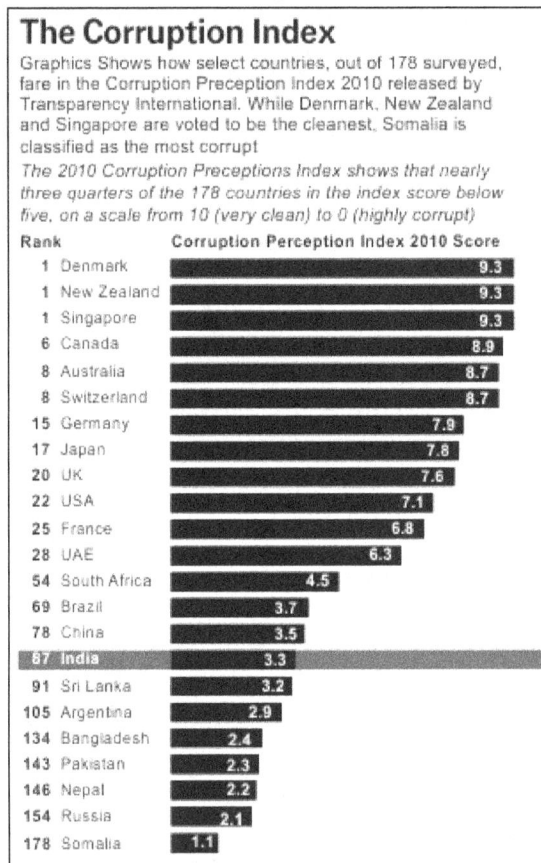

The Corruption Index

Graphics Shows how select countries, out of 178 surveyed, fare in the Corruption Preception Index 2010 released by Transparency International. While Denmark, New Zealand and Singapore are voted to be the cleanest, Somalia is classified as the most corrupt

The 2010 Corruption Preceptions Index shows that nearly three quarters of the 178 countries in the index score below five, on a scale from 10 (very clean) to 0 (highly corrupt)

Rank	Country	Corruption Perception Index 2010 Score
1	Denmark	9.3
1	New Zealand	9.3
1	Singapore	9.3
6	Canada	8.9
8	Australia	8.7
8	Switzerland	8.7
15	Germany	7.9
17	Japan	7.8
20	UK	7.6
22	USA	7.1
25	France	6.8
28	UAE	6.3
54	South Africa	4.5
69	Brazil	3.7
78	China	3.5
87	India	3.3
91	Sri Lanka	3.2
105	Argentina	2.9
134	Bangladesh	2.4
143	Pakistan	2.3
146	Nepal	2.2
154	Russia	2.1
178	Somalia	1.1

Source: Hitavada, October 27, 2010.

India has slipped to 87th position in Transparency International's latest ranking of nations based on the level of corruption, with the global watchdog asserting that perceptions about corruption in the country increased in the wake of the scam-tainted Commonwealth Games, 2G, 3G Spectrums and Adarsh Housing. Transparency International's Corruption Perception Index's report covering the public sector in 178 countries shows that India fell by three positions from its ranking of 84th in 2009. Top three countries with the lowest level of corruption globally, as ranked by Transparency

International, are Denmark, New Zealand and Singapore. Pakistan climbed up the corruption index from 42nd position in 2009 to 34th in 2010.

Dimensions of Corruption

The dimensions of corruption are being changed constantly. Bribe, patronage, nepotism, favouratism, misappropriation, transfers and appointments of officials to lucrative posts, procuring goods or services at rates higher than those prevailing in market with a view to getting commission, forming baseless and unprincipled conditions, trying to get cheap popularity at the cost of State exchequer including installing statutes of their political mentors and forming trust in their names and getting forcible donation of real estate to it, misuse of governmental machinery and illegal occupation of government accommodations etc, are some of the manifest forms of corruption. There can be many more manifestation form of corruption which changes from time to time.

Causes of Corruption

There are number of factors that have been responsible for corruption. The first cause is the emergence of political elite who believe in interest-oriented rather than nation-oriented programmes and policies. After independence in the first two decades the political elites were somewhat honest, dedicated to nation-building. They worked for the country's progress and development. But after two decades, political elites worked only on the basis of some vested interest, namely self-interest, family, caste, region, party and so forth. The planning and programmes were not nation-oriented but they were self-oriented. Even the bureaucrats were concerned with more perks and privileges rather than development-oriented policies for society. Corruption also emerges from power of the government officials of taking decisions like issuing licenses, assessing income tax, giving extensions and so on. Many officials pay thousands and lakhs of rupees to get themselves posted in particular places only because those places enable them to earn thousands and lakh of rupees every month as illegal gratification. This can be considered as causes of corruption.

Secondly, corruption is caused by scarcity. When things required are in short supply, people in power demand consideration to ensure their regular supply or increase their cost. This happens whenever there is high demand but low supply of commodity of daily needs like onion, *Toor dal*, sugar etc. In fact there may not be shortage of goods; it is not properly supplied to people. It is kept in the godown to wait for price-hike. Thirdly, corruption is caused as well as increased because of the change in the value system and ethical qualities of men who administer. Fifthly, corruption can be traced to ineffective administrative organization. Lack of vigilance, enormous power to the ministerial staff, unaccountability, defective information system, etc., all give scope to officials not only to be corrupt but remain unaffected even after following corrupt practices.

Impact of Corruption

Corruption also comes when the price is paid but for which no service has been provided. Adulteration in food or spurious drugs sold to patients is corrupt practices seen in society. Such cases in our daily life are not regarded as corruption because it has become regular phenomenon. In the office it is found that many officials come to office, sign the register and leave office. They become available only when they are offered money for file that they move. No doubt this is corruption. Corruption is found even in most developed countries like the United States of America, Japan, England, France, Canada and Germany. One must not think that corruption is prevalent in India alone. Corruption in its form differs in developed countries. Corruption in developed countries exists only among the highest echelons of business giants, while in India corruption can be seen in every spectrum of our daily life like paying for the railway reservation, for getting admission not only in a professional institution but even for a child in a good primary school, for buying a cinema ticket, for purchasing a gas cylinder, for driving the scooter without a helmet, for getting the arrear-bill passed and so on. All these affect the day to day living of the common man and in some way violate human rights. Let us study the effect of corruption in our daily life. 1) It retards economic development of the country in general. 2) It creates violence and lawlessness in society since corrupt man has the money power to influence the executers of law to serve him. 3) It has given rise to casteism and communalism. 4) It affects individuals' character. 5) It develops nepotism. 6) It reduces the credibility of the officials in the eyes of the masses. 7) It increases black money in open market. 8) It creates adulteration of eatables, spurious drugs and shortage of daily needs. 9) It destabilizes the government. Let us study how corruption has some relation to human rights in general and how it becomes a means for human rights violation.

Whole world is concerned about the extent of corruption everywhere. No country is exception to the cancer of corruption. In order to halt the practice of corruption in the world, the world leader came collectively to put a halt the practice of corruption. All agreed that the corruption is violation of human rights. In the words of former UN Secretary-General Kofi Annan, 'Corruption hurts the poor disproportionately by diverting funds intended for development, undermining a government's ability to provide basic services, feeding inequality and injustice, and discouraging foreign investment and aid.' The UN Convention against Corruption (UNCAC) came into force on December 14, 2005, and UN's Article 68(1) has been ratified by 140 countries. Various movements have been launched to bring the attention of government on the issue of corruption. In spite of all these, corruption has touched its height.

CORRUPTION: A MECHANISM FOR HUMAN RIGHTS VIOLATION

There is a close connection between corruption and human rights. Increasing empirical evidence around the world reveals a linkage between corruption and the infringement of human rights. Corrupt state officials use their power to silence critics, so that justice would be subverted. It could be said that corruption causes a lack of respect for human rights and the rule of law.

In India, corruption attacks the fundamental values of human dignity and political equality of the people and hence, there is a pressing need to formulate an act to make a corruption-free society.

Human rights have indeed acquired a special position in the contemporary world because of the increasing tendency of national governments to include these rights in their respective constitution as well as laws. This has resulted in several judiciaries around the world interpreting different human rights as a part of their own national laws or for that matter as a part of the International Law, which their respective country has been a signatory to, through treaties and other conventions. Thus the Universal Declaration of Human Rights (UDHR), the International Covenant on Civil and Political Rights (ICPR) and the International Covenant on Economic, Social and Cultural Rights (ICESCR) have acquired greater legitimacy in the last few decades as more and more nations have realized the importance of these human rights as instruments for better governance. Probity in governance is an outcome for an efficient system of governance and for socio-economic development. An important requirement for ensuring probity in governance is the absence of corruption. The other requirements may be effective laws, rules and regulations that govern every aspect of public life coupled with effective law enforcement and criminal justice systems.

The right to life, dignity and equality and other important human rights and values depend significantly upon this right. That is, it is a right without which these essential rights lose their meaning. As a fundamental right, the right to a corruption-free society cannot be discarded easily.

Right to Development, Human Rights and Corruption Free-Society

The Declaration on the Right to Development, which stated unequivocally that the right to development is a human right, was adopted by the UN in 1986. The Declaration has four main propositions: 1) The right to development is a human right; 2) The human right to development is a right to a particular process of development in which all human rights and fundamental freedoms can be fully realized, 3) The meaning of exercising these rights consistently with freedom implies free, effective, and full participation of all the individuals concerned in decision-making and in the implementation of the process, and therefore, the process must be transparent and accountable, and individuals must have equal opportunity of access to the resources for development and receive a fair distribution of the benefits of development 4) The right confers an unequivocal obligation on duty-holders, individuals within the community, states at the national level, and states at the international level. Nation states have the responsibility to help realize the process of development by initiating appropriate development policies. International agencies have the obligation to cooperate with the nation states to facilitate the realization of the process of development. It is in this context that the fundamental right to a corruption-free society adds a new and necessary dimension to the right to development. No development process will have any meaning and relevance if corruption as an institutionalized process interferes with people's struggles to realize their right to development. Corruption retards the right to development.

HUMAN RIGHTS AND CORRUPTION: AN INTER-RELATIONSHIP

If corruption is shown to violate human rights, this will influence public attitudes. Identifying the specific links between corruption and human rights may persuade key actors—public officials, parliamentarians, judges, prosecutors, lawyers, business people, bankers, accountants, the media and the public in general—to take a stronger stand against corruption. This may be so even in countries where reference to human rights is sensitive.

Connecting acts of corruption to violations of human rights also creates new possibilities for action, especially if, as we will argue, acts of corruption can be challenged using the different national, regional and international mechanisms that exist to monitor compliance with human rights. In the last sixty three years, the Universal Declaration of Human Rights (UDHR) and many more mechanisms have been created to hold states and individuals accountable for human rights violations. When acts of corruption are linked to violations of human rights, all these institutions could act to force accountability and so create disincentives for corruption.

Vulnerability and Disadvantage

While corruption violates the rights of all those affected by it, it has a disproportionate impact on people that belong to groups such as minorities, indigenous peoples, migrant workers, disabled people that are exposed to particular risks. It also disproportionately affects women and children. Corruption in such cases can magnify and intensify human rights problems of such groups.

Corruption and Violation of Women Rights

Corruption impacts men and women differently and reinforces and perpetuates existing gender inequalities. Women's lack of access to political and economic power excludes them from networks that permit access to decision-making bodies. Where institutions are controlled by men, women do not have enough power to challenge corruption. Women's access to justice is compromised in other ways. Many women also have fewer opportunities than men to acquire higher education, or obtain land, credit and other productive assets. When they have access to work, they are often paid lower salaries. They tend to assume the domestic responsibilities of taking care of children and older adults, which means they are financially dependent, cannot work or are poorer. For all these reasons—but essentially because women are over-represented in the poorest social segments of society and under-represented in decision-making bodies—corruption affect them in particular ways, often disproportionately.

Corruption and Children's Rights

Corruption may also have a disproportionate impact on children. While children possess in general the same civil, political, economic, social and cultural rights as adults, they also have certain rights specific to them. Most of these are identified in the 1989 United Nations Convention on the Rights of the Child (CRC), in Article 24 of the International Covenant on Civil and Political Rights (ICCPR), and in Article 10(3) of the International Covenant on Economic, Social and Cultural Rights (ICESCR). Corruption can violate many of the rights that children share with adults, including the right to life and the right to health. In addition, some rights, such as the right to education, are particularly important to children. Corruption in the education sector very often violates the rights of children.

Corruption, Poverty and Human Rights

Corruption has a severely detrimental impact on the lives of people living in poverty when compared with higher income groups. Corruption not only affects economic growth and discourages foreign investment, thereby indirectly affecting the poor, but reduces the net income of those living in poverty, distorts policies, programmes and strategies that aim to meet their basic needs, and diverts public resources from investments in infrastructure that are crucial elements of strategies to lift them out of poverty. Whenever corruption is generalized, poor people are as exposed as others to the small-scale bribery of public officials (notably in the healthcare, law enforcement and judicial sectors) but the effect on their purse will be heavier. Large-scale corruption, meanwhile, damages the quality of public services on which the poor depend particularly, to meet basic needs. Hence, corruption breeds poverty and infringes human rights globally.

Corruption, Indigenous People and Minorities and Human Rights

Indigenous people and minorities suffer particularly from corruption. They are often among the poorest and most disadvantaged groups in society. Indigenous women are additionally exposed to risk. Indigenous communities that are closely linked to land they live on collectively are especially vulnerable to corruption of infrastructure programmes that displace them, and smaller-scale corruption associated with land sales and registration. Many indigenous communities also lack access to education and are consequently less aware of their legal rights. Mechanisms for reporting and tackling corruption are often out of their reach. Since indigenous voices are rarely heard in policy discussions, these populations often have little influence on the design and imple- mentation of anti-corruption policies and programmes that could improve their status. Today farmers are facing a lot of problems due to the land scams everywhere. Corruption, land scam take away the rights of farmers to cultivate.

Corruption Violates Socio-Economic and Cultural Rights

Corruption is likely to violate enjoyment of cultural rights. States have a wide range of duties to provide or regulate public services in relation to health, housing, water and education. These services generate large public contracts which not only create opportunities for corruption but have a disproportionate impact on vulnerable and disadvantaged groups, in particular women. Widespread corruption in health or educational services deters the poor from seeking healthcare and education and depresses living standards and opportunities for poorer people in particular. Corruption will have an impact on the enjoyment of all economic, social and cultural rights.

Corruption and Right to Food

The right to food also referred to as the right of everyone to be free from hunger, is a component of the more general right to an adequate standard of living (ICESCR, Article 11(2)). The right to adequate food asserts that all people should be in a position to feed themselves. It should be made clear that the right to food does not imply that states must provide food to everyone. The obligation on a state is to take steps that will gradually make it possible for all people to feed themselves, will provide access to food in an equal and non-discriminatory way, and will assist people to obtain food if they are not in a position to feed themselves. The food-grains which are to be sold in Public Distribution Scheme are being sold on higher price. Price-hike of food-grain in some way is due to corruption and that violates right to food of poor mass.

Corruption may also affect other elements of the right to food. Food security may be compromised if food producers obtain licenses by bribing the authorities; and the right to health (and life) may be compromised, if such food producers subsequently put adulterated or unsafe products on the market. Corruption in food programmes and schemes designed to meet the needs of socially vulnerable people may also prevent them from obtaining food; when a person embezzles funds from a food programme, or diverts food into the black market for personal profit, the right to food of those who are embezzled is clearly compromised.

Corruption Violates the Right to Adequate Housing

The right to adequate housing derives from the right to an adequate standard of living. It focuses on the obligation to ensure that everyone has housing that is safe, healthy and adequate (ICESCR, Article 11(1)). In addition, the right forbids discrimination in the field of housing, as well as forced or arbitrary evictions or acts of unjust dispossession. The right to adequate housing does not entail that the government has to build housing for the entire population or that housing must be provided free of charge to whoever requests it. It is primarily a right of access. What constitutes adequate is dependent on social, economic, climatic, ecological and other factors. However, certain minimum elements are integral to the right and should always be taken into account. Corruption may violate this right by restricting one or more of its elements. The *Adarsh* apartment scam in Mumbai is the glaring example before us. Those who are supposed in their house are living in *juggi-jhopadi*.

Corruption and Health

Corrupt practices in the pharmaceutical industry are prevalent everywhere. Unethical drug promotion can generate conflicts of interest for physicians and ultimately can harm patients' health. If drug marketing by pharmaceutical companies is not well regulated, it may not benefit to patients. If states do not guard against this kind of abuse, they will violate their duty to protect the right to health. In general terms, corruption in the health sector, occurs in three main forms: in management of financial resources (budget allocation, etc.); in the distribution of medical supplies (purchasing, marketing); and in the relationships of health workers with patients.

CONCLUSION

Human rights and corruption are related in ways in which corruption leads to violations of human rights. Acts of corruption can directly and indirectly violate human rights, especially those of the disadvantaged. Anti-corruption measures need a human rights perspective. Similarly, effective human rights protection measures need to incorporate and integrate anti-corruption measures as well.

When violations of human rights are portrayed as a result of corruption, it will raise the awareness of people concerning the consequences of corruption on the well-being of individuals. This perspective helps to demonstrate clearly to the public the destructive effects of corruption on human beings. Trafficking in human beings is so inhumane that it might create a common spirit and public support for the cause of attempting to limit or eliminate corruption. The negative impacts of corruption on humanity would thus be more convincing and tangible to the public. People will have more understanding about the detrimental effects of corruption when they see that it can threaten their lives. They will have greater sympathy for the victims of corruption because they are the same victims of human rights violations. Any individual could become one of the unfortunate victims if the state is not able to protect them and if the public remains passive and unaware. Public support for combating corruption will create demands and put pressure on the government to be committed more seriously to this cause and generate the true political will to eradicate corruption. Giving a human face to corruption may lead to more effective anti-corruption strategies through better awareness of the destructive effects of corruption, which should no longer be tolerated.

Considering the issues of corruption and human rights through the lens of power relations enables us to see them as relationship between different social groups or individuals who are able to access power differently. Let's launch a mass movement to combat corruption from this universe.

REFERENCES

[1] Choudhry, P.C., "Corruption" in *Seminar* No. 421, September, 1994.

[2] Ahuja Ram, Social Problems in India, Rawat Publication, Jaipur, 1997, and 2003, pp. 449–474.

[3] Anukansai, Kanokkan, "Corruption: The Catalyst for violation of Human Rights, *BACC Journal,* July 2010, pp. 6–15.

[4] Corruption and Human Rights: Integrating Human Rights into the Anti-corruption Agenda: Challenges, Possibilities and Opportunities. Draft Report February 2009, *International Council on Policy,* Human Rights, Switzerland.

[5] Santhanam Committee Report on "Prevention of Corruption", Government of India 1964.

[6] The Impact of Corruption on the Human Rights based Approach to Development, United Nations Development Programme Oslo Governance Centre 2004.

Understanding Corruption from a Human Rights Perspective

Anamika Ajay

Institute of Commonwealth Studies, University of London

E-mail: anamajay@gmail.com

INTRODUCTION

The International Bill of Human Rights, numerous other human rights conventions/ declarations and laws that have come into existence at the national and international levels, reflect the belief that it is the responsibility of the States to respect, protect and promote human rights. States are responsible for taking initiatives to the fullest of their abilities and resources so as to realize the rights of the people. For instance, state obligations with regard to promotion of human rights is clearly elucidated in the International Covenant on Economic, Social and Cultural Rights states that:

> *"Each State Party to the present Covenant undertakes to take steps, individually and through international assistance and co-operation, especially economic and technical, to the maximum of its available resources, with a view to achieving progressively the full realization of the rights recognized in the present Covenant by all appropriate means, including particularly the adoption of legislative measures."*[1]

With this understanding, it would not be imprudent to assume that corruption and related acts committed by public institutions or officials reduce the state's will, abilities and resources that are necessary for the realization of human rights. Corruption is popularly defined as the 'abuse of public office for private gains'.[2] This implies that

---

[1] United Nations (1966a). International Covenant on Economic, Social and Cultural Rights. in Ghandi P.R., 2002. ed., *Blackstone's International Human Rights Documents*, 3rd ed. Oxford: Oxford University Press.

[2] World Bank (1997). *Helping Countries Combat Corruption: The Role of the World Bank*. Report. Available at: http://www1.worldbank.org/publicsector/anticorrupt/corruptn/corrptn.pdf [last accessed on 12/07/2011]

corruption redirects the public good and resources for the welfare of the people to a few hands. Corruption is founded on injustice and inequality,[3] both of which undermine the spirit of human rights. In the present context of liberalization, the gaps between the well-to-do and the disadvantaged are stark. Especially in the recent past, there is an increased awareness among the international community regarding the negative effects of corruption on human rights and development.[4] In addition to this realization, there is a belief that human rights approach should be central to all anti-corruption strategies. Rights based approach has emerged as a system and a movement that has the potential to address all the major contemporary issues.

In the Indian context, there is an increased demand for transparency in governance. The corruption scams are on a rise and the longstanding demand for a strong anti-corruption agency (Lokpal) from the civil society has reached new heights. The importance of ethics in governance, the need to curb corruption at all levels of governance and the importance of respect for rule of law and human rights have been discussed in great detail by the Second Administrative Reforms Commission.[5] According to Rajkumar, "Corruption in India not only poses a significant danger to the quality of governance but also threatens in an accelerated manner the very foundations of its democracy and statehood."[6] Most of the anti-corruption strategies in the country have failed to address the root causes. Rights of the vulnerable and disadvantaged are further violated by corruption. The fight against corruption and human rights violations are interlinked and both these require independent and accountable systems, political will and respect for rule of law. With corruption levels reaching the peak in India it is likely that the ability of the Government to respect and fulfill its obligations with respect to human rights is diminishing.

Thus from the above discussion, understanding corruption from a human rights perspective is important in two ways. Firstly, human rights perspective allows us to understand the perils caused by corruption with both short and long term effects. Secondly, human rights could provide for comprehensive solutions to tackle corruption

---

[3]International Council on Human Rights Policy (2009a). *Corruption and Human Rights: Making the Connection.* Report. Available at: http://www.ichrp.org/files/reports/40/131_web.pdf [last accessed on 12/07/2011]

[4]International Council on Human Rights Policy (2009b). *Corruption and Human Rights- Integrating Human Rights into Anti-Corruption Agenda: Challenges, Possibilities and Opportunities.* Report. Available at: http://hrbaportal.org/wp-content/files/1247495995_8_1_1_resfile.pdf [last accessed on 12/07/2011]

[5]Government of India-Second Administrative Reforms Commission (2005). *Citizen Centric Administration.* Twelfth Report. Available at: http://arc.gov.in/arc_12th_report/arc_12th_Report.pdf [last accessed on 12/07/2011]

[6]Rajkumar, C. (2002). *Corruption and Human Rights.* Frontline Vol. 19 (19). Available at: http://www.hindu.com/fline/fl1919/19190780.htm [last accessed on 12/07/2011]

menace by emphasizing on the rule of law and law enforcement. The paper is aimed at answering a key research questions:

- How does corruption in India violate human rights?
- Why do the current anti-corruption agencies fail to combat corruption in India?
- How does a Rights based approach serve as a plausible way forward to effective anti-corruption strategies?

While it is realised that the State has the prime responsibility to ensure accountability and rule of law, with a prominent role played by private actors in the process of governance in the context of liberalisation and globalisation, the present paper aims to discuss the issues of corruption in the public and private sector and how these malpractices have an impact of human rights. The paper discusses in detail the specific human rights violations caused by corruption in the judiciary, government bodies/institutions and the private sector.

IMPORTANCE OF HUMAN RIGHTS PERSPECTIVE IN UNDERSTANDING CORRUPTION

Corruption, as a subject, is receiving a lot of attention from academicians, governments, international organizations and financial institutions. This could be attributed to the concerns regarding the impact unethical and unlawful behavior of officials has on the quality of governance. Corruption is pervasive at all levels of governance and exists in different forms. The India Corruption Study conducted by Transparency International and the Centre for Media Studies in 2005 revealed that corruption is prevalent in all the sectors of governance and have impacted the quality of life of the people. The study measured citizens' perception about the levels of corruption prevalent in 11 need based and basic public services which are rural financial institutions, municipalities, income tax office, land administration, judiciary, police, school, water supply, Public Distribution System (PDS), electricity and government hospitals. Among these the people rated police to be the most corrupt followed by judiciary, office for land administration and hospitals in that order.[7] Thus it is very clear that corruption has crept into all the institutions in the public domain. The impact of corruption in these sectors is dangerous as they are services that are required to ensure basic human rights. These institutions are vital in respecting and fulfilling right to life, fair trial, health, education and other basic facilities. Therefore corruption in these sectors poses serious concerns about the extent to which citizens enjoy their rights. Table 1 below, illustrates the different forms of corruption that are prevalent in India.[8]

---

[7]Transparency International and Centre for Media Studies (2005). *India Corruption Study*. Report. Available at: http://www.transparency.org/regional_pages/asia_pacific/newsroom/news_archive2/india_corruption_study_2005 [last accessed on 12/07/2011]

[8]Table 1 covers the broad aspects of corruption in India. Acts like embezzlement, bribery would be covered under these broad categories.

Table 1: Description of Different Types of Corruption

Type of Corruption	*Description*	*Examples from India*
Grand Corruption	Corruption involving head of the state, ministers, top level officials and bureaucrats. The monies involved in such cases are enormous.[9]	Commonwealth Games Scam and 2G scam
Political Corruption	Involves political party members or legislators who seek bribes or funds for their political and personal benefit and provide favours to their supporters at the expense of broader public benefits.[10]	Cash-for-vote Scam
Judicial Corruption	Acts or omissions that constitute the use of public authority for the private benefit of court personnel, and result in the improper and unfair delivery of judicial decisions.[11]	Jessica Lal case
Corporate Corruption	Illegal behaviour by corporate officials for private gain.[12]	Sathyam Scam, Fake Certificate scandal
Administrative Corruption	Institutionalized personal abuse of public resources by civil servants. It involves influencing public officials to evade tax payments, escape trade regulations and gain procurement contracts.[13]	Office of Drug Controller, Karnataka case
Petty Corruption	Corruption that people experience in their encounters with public officials while accessing public services like health and education.[14]	Numerous cases like bribing the RTO for driving license

Source: Author's interpretation.

Accountability and respect for the rule of law are two fundamental principles of good governance.[15] However, according to Global Integrity Report, India's fight for corruption is hindered by a weak anti-corruption agency, lack of respect for rule of law

---

[9]Anti-Corruption Resource Centre, Corruption Glossary. Available at http://www.u4.no/document/glossary.cfm [last accessed on 12/07/2011]

[10]Heidenheimer, A. J., *et al.*, eds. *Political Corruption: Concepts and Texts.* New Brunswick: Transaction Publishers, 2002.

[11]Transparency International (2007). *Global Corruption Report- Corruption in Judicial Systems.* Available at: http://www.transparency.org/publications/gcr/gcr_2007 [last accessed on 12/07/2011]

[12]Clinard, Marshall and Peter Yeager (2005). *Corporate Crime.* New Brunswick: Transaction Publishers.

[13]Johnston, Michael. *Syndromes of Corruption: Wealth, Power and Democracy.* Cambridge: Cambridge University Press, 2005.

[14]Anti-Corruption Resource Centre website (ibid 9).

[15]UNDP (1997). Governance for Sustainable Human Development. Policy Document. Available at: http://mirror.undp.org/magnet/policy [last accessed on 12/07/2011]

and inefficient law enforcement.[16] Corruption minimizes the state's ability to uphold the rights of its people. While there is a direct violation of economic and social rights when the public officials are engaged in corruption, there is also a less obvious violation of civil and political rights due to corruption. Corruption prevails in societies that have polar power structures.[17] Corruption also has the ability to further polarize groups by breeding conditions of inequality and injustice, that is, in a corrupt system the more powerful (power could be in terms of social or economic status) access and enjoy privileges and services that are under normal circumstances entitled to all equally. A unique characteristic of corruption is that it can occur at all levels of the power structure. India is a quintessential breeding ground for corruption of all types. Right from grand corruption to petty corruption, the people at power abuse their position for private gains which results in huge economic, political, and social losses.

The description of different kinds of corruption in Table 1 reveals that corruption is likely to occur when public officials are exposed with opportunities to make private gains at the expense of public 'good'. One of the major reasons for the failure of anti-corruption strategies could be attributed to the lack of awareness about the human rights violations it leads to. The effects and losses caused by corruption is usually understood in economic terms, undermining its direct and indirect negative effects on the civil, political, economic, social and cultural rights of the citizens which are guaranteed by the Constitution of India and many international human rights treaties. According to Rajkumar, institutionalised corruption can result in widespread victimisation, destabilize the rule of law, affect democratic governance and tamper the social fabric of the nation.[18] Corruption can result in colossal damages to the economic well-being of a nation, it directly violates right to life, fair trial, right to equality, right to public services and right to political participation.[19] The relevance of a rights based analysis of corruption in India is essential due to two reasons:

1. Identifying the specific human rights that are directly violated by corruption will reveal the extent and intensity of damage/harm caused. Such identification is important because if an act or omission of act results in the violation of the fundamental rights guaranteed by the Constitution then the trial of such cases, punishment of corrupt acts and compensation of the victims can be made more effective. This is especially important in India's case because in the current scenario, the Prevention of Corruption Act (1988) and other anti-corruption related laws deal

---

[16]Global Integrity (2009). Global Integrity Report- India. Available at: http://report.globalintegrity. org/India/2009 [last accessed on 12/07/2011]

[17]Rogow, A.A. and Lasswell, H.D. (1963). *Power, Corruption and Rectitude*. Westport: Greenwood Publishing Group.

[18]Rajkumar, 2002.

[19]International Council on Human Rights Policy, 2009a.

with corrupt acts as a matter of deteriorating ethics in governance without any reference to victims of corruption. Such an understanding undermines the extent of inequality, injustice and human rights violations implanted by corruption. Therefore, human rights based understanding of corruption will provide more clarity into matters of the consequences of corruption and also identifies victims of corrupt acts.

2. Human rights could provide an alternative framework to combat the menace of corruption in India as it would reduce opportunities available to public servants to abuse their official power for private gains.[20] Rights based measures like creating awareness among people about the human rights violation resulted by corruption, better exercise of political rights by the citizens, widespread use of right to information and guaranteeing protection of whistleblowers will motivate many more people to act as watchdogs and help in reducing corruption considerably.[21] Also, tackling corruption as a human rights issue is particularly beneficial considering the development of human rights law and the extent to which these standards have been enforced in the national and international courts.

Thus it would not be imprudent to argue that human rights would help to understand the magnitude of the problem of corruption, bringing perpetrators to corruption, providing reparations to victims of corruption and most importantly, it would act as an effective preventive measure. In order to reveal the magnitude of corruption problem in India, the paper specifically analyses cases of judicial corruption, corporate corruption and administrative corruption using the human rights framework provided by Constitution of India and international treaties.

IDENTIFYING DIRECT HUMAN RIGHTS VIOLATIONS THROUGH DIFFERENT TYPES OF CORRUPTION

Judicial Corruption and Violation of Right to Fair Trial

According to Transparency International, judicial corruption could be defined as "acts or omissions that constitute the use of public authority for the private benefit of court personnel, and result in the improper and unfair delivery of judicial decisions".[22] Such acts include bribery, extortion, intimidation, influence peddling and the abuse of court procedures or personnel for personal gain. This definition could be interpreted to include influencing judges, lawyers, court personnel police personnel and even the witnesses who play a very key role in criminal justice administration. There is a rise in

---

[20]International Council on Human Rights Policy, 2009a.
[21]International Council on Human Rights Policy, 2009b.
[22]Transparency International (2007).

the instances where the judicial integrity in India has been questioned. Use of bribes, extortions or threats to influence the appointment of judges, influencing the trial process, exclusion or manipulation of evidences that otherwise would result in conviction of an accused, influencing any actor within the justice system to affect the impartial and independent nature of justice delivery have led to public outcry in India.[23]

Article 21 of the Constitution of India states that "No person shall be deprived of his life or personal liberty except according to procedure established by law."[24] In Maneka Gandhi case, Justice Bhagwati explains that a law cannot be fair until it fulfils the audi alteram partem rule also says that. He says that in a trial the persons affected must have reasonable opportunity of being heard and the hearing must be a genuine hearing and not an empty public relations exercise.[25] This judgement suggested that the right to life envisioned in Article 21 also includes right to fair trial. A minimum standard for fair trial procedures can be found in the Criminal Procedure Code (1973) which lays out equality of arms for all the parties involved in a trial. In the international human rights framework, Article 14 of the International Covenant on Civil and Political Rights (ICCPR) states that right to fair trial is one of the fundamental and inalienable rights that the State has to respect, protect and ensure at all time.[26] In John Campbell v Jamaica, the Human Rights Committee suggested that an indispensible aspect of the fair trial principle is the equality of arms between the prosecution and the defence.[27]

The extent of corruption in Indian judiciary can be revealed through the Jessica Lal case and the Priyadarshini Mattoo case. In the former case, a model named Jessica Lal was shot and killed at a private party in South Delhi on April 30, 1999. Three eye witnesses identified Manu Sharma, son of a senior party politician and Union Minister. After a few days the main accused surrendered to the authorities in Chandigarh. However in a few days, the accused and the key eye witnesses retracted the statements and the plea of non-guilty was filed for trial. In the year 2006, the main accused and eight other co-defendants were acquitted of all charges. Due to huge public outcry that followed this decision, the President of India promised action. The decision was appealed in the Delhi High Court which reversed the lower court decision with respect to the main accused, Manu Sharma, who was convicted of murder and sentenced to

---

[23]O'Flaherty, Brenden and Sethi, Rajiv (2009). Public Outrage and Criminal Justice: Lessons from the Jessica Lal case. Available at: http://www.columbia.edu/~rs328/Jessica.pdf [last accessed on: 12/07/2011]

[24]Government of India (1950). Constitution of India, in Bakshi P.M., 2005. The Constitution of India (5th ed). New Delhi: Universal Law Publishing Co. Ltd.

[25]Maneka Gandhi v Union of India, 1978. Case No. AIR1978SC597.

[26]United Nations, 1966a. International Covenant on Civil and Political Rights in Ghandi, P.R., 2002. ed., *Blackstone's International Human Rights Documents*, 3rd ed. Oxford: Oxford University Press.

[27]John Campbell v Jamaica, 1988, Communication No. 307/1988.

life imprisonment. This judgment has also been appealed to the Supreme Court.[28] In the Priyadarshini Mattoo case, a 25 years old girl was brutally raped and murdered at her residence in New Delhi in 1996. All the physical and circumstantial evidences and also DNA tests pointed towards Santhosh Kumar Singh, a son of a Senior Police officer. However, the nation was shocked with the judgment that acquitted the main accused. Like in the Jessica Lal case, a huge public outcry at the acquittal resulted in the appeal to the Delhi High court in 2000. The pressure on the judiciary built on by the verdict with respect to Jessica Lal case in 2006 which resulted in the Delhi HC to convict Santosh Kumar Singh for murdering Priyadarshini Mattoo and was sentenced to death and later commuted to life imprisonment by the Supreme Court.[29] A look at both these cases reveals a few similarities. Both these cases involved high profile individuals, the trial of both the cases were influence by political or other official powers, both led to public outcry after an active civil society campaign which resulted in appeals to higher courts. While in the Jessica Lal case, the witnesses retracted their statements under influence of political power possessed by the defendants, in the Priyadarshini case the defendant's father abused his official power to influence the police and the court processes. Abuse of official power for private gain in both these cases makes corruption in judiciary a reality in India.

As discussed earlier, every individual has a right to fair trial. Paying bribes to the witnesses or influencing the police or court personnel would render the trial process unfair and partial. In both the cases, what seemed like an open and shut case with very straightforward evidences against the accused resulted in their acquittal in the lower courts denying justice to the victims. The influences in both the cases violated the standards set for fair justice administration. It was only due to the civil society campaigns that the verdict of the lower court was challenged which finally led to a fair trial. However, it must be realized that these cases received the attention they did from the media in specific and civil society in general because they were high profile in nature. There may be numerous low profile cases where judicial integrity is tampered with power and corruption, but the victims have no support resulting in violation of the rights of victims. The State failed to respect and fulfill its obligation with respect to fair trial of the victims.

Business and Human Rights: Corruption in Private Education and Violation of Right to Life and Education

Economic growth in India has resulted in the entry of the private sector in major service delivery domain. As their counterparts in the public domain, private actors are

---

[28]O'Flaherty, Brenden and Sethi, Rajiv (2009).
[29]Ibid 28.

also found to be corrupt and unethical to a great extent. Corruption by private actors is clearly evident from the nation's experiences of privatizing educational institutions. Privatization of educational institutions is on a rise in India. With Supreme Court judgments like P.A. Inamdar case (2005)[30] and Islamic Academy Case (2003),[31] the Supreme Court bestows greater autonomy with the private actors in terms of autonomy to start educational institutions for specific groups or minorities. However it can be seen that the private institutions engage in corrupt acts like charging exorbitant fees in the form of capitation fees,[32] stealing certificates from the students, i.e., the students are asked to submit their certificates while getting admitted into the college and these are not returned until they finish their course. This is a kind of entrapment which makes it impossible for the students to shift to other better institutions.[33]

A landmark judgment by the Supreme Court of India in the case Mohini Jain v State of Karnataka has held that "the Right to Education is a Fundamental Right under Article 21 of the Constitution, which cannot be denied to a citizen by charging higher fee known as capitation fee".[34] Moreover, at an international level, Articles 13 and 14 of the ICESCR guarantees right to education to all citizens.[35] States are required to take necessary steps to make primary, secondary and higher levels of education available and accessible to all. These articles could be interpreted to include that right to education includes giving reasonable institutional autonomy and also the freedom to individuals/parents/guardians to choose an institution that align to their beliefs or preferences. Moreover, Article 38 of the Directive Principles of State Policy provided by the Constitution requires that the State to promote welfare of the people by securing and promoting social order that shall inform all institutions in terms of justice, social, economic and political.[36]

Thus, according the standards set by the national and international human rights framework it is clear that by charging exorbitant fees from students the private institutions violate the right to education of the students which is an integral part of the fundamental right to life provided by Article 21 of the Constitution. Right to education is also violated in cases where the students were denied the right to seek admissions to the institutions of their choice by confiscating their certificates. The private institutions by

---

[30]P.A. Inamdar and others v. State of Maharashtra Case No.: Appeal (Civil) 5041 of 2005.

[31]Islamic Academy and others v State of Karnataka, Writ Petition (Civil) No. 350 of 1993.

[32]Financial Express (2010). *Private Colleges defend capitation fees*. Online Article. Available at: http://www.financialexpress.com/news/pvt-colleges-defend-capitation-fee/593749 [last accessed on 12/07/2011]

[33]Transparency International (2009). Global Corruption Report: Corruption and Private Sector. Available at: http://www.transparency.org/publications/gcr/gcr_2009 [last accessed on 12/07/2011]

[34]Mohini Jain v. State of Karnataka, Case no. 1992 SCR (3) 658.

[35]United Nations, 1966a.

[36]Government of India,1950.

engaging in malpractices directly and the State by failing to regulate such malpractices violate the right to education of the students laid under the Fundamental Rights and Directive Principles of the State Policy as in the Constitution and also violation of Article 13 of the ICESCR to which India is a party.

Administrative Corruption and Violation of Right to Basic Services

There are a numerous cases in India, where bribes are solicited or accepted by public officials to help individuals/organisations to reduce taxes or evade trade regulations. Such acts have the potential to violate fundamental human rights like right to life and right to health. Article 21deal with "No person shall be deprived of his life or personal liberty except according to procedure established by law." Article 12 of the ICESCR established the "right to the highest attainable standard of physical and mental health", defined as the "right to the enjoyment of a variety of facilities, goods, services and conditions necessary for the realization of the highest attainable standard of health". In 1997, the Supreme Court held that right to health and medical care is a fundamental right covered by Article 21 and the state has the constitutional responsibilities to provide health facilities.[37] The state has an obligation under Article 21 to safeguard the right to life of every person, preservation of human life being of paramount importance. The Supreme Court has in the case of *Parmanand Katra vs Union of India,*[38] held that whether the patient be an innocent person or be a criminal liable to punishment under the law, it is the obligation of those who are in charge of the health of the community to preserve life so that innocent may be protected and the guilty may be punished. Also Articles 47 of the Constitution under the Directive Principles of the State Policy, provides that the State has the responsibility to ensuring public health services to all citizens.

One of the best examples to elucidate the extent to which corruption is institutionalised in the public sector is the case involving the Office of the Drug Controller (ODC) in Karnataka. In this case, a doctor and an activist from Drug Action Forum (DAF) which aims at creating awareness about drugs promotion and policy filed a complaint to the Karnataka Lokayukta in 2003 accusing the ODC of corruption and malpractices. Investigation conducted by the Lokayukta revealed that many drugs circulated to the hospitals were of sub-standard which violates the Office mandate that the drugs permitted for circulation should be of a minimum quality standards. It was found that companies that paid bribes to the ODC were allowed to evade regulations. It was revealed that one of the blood banks that were permitted by the ODC provided HIV-positive blood. Three lower level officials who assisted the Lokayukta in the

---

[37]Mohinder Singh v State of Punjab, AIR 1997 SC 1225.
[38]AIR 1989 SC 2039.

investigations were suspended by the ODC which later on led to Lokayukta threatening to hold the government responsible for interfering in the process of justice. The final report of the Lokayukta implicated three top officials of the ODC who were suspended in 2004 for misconduct and also the reinstating the officials who supported the Lokayukta in its investigations.[39]

In the above case, ODC's collusion with the private companies that led to the supply of counterfeit drugs is an example of the cases in which the State fails to respect, protect and fulfil its obligation with regards to right to health of the citizens. By allowing the supply of counterfeit drugs to the hospitals that would be circulated to the patients in the hospital violates the right to life of citizens as low quality drugs could cause grievous harm to a person's life. Article 21 prohibits the ODC from violating right to life by circulating harmful drugs to the patients and also puts a positive obligation on the State to respect, protect and fulfil its responsibilities to ensure right to life to all citizens by regulating the production and supply of counterfeit drugs. The ODC and the Government of Karnataka should and was held responsible for corrupt practices, but they are also responsible for violating the right to life and health of the citizens. The private companies that paid bribe to the ODC for circumventing the regulations are also responsible for human rights violations.

Thus all the above case studies reveal that the corruption at different levels involving both public and private actors directly violate a range of human rights that are envisioned in the Constitution of India and the international human rights treaties like the ICCPR and the ICESCR. Moreover, human rights based understanding of the corrupt acts discussed in this section helped in understanding the extent of harm these acts instill both in the short term and in the long term. This could help in designing strategies to prevent corruption or redress corruption-induced injustices. A better awareness about rights, high levels of political participation, engaging with the government, use of tools of transparency like right to information and so on are rights based approaches that can reduce occurrences of corruption.

CONCLUSION

A state that respects, protects and fulfills human rights is very unlikely to tolerate and breed corruption. Similarly, a state that has a bad track record in terms of corruption is most likely to have a poor track record of human rights. Corruption reduces the ability of the State to fulfill its obligations to uphold human rights. Also, corruption is perceived to have a negative impact on human rights. However there have been only few efforts

---

[39]Transparency International(2006). *Global Corruption Report-Corruption and Health*. Available at: http://www.transparency.org/global_priorities/other_thematic_issues/health [last accessed on 12/07/2011]

to identify the specific situations in which human rights are directly violated by a corrupt act. This will help in understanding the magnitude of damage corruption results in which will help in determining a just restitution for the victim and punishing the perpetrators. Human rights could also provide an effective framework for preventing corruption. This is based on the argument that corruption is dominant in societies that are unjust and unequal. It exists where people are exposed to opportunities for furthering their personal gains at the cost of the public good. Awareness about the ill-effects of corruption in terms of its impact on human rights, better political participation, engaging with the governments and holding them accountable and better law enforcement are some of the rights based approaches to preventing corruption. These measures could be more effective unlike the present day anti-corruption strategies as rights based solutions tend to tackle the root causes of the problem.

India, in the last decade has witnessed numerous scams at all levels of governance. The fight against corruption in India has been rendered unsuccessful in bringing about transparent governance because of lack of respect for rule of law, political interferences in the functioning of the anti-corruption agencies and weak rule of law. Corruption is prevalent and pervasive across domains of public life. The situation is made complex by the entry of private actors, post-liberalisation, in the public service delivery sector. The definition of corruption as per Indian anti-corruption laws does not include private companies under its purview and therefore could lead to impunity in terms of corrupt practices by private actors.

The paper aimed to understand and identify the specific human rights that have been violated by different forms of corruption. The paper analysed three different types of corruption, i.e., judicial corruption, corporate corruption and administrative corruption using the human rights framework provided by the Constitution of India and the international treaties. Case studies were used to identify the specific human rights that could be violated by corruption. Analysis revealed that corruption can directly violate fundamental rights like right to life, fair trial, right to education and health. While the paper was limited in its scope in terms of the analysis of different types of corruption, the findings of the paper could be indicative of the fact that all forms of corruption leads to direct victimisation of individuals or group. Tacking corruption solely as an economic crime would undermine the violation of the civil, political, social and cultural rights. It is therefore a necessity to analyse all the acts of corruption from a human rights perspective—this will provide clarity into who are the victims and the perpetrators, why and how were the rights violated and how can it be redressed. The establishment of human rights law as a widely accepted and followed framework would reinforce this approach to fight against corruption. Human rights therefore should be considered both as the means and an end with regard to fight against corruption.

Corruption Dynamics: Scope and Cures

P.S. Vivek

Department of Sociology, University of Mumbai

INTRODUCTION

In recent years, the subject of corruption has been given much more attention. Work on governance has brought it to light and the subject is no longer taboo. It is being addressed directly by financial institutions, government agencies, bilateral donors, international organizations, NGOs and development professionals. The causes of corruption have been measured empirically, as have the impacts on human development. Institutions and administrative procedures have been overhauled; countries have negotiated and signed international anti-corruption conventions; Transparency International (TI) has created a large forum for discussion and advocacy around its many forms; and an international coalition of NGOs has emerged, challenging corruption "from below".

The International Council's project on corruption and human rights is designed to identify, explore, and clarify links between corruption and human rights; to assess the direct impact of corruption on human rights; to assess the strengths and weaknesses of anti-corruption strategies from a human rights point of view; and to assess where fuller use of human rights norms, principles and methods would make such strategies more effective in practice. The project does not advocate human rights as a policy panacea for every challenge faced by anti-corruption specialists. Rather it examines when and how the use of human rights might improve performance in certain areas; it will also identity the limits of a human rights approach to corruption. The goal is to provide an operational framework for applying human rights principles and methods to anti-corruption programmes.

While it is important to develop a clear description of the conceptual links between human rights and corruption, a conceptual model alone will not be enough. It is now widely accepted that to effectively combat corruption and design appropriate policies it is essential to deal with corrupt practices in the private sector and increasingly accepted that human rights law should apply to private companies. There is a significant connection that exists between corruption, human rights, and the private sector. Corruption by private companies is without doubt directly relevant to the study of public or official corruption. This is already widely understood by those involved in "corporate social responsibility" ("CSR"). The CSR initiative of the United Nations, the Global Compact, also contains an Anti-Corruption Principle: "Business should work against corruption in all its forms, including extortion and bribery." This principle was not enunciated when the Global Compact was launched in 2000 at the behest of United Nations. It became the Compact's "tenth principle" in 2004, after it was realised that work on this issue was essential. Companies that participate in the Compact had to oppose corruption in their strategy, culture, and day-to-day operations.

The degree of attention now paid to corruption leads naturally to the question of why. Why so much attention now? Is it because there is more corruption than in the past? Or is it because more attention is being paid to a phenomenon that had always existed but had been largely, though not completely, ignored? The answer is not obvious, and there are no reliable statistics that would make possible a definitive answer. Several arguments can be advanced that suggest that corruption is simply attracting more attention now than in the past.

Understanding Corruption

Corruption has been defined in many different ways, each lacking in some aspect. A few years ago, the question of definition absorbed a large proportion of the time spent on discussions of corruption at conferences and meetings. However, like an elephant, while it may be difficult to describe, corruption is generally not difficult to recognize when observed. In most cases, different observers would agree on whether a particular behaviour connotes corruption. Unfortunately, the behaviour is often difficult to observe because acts of corruption do not typically take place in broad daylight. The most popular and simplest definition of corruption is that it is the abuse of public power for private benefit. This is the definition used by the World Bank.

From this definition it should not be concluded that corruption cannot exist within private sector activities. Especially in large private enterprises, corruption clearly does exist, as for example in procurement or even in hiring. It also exists in private activities regulated by the government. Sometimes, the abuse of public power is not necessarily for one's private benefit but for the benefit of one's party, class, tribe, friends, family, and so on. In fact, in many countries some proceeds of corruption go to finance the activities of the political parties.

Not all acts of corruption result in the payment of bribes. For example, a public employee who claims to be sick but goes on vacation is abusing his public position for personal use. Thus, he is engaging in an act of corruption even though no bribe is paid. The president of a country who has an airport built in his small hometown is also engaging in an act of corruption that does not involve the payment of a bribe. It is important to distinguish bribes from gifts. In many instances, bribes can be disguised as gifts. A bribe implies reciprocity while a gift should not.

However, even though the distinction is fundamental, it is at times difficult to make. At what point does a gift become a bribe? Does the distinction depend on the size of the gift? What about cultural differences that can explain different sizes of gifts? What if a large gift is given not to the person who provides the favour but to a relative of that person? Does the distinction depend on whether the gift is given in broad daylight, for every-one to see, or privately? Clearly, the identification of a bribe is not always simple. Acts of corruption can be classified in different categories. Corruption can be:

1. bureaucratic (or "petty") or political (or "grand"); for example, corruption by the bureaucracy or by the political leadership;
2. cost-reducing (to the briber) or benefit enhancing;
3. briber-initiated or bribee-initiated;
4. coercive or collusive;
5. centralized or decentralized;
6. predictable or arbitrary; and
7. involving cash payments or not.

Undoubtedly, other classifications could be added to this list.

Factors Contributing to Corruption

Corruption is generally connected with the activities of the state and especially with the monopoly and discretionary power of the state. Therefore, as Gary Becker, Nobel Laureate in economics, pointed out in one of his Business Week columns, if we abolish the state, we abolish corruption (Becker, 1968: 201). But, of course, quite apart from the fact that corruption can exist in the private sector, a civilized society cannot function without a state, and in modem, advanced societies, the state must have many functions. The Becker argument seems to collide with the reality that some of the least corrupt countries in the world, such as Canada, Denmark, Finland, the Netherlands, and Sweden, have some of the largest public sectors, measured as shares of tax revenue or public spending in gross domestic product. Thus, the solution to the problem of corruption may not be as simple as just reducing the level of taxation or public spending. Rather, the way the state operates and carries out its functions is far more important than the size of public sector activity measured in the traditional way. Particular aspects of governmental activities create a fertile ground for corruption.

Regulations and Authorizations

In many countries, and especially in developing countries, the role of the state is often carried out through the use of numerous rules or regulations. In these countries, licenses, permits, and authorizations of various sorts are required to engage in many activities. Opening a shop and keeping it open, borrowing money, investing, driving a car, owning a car, building a house, engaging in foreign trade, obtaining foreign exchange, getting a passport, going abroad, and so on require specific documents or authorizations. Often several government offices must be contacted to authorize the activity. The existence of these regulations and authorizations gives a kind of monopoly power to the officials who must authorize or inspect the activities. These officials may refuse the authorizations or may simply sit on a decision for months or even years. Thus, they can use their public power to extract bribes from those who need the authorizations or permits. In India, for example, the expression "licence raj" referred to the individual who sold the permits needed to engage in many forms of economic activities. In some countries, individuals become middlemen or facilitators for obtaining these permits. The fact that in some cases the regulations are non transparent or are not even publicly available and that an authorization can be obtained only from a specific office or individual—that is, there is no competition in the granting of these authorizations— gives the bureaucrats a great amount of power and a good opportunity to extract bribes.

The existence of these regulations generates the need for frequent contacts between citizens and bureaucrats. It also requires an enormous amount of time to be spent by the citizens in acquiring these permits and in dealing with public officials. Surveys from different countries and especially from developing and transition countries indicate that much of the time of the managers of enterprises, and especially of small enterprises, is spent dealing with public bureaucracies. This time that is taken away from managing the enterprises can be reduced through the payment of bribes.

Taxation

Taxes based on clear laws and not requiring contacts between taxpayers and tax inspectors are much less likely to lead to acts of corruption. However, when the following situations arise, corruption is likely to be a major problem in tax and customs administrations (Tanzi, 1998: 120):

1. the laws are difficult to understand and can be interpreted differently so that taxpayers need assistance in complying with them;
2. the payment of taxes requires frequent contacts between taxpayers and tax administrators;
3. the wages of the tax administrators are low;
4. acts of corruption on the part of the tax administrators are ignored, not easily discovered, or when discovered penalized only mildly;
5. the administrative procedures(e .g., the criteria for the selection of tax-payers for audits) lack transparency and are not closely monitored within the tax or customs administrations;

6. tax administrators have discretion over important decisions, such as those related to the provision of tax incentives, determination of tax liabilities, selection of audits, litigations, and so on; and

7. more broadly, the controls from the state (the principal) on the agents charged with carrying out its functions are weak.

Reports from several countries indicate that the number of applicants for poorly paid jobs in administering taxes or in customs has been unusually large, pointing to the possibility that applicants know these jobs create opportunities for extra incomes.

Spending Decisions

Corruption can also affect public expenditure. Investment projects have lent themselves to frequent acts of high-level corruption. Because of the discretion that some high-level public officials have over decisions regarding public investment projects, this type of public spending can become much distorted, both in size and in composition, by corruption (Tanzi and Davoodi, 1997).

Public projects have, at times, been carried out specifically to provide opportunities to some individuals or political groups to get "commissions" from those who are chosen to execute the projects. This has reduced the productivity of such expenditure and has resulted in projects that would not have been justified on objective criteria of investment selection such as cost-benefit analysis.

Procurement spending, that is, the purchase of goods and services on the part of the government, is another area affected by corruption. To reduce corruption possibilities, some countries have developed complex and costly procedures that may have reduced corruption at the cost of sharply increasing the prices at which some goods are purchased.

Extra budgetary accounts are common in many countries. Some of them have legitimacy and are set up for specific purposes (pension funds, road funds, etc.). Others are set up to reduce the political and administrative controls that are more likely to accompany spending that goes through the budget. In some countries, the money received from foreign aid or from the sale of natural resources such as oil is channelled toward special accounts that tend to be less transparent and less controlled than the money channelled through the budget.

Some of this money may go into illegitimate uses or pockets. In all these areas, lack of transparency and of effective institutional controls is the main factors leading to corruption.

Below-Market Price Provisions

In most countries, the government engages in the provision of goods, services, and resources at below-market prices for example, electricity, water, public housing, some rationed goods, access to educational and health facilities, access to public land, and so on. Even access to some forms of pensions, such as those for disability, fall into this category because the individuals who get them have paid less in contributions to the pension funds over time than the pension they get once their disability status is approved.

Sometimes, because of limited supply, rationing or queuing becomes unavoidable. Excess demand is created and decisions have to be made to apportion the limited supply. These decisions are often made by public employees. Those who want these goods (the users) would be willing to pay a bribe to get access (or a higher access) to what the government is providing. It is thus not surprising that in all these areas cases of corruption have been reported.

Besides, public officials in many countries can find themselves in positions where they have discretion over important decisions; in these situations, corruption, including high-level or political corruption, can play a major role.

Indirect Causes of Corruption

Besides the factors that promote corruption directly, other factors can contribute to corruption indirectly. *Quality of the Bureaucracy*: The quality of the bureaucracy varies greatly among countries. In some, public sector jobs give a lot of prestige and status; in others, much less so. Many factors contribute to that quality. Many years ago Max Weber (1947), the German sociologist, described what should be the characteristics of an ideal bureaucracy. He was aware that most bureaucracies are not ideal. Tradition and the effect that it has on the pride that individuals have in working for the government may explain why, all things being equal, some bureaucracies are much more efficient and much less vulnerable to corruption than others. Rauch and Evans (1997) have gathered information on the degree to which civil servants' recruitment and promotions are merit based for 35 developing countries. Their results indicate that the less recruitment and promotion are based on merit, the higher is the extent of corruption.

Absence of politically motivated hiring, patronage, and nepotism, and clear rules on promotions and hiring, all contribute to the quality of a bureaucracy. The incentive structure plus tradition go a long way toward explaining why some bureaucracies are much less corrupt than others.

Level of Public Sector Wages

Over the years many observers have speculated that the wages paid to civil servants are important in determining the degree of corruption. For example, Assar Lindbeck (1998: 160) attributes the low corruption in Sweden in this century partly to the fact that at the turn of the century, high-level administrators earned 12-15 times the salary of an average industrial worker. One can speculate that there may be corruption due to greed and corruption due to need. Regardless of the wage level, some public officials will be corrupt perhaps because of their own psychological or moral makeup, or because some of the bribes offered may be too large for some officials to resist. Thus, it implies, realistically, that not all officials respond in the same way to the same incentives. In theoretical jargon, agents are heterogeneous.

The relationship between wage level and corruption index has been tested empirically by Rijckeghem and Weder (1997) and, also, Haque and Sahay (1996). With the use of cross-sectional data, they have been able to support the common intuition by finding a statistically significant relationship between corruption and wage levels. They have speculated that while an increase in the wage level is likely to reduce corruption, a very large increase would be necessary to reduce it to minimal levels. In other words, the fight against corruption, pursued exclusively on the basis of wage increases, can be very costly to the budget of a country and can achieve only part of the objective. Furthermore, even at high wages some individuals may continue to engage in corrupt practices.

In recent years, several countries (Argentina, Peru, etc.) have attempted to reduce corruption in particularly sensitive areas, such as customs and tax administrations, by increasing the level of salaries for the public employees in these areas. These countries have also increased salary differentials to be able to retain and attract more able, productive, and honest individuals. Over the years, Singapore has pursued a wage policy aimed at reducing the temptation for public officials to engage in acts of corruption. Reportedly, the salaries of ministers and other high-level officials in Singapore are among the highest in the world. A common belief is that in situations of low wages but high possibilities of corruption, less honest individuals will be attracted to the civil service.

Penalty Systems

Following Gary Becker's (1968: 205) classic analysis of crime prevention, given the probability that the perpetrator of a crime would be caught, the penalty imposed plays an important role in determining the probability that criminal or illegal acts would take place (Tulden, van and van der Torre, 1997: 69). In theory, all things being equal, corruption could be reduced by increasing the penalties on those who get caught. This analysis implies that the penalty structure existing in a country is an important factor in determining the extent of corruption in that country. But once again, at least theoretically, higher penalties may reduce the number of acts of corruption, but they may lead to demands for higher bribes on the corrupt acts that still take place. In the real world, relatively few people are punished for acts of corruption, in spite of the extent of the phenomenon.

Furthermore, with the exception of a few countries, there seems to be a wide gap between the penalties specified in the laws and regulations and the penalties that are effectively imposed. Many acts of corruption also go unpunished, so that uncertainty prevails on the treatment of individuals accused of corruption. This may lead to the perception that penalties are applied selectively or arbitrarily. Generally, effective penalties tend to be more lenient than the statutory ones. The administrative procedures followed before a public employee is punished for acts of corruption are slow and cumbersome. Often legal, political, or administrative impediments prevent the full or quick application of the penalties. Due process and the need to provide incontrovertible evidence are major hurdles. The potential accusers are often reluctant to come forward and to spend the time and effort to go through the full process required to punish someone.

Also, when corruption is widespread, the costs to the accusers in terms of social capital, such as lost friends, can be high. Even in countries with relatively little corruption, so-called "whistle blowers" do not seem to have an easy time. Furthermore, the judges who will impose the penalties may themselves be accessible to corruption or may have political biases, so that they may be bought by the accused or may put obstacles in the way of the proceedings. All these factors limit the role that penalties actually play in many countries, especially when corruption is partly politically motivated. Reluctance to apply harsh penalties may also be due to concerns that the penalties might be applied selectively, to political opponents. This attitude brings toleration for small acts of corruption that can in time encourage bigger acts.

Examples by the Leadership

A final contributing factor is the example provided by the leadership. When the top political leaders do not provide the right example, either because they engage in acts of corruption or, as is more often the case, because they condone such acts on the part of relatives, friends, or political associates, it cannot be expected that the employees in the public administration will behave differently. The same argument applies within particular institutions such as tax administration, customs, and public enterprises. These institutions cannot be expected to be corruption free if their heads do not provide the best examples of honesty.

In some countries, the leadership has been somewhat indifferent o this problem. In an African country, a president refused to fire ministers widely reputed to be corrupt.

In an Asian country, a minister that was accused of corruption was simply moved to head another ministry. In a Latin American country, a president who was planning to create an anticorruption commission proposed to appoint as head of this commission an individual widely reported to be corrupt. Examples such as these do not help create the climate for a corruption-free society.

If corruption could be measured, it could probably be eliminated. In fact, conceptually it is not even clear what one would want to measure. Simply measuring bribes paid would ignore many corrupt acts that are not accompanied by the payment of bribes. An attempt to measure acts of corruption rather than the amounts of bribes paid would require counting many relatively unimportant actions and identifying each act—information that is simply not available. While there are no direct ways of measuring corruption, there are several indirect ways of getting information about its prevalence in a country or in an institution. Useful information can be obtained from the reports on corruption available from published sources including news-papers. And also, it can be obtained from the case studies of corrupt agencies such as tax administrations, customs, and police. Unfortunately, while there are many such studies, often the reports are internal and are kept confidential.

Economic Effects of Corruption

The recent fairly broad consensus seems to be that corruption is unqualifiably bad. However, in past years, the views on corruption had been more divergent and some economists had even found some redeeming value in it. Economist like Braguinsky (1996: 20) argues that, within well confined circumstances, corruption may promote faster growth. Until the 1997 financial crisis, some countries from Southeast Asia seemed to provide support for the view that corruption might promote growth. Thus, corruption "oils the mechanism" or "greases the wheel" This reasoning was often used to explain the high rates of growth in some countries of South East Asia.

Beck and Maher (1986) and Lien (1986) have developed models that show that, in bidding competitions, those who are most efficient can afford to offer the highest bribe. Therefore, bribes can promote efficiency by assigning projects to the most efficient firms. Lui (1985: 776) has argued that time has different values for different individuals, depending on their level of income and the opportunity cost of their time. Those for whom time is most valuable will offer bribes to public officials to be allowed to economize on time by jumping in front of the line, that is, by getting decisions more quickly. Thus, corruption can be efficient because it saves time for those for whom time has the greatest value. While corruption may improve the allocation of resources in some circumstances, it reduces growth because it provides some individuals the incentive to acquire the kind of human capital that can be used to improve corruption opportunities (Lui, 1996: 27).

The argument which seemingly favours corruption can be countered in many ways. First, rigidities and rules are not exogenous and unmovable features of a society; a society is not born with these rigidities. They are created, and, in fact, they may be intentionally created by public officials, to extract bribes. When rules can be used to extract bribes, more rules will be created. Furthermore, these rules are often kept intentionally opaque so that more power will remain on the side of those who enforce them. Knowledge gives power to those who have it.

Second, those who can pay the highest bribes are not necessarily the most economically efficient but rather the most successful at rent seeking. If bribes are seen as investments, those who pay them must consider that they are investments with a high rate of return.

Third, payment of speed money may be an inducement for the bureaucrats to reduce the speed at which most practices are being processed. Bribes may change the order in which public officials perform the process, say, of providing permits, but they may also slow down the average time for the whole process (Myrdal, 1968: 107). And while corruption and rent seeking may be helpful as political glue or as wage supplements in the short run, they may lead to major problems over the longer run.

Qualitative Effects

Corruption reduces public revenue and increases public spending. It thus contributes to larger fiscal deficits, making it more difficult for the government to run a sound fiscal policy. Corruption is likely to increase income inequality because it allows well-positioned individuals to take advantage of government activities at the cost of the rest of the population. There are strong indications that the changes in income distribution that have occurred in recent years in previously centrally planned economies have partly been the result of corrupt actions such as privatisation. Corruption distorts markets and the allocation of resources for the following reasons, and is therefore likely to reduce economic efficiency and growth:

1. It reduces the ability of the government to impose necessary regulatory controls and inspections to correct the market failures.
2. It distorts incentives. In a corrupt environment, able individuals allocate their energies to corrupt practices and not to productive activities.
3. It reduces the fundamental role of the government in such areas as enforcement of contracts and protection of property rights.
4. It reduces the legitimacy of the market economy and perhaps also of democracy. Thus, corruption may slow down or even block the movement toward democracy and a market economy.
5. Finally, corruption is likely to increase poverty because it reduces the income earning potential of the poor.

Indian Context

Corruption in India has I attracted much commentary given the large number of members in Parliament and state legislative assemblies facing criminal charges. More recently, Kaushik Basu, the chief economic adviser in the ministry of finance, has proposed that bribe givers in a particular class of bribery cases be given immunity from prosecution to encourage more "whistleblowing" (Panagaria, 2011). Given that the proposal has come under fire mostly for the wrong reasons, a more careful examination of it is required.

Economists distinguish between two types of bribes: Type 1 given to (often low-level) bureaucrats to do what they are supposed to do and Type 2 given to (usually high-level) public officials and politicians to do what they are not supposed to do. In the former case, the bribe giver is the victim with no loss to the state; in the latter case, he is a partner in crime and shares in the profits created by defrauding the state.

Thus, when a railway official extracts a payment over and above the price of a train ticket to issue the ticket, he is taking a bribe for a service legitimately due to the passenger. This is a Type 1 bribe. If, instead, the official takes a bribe and lets the passenger travel with no ticket issued, he and the passenger jointly benefit by defrauding the state. This is a Type 2 bribe. The 2G, Adarsh Society and Commonwealth Games scandals are the more high-profile examples in this category.

The proposal by Basu would make giving (but not receiving) Type 1 bribes legal. He calls these bribes "harassment bribes," which is a misnomer since all bribes involve harassment of the citizenry *vis-a-vis* a smooth-functioning corruption-free state. The rationale behind the proposal is that such legalisation will free bribe givers from the fear of prosecution and lead them to massively report the corrupt officials to the appropriate authorities. Indeed, one can go a step further and argue that, anticipating the increased prospects of being reported, public officials might stop extracting bribes in the first place.

But this seemingly plausible argument is flawed on three counts:

> First, getting service from a government office is not a one-time affair; in most cases, a citizen must repeatedly return to the same office for the service. Therefore, a potential whistleblower must consider the impact his action will have on his ability to access the same service in the future. Two factors make it likely that he will suffer on this count. One, given the slow pace with which our administrative and judicial system moves, whistle blowing will result in either no action or very slow action. Therefore, the probability that the whistleblower will find the same official behind the desk when he returns for the service is high. Two, Type 1 cases overwhelmingly involve low-level public officials who are highly organised in India. Therefore, even if a particular official is successfully suspended on charges of bribery, the successor officer, in solidarity with other members of his service, will retaliate by denying the whistleblower the service the next time the latter returns.

Second, even assuming that whistle blowing does not impair future access to the service, the potential whistleblower must take into account the cost incurred in delivering testimony to the courts. In our legal system, officials charged with bribery can themselves use Type 2 bribes *in* the lower courts and in any case exploit multiple appeals to delay the decision for years. This means that the whistleblower must be prepared to spend a great deal of time and personal expense to see the case through.

Add to this the non-negligible probability of the accused official sending goons to inflict violence on him and his family and the option of paying the petty bribe each time without blowing the whistle begins to look attractive. It is presumably for these reasons that a law exempting bribe givers from prosecution in the Philippines, which has been on the books since 1975, has been rarely used.

Finally, there is even a possibility that the immunity from prosecution would increase rather than decrease the incidence of bribes. Under the current system, at least someone like me is afraid to offer a bribe for fear that the official behind the desk might turn out to be honest with embarrassing consequences. But once the proposed immunity is in place, everyone will feel free to offer the bribe rather than go an extra mile to avoid it. Indeed, those able to afford it will likely openly compete with offers of ever-higher bribes to get ahead in the queue.

What then can India do to combat Type 1 bribes? Three avenues come to mind. First, NGOs and the press may be mobilised to more vigorously blow the whistle on corrupt officials. Second, we must push for administrative and judicial reforms for better enforcement of laws against bribes. Finally, it is important continue to expand the use of technology, which allows customers to access services electronically as, for example, is the case with respect to the sale of railway tickets.

Alternatives and Conclusion

This paper has discussed the phenomenon of corruption which affects many countries. It has highlighted the damages that it brings to economies and democracies. When corruption is wide-spread and especially when it contaminates the actions of the policymakers in democratic, market-oriented economies, it becomes more difficult to argue in favour of such economic and political arrangements. (It should be remembered that many dictators or potential dictators make the fight against corruption as one of the reasons why they should be given the reigns of a country. The disillusion among the population of some economies in transition and some developing countries with both market economies and democratic processes is very much caused by the widespread corruption that prevails in these countries and is wrongly attributed to the market economy and the democratic process.

As has been argued that corruption is closely linked to the way governments conduct their affairs in modern societies, and therefore also to the growth of some of the government's activities in the economy. It is unlikely that corruption can be substantially reduced without modifying the way governments operate. The fight against corruption is, thus, intimately linked with the reform of the state. In any case, any serious strategy to attempt to reduce corruption will need action on at least four fronts:

1. Honest and visible commitment by the leadership to the fight against corruption, for which the leadership must show zero tolerance;
2. Policy changes that reduce the demand for corruption by scaling down regulations and by making those that are retained with transparency and nondiscretionary as possible;
3. Reducing corruption by increasing public sector wages, increasing incentives toward honest behaviour, and instituting effective controls and penalties on the public servants; and
4. Solving the problem especially of financing of political parties.

Societies can do much to reduce the intensity of corruption, but no single action will achieve more than a limited improvement and some of the necessary actions may require major changes in existing policies.

It may be necessary to point out here that Mahatma Gandhi (Naik, 2000:18) while commenting on need for social reform in India to have corruption free and just society suggested conscious decisions by the citizens to avoid the following *social sins* in society: 1. Politics without Principles; 2. Commerce without Morality; 3. Wealth without Work; 4. Education without Character; 5. Science without Humanity; 6. Pleasure without Conscience; 7. Worship without Sacrifice.

Corruption is essentially an activity carried out by groups with power. Therefore, in order to design and implement effective anti-corruption policies, one must identify and analyse the relationship between corrupt practices and the different ways power operates in that society. From this perspective, the conceptual framework and the tools for studying and confronting corruption should incorporate a structural perspective of power that can explain the social causes that allow certain groups of people, governments and companies to control others economically, politically and socially.

In this approach, corruption is not seen as a selfish act—isolated and opportunistic— but rather a profoundly social activity, shaped by cultural notions of power, privileges and social status. When this structural perspective of power is used as a lens, corruption can be addressed as an instrument that helps to define, sustain, expand or reduce the social order on the basis of unequal relationships between polar categories of people: men and women, heterosexual and homosexual, Dalit and non-Dalit, dominant and minority group, etc. Then, these categories are included in social rankings: good and bad, right and wrong, normal and abnormal, in order to finally link these concepts to biology to imply that rankings are fixed, permanent and embedded in nature.

Within this social framework, corruption benefits those with access to power, while it affects and victimises mainly those who suffer discrimination (Weber, 2004: 128) on the basis of race, gender, handicap, sexuality, ethnic origin, etc.

REFERENCES

[1] Beck, Paul J. and Michael W. Maher (1986). "A Comparison of Bribery and Bidding in Thin Markets," *Economic Letters*, Vol. 20, No. 1, pp. 1–5.

[2] Becker, Gary S. (1968). "Crime and Punishment: An Economic Approach," *Journal of Political Economy*, Vol. 76 (March/April), pp. 169–217.

[3] Becker, Gary S., and George J. Stigler (1974). "Law Enforcement, Malfeasance, and Compensation for Employees," *Journal of Legal Studies* (January), pp. 1–18.

[4] Braguinsky, Serguey (1996). "Corruption and Schumpeterian Growth in Different Economic Environments," *Contemporary Economic Policy*, Vol. 14 (July), pp. 14–25.

[5] Global Compact, see www.globalcompact.org/AboutTheGC/index.html. Accesses on 27/5/2011.

[6] Haque, Nadeem and Ratna Sahay (1996). "Do Government Wages Cuts Close Budget Deficits? Costs of Corruption," Staff Papers, International Monetary Fund, Vol. 43 (December), pp. 754–78.

[7] Lien, Da Hsiang Donald (1986). "A Note on Competitive Bribery Games," *Economic Letters*, Vol. 22, No. 4, pp. 337–41.

[8] Lindbeck, Assar (1998). *Swedish Lessons for Post-Socialist Countries,* Stockholm, University of Stockholm Institute for International Economic Studies.

[9] Lui, Francis T. (1985). "An Equilibrium Queuing Model of Bribery," *Journal of Political Economy*, Vol. 93 (August), pp. 760–81.

[10] Lui, Francis T. (1996). "Three Aspects of Corruption," *Contemporary Economic Policy*, Vol. 14 (July), pp. 26–9.

[11] Lukes, S. (1974). *Power: A Radical View*, London, Macmillan

[12] Myrdal, Gunnar (1968). *Asian Drama: An Inquiry into the Poverty of Nations*, New York: Twentieth Century Fund.

[13] Naik, J.V. (2000). "Relevance of Gandhi" in S.N. Datye (ed), Rethinking Mahatma Gandhi: Relevance of Gandhian Thought and Leadership in 21ˢᵗ Century, Delhi, Kalinga Publication.

[14] Panagariya, Anrind (2011). 'The Art of Graft: It will take more than legalizing bribe giving to reduce petty corruption.' *The Times of India*, Mumbai, May 9, p. 18.

[15] Rauch, James E., and Peter B. Evans (1997). "Bureaucratic Structure and Bureaucratic Performance in Less Developed Countries", California; University of California.

[16] Rijckeghem, Van Caroline and Beatrice Weder (1997). "Corruption and the Rate of Temptation: Do Low Wages in the Civil Service Cause Corruption?" IMF Working Paper 97/73, Washington, International Monetary Fund.

[17] Tanzi, Vito (1998). "Corruption and the Budget: Problems and Solutions," in Arvind K. Jain (ed), *Economics of Corruption*, Boston, Massachusetts: Kluwer Academic Publishers, pp. 111–28.

[18] Tanzi, Vito and Hamid Davoodi (1997). "Corruption, Public Investment, and Growth," IMF Working Paper 97/139, Washington: International Monetary Fund.

[19] Tulden, van Frank, and Abraham van der Torre (1997). "Crime and the Criminal Justice System: An Economic Approach," paper presented at the 53rd Congress of the International Institute of Public Finance, Kyoto, Japan, August.

[20] Weber, L. (2004). "A conceptual framework for understanding race, class, gender, and sexuality". In Hesse Biber, S. and Yaiser, M. (ed.), *Feminist perspectives on social research*, Cambridge, Oxford University Press.

[21] Weber, Max (1947). *The Theory of Social and Economic Organization*, London: The Free Press of Glencoe.

Effects of Corruption on Human Rights

S. Saravana Kumar

Department Political Science, Gopi Arts and Science College, Gopichettipalayam, Tamil Nadu

INTRODUCTION

The term "corruption" comes from the Latin word *corruptio* which means "moral decay, wicked behaviour, putridity or rottenness". The concept may have a physical reference, as in "[t]he destruction or spoiling of anything, especially by disintegration or by decomposition with its attendant unwholesomeness and loathsomeness; putrefaction"; or moral significance, as in "moral deterioration or decay... [the] [p]erversion or destruction of integrity in the discharge of public duties by bribery or favour...".

These definitions are representative of two common shortcomings: they define corruption only in terms of bribery, or in terms that are very general. As a result, corruption definitions tend either to be too restrictive or excessively broad. In fact, this is not as contradictory as it may seem. Corruption has indeed broad causes and consequences. As Michael Johnston, a Professor at Colgate University, has stated: "In rapidly changing societies the limit between what is corrupt and what is not is not always clear and the term corruption may be applied broadly".

Corruption is a universal phenomenon. It is not something new either. Corruption in one form or another existed since time immemorial. A review of penal codes utilized in various ancient civilizations clearly demonstrate that bribery was a serious problem among the Jews, the Chinese, the Japanese, the Greeks, the Romans as well as the Aztees of the New World . In ancient India large-scale corruption dominated public life. As has been observed "corruption prevailed on a larger scale in India during the ancient period and the ones that followed". From this one can assume the nature and scale in the increase of corruption from medieval to the present time in the countries of the Indian sub-continent. One of the greatest evils of medieval administration in India was the extortion of perquisites and presents. Corruption was evident during the British rule in India. There was almost regular and systematic corruption involving almost all officials at different levels in the political and administrative hierarchy. There was an underlying belief among officials of "making hay while the sun of British Raj shone".

Fighting corruption has emerged as a key development issue in India in recent years. More and more policymakers, businesses, and civil society organizations, have begun to confront the issue openly. As per Transparency Internationals Corruption Perception Index India ranks 84th among 189 countries in the list of most corrupted country. Corruption has become a global threat with global effects; it has become challenge to the whole community of civilized nations.

Every one of us expects and aspires that our government should be good and effective. In fact, we also know that it was for the purpose of securing conditions for safe and happy life that the state came into existence and its continuity is justified in terms of promoting and preserving the quality of life. Kautilya considered it as the bounden duty of the government to act in a manner that realizes the material, mental, moral and cultural well being of the people.

The fight against corruption is central to the struggle for human rights. Corruption has always greased the wheels of the exploitation and injustice which characterize our world. From violent ethnic cleansing to institutionalized racism, political actors have abused their entrusted powers to focus on gains for the few at great cost for the many. For too long the anti-corruption and human rights movements have been working in parallel rather than tackling these problems together.

As identified in the ICHRP report, it is the vulnerable and marginalized—women, children and minority groups—who often suffer corruption's harshest consequences. In dealings with police, judges, hospitals, schools and other basic public services, poor citizens tend to suffer more violations than the rich and see a larger share of their resources eaten away. In Mexico, it is estimated that approximately 25 percent of the income earned by poor households is lost to petty corruption. Those with the least influence are left with little recourse against bribery. In Bangladesh, surveys show that nearly one-third of girls trying to enroll in a government stipend scheme for extremely poor students had to pay a bribe, while half had to make a 'payment' before collecting their awarded scholarship. In Madagascar, one-quarter of all households are forced to cover school 'enrolment' fees although all primary education is 'free'. These daily realities are a direct contravention of many human rights conventions, undermining basics principles such as non-discrimination that are enshrined in the UN Declaration of Human Rights (UDHR) and which have been expanded through the International Covenant on Civil and Political Rights (ICCPR) as well as subsequent international laws. Human rights conventions set out the legal obligations of a government, including ensuring that all people living in a country enjoy equality, a fair justice system, and access to goods and public services, among other rights. A government's ability to respect, protect and fulfil these rights—social, cultural, political, economic and civil—will ultimately be defined by the levels and systemic nature of corruption in those states.

Corruption affects the poor disproportionately, due to their powerlessness to change the status quo and inability to pay bribes,creating inequalities that violate their human rights. The Human Rights Based Approach (HRBA) with its main elements of Express Linkages to Rights, Accountability, Empowerment, Participation and Attention to Disadvantaged Groups, has been developed specifically to address these inequalities and to ensure that the poor and disadvantaged are also equal partners in development. However, if corruption creates fundamental inequalities in the poor's access to justice and to development services, the results envisaged by the HRBA cannot be achieved. Therefore, anti-corruption should be added to the main elements of the HRBA that have now generally been agreed upon. When applying a HRBA to accessing justice, it is even more crucial that issues of corruption in the justice sector be addressed as a priority. In this case, justice sector includes normative protection; implementation and enforcement including the judiciary, police and prisons; and empowerment mechanisms such as lawyers, civil society organizations and watchdog institutions. If there is corruption in any of these sectors, a HRBA to accessing justice cannot be successfully applied. Therefore, in developing strategies for Access to Justice Projects, there must be clear outcomes targeting both duty bearers and claim holders to tackle the issue of corruption.

In 1986, the United Nations declared that the right to development is an inalienable human right by virtue of which every human person and all peoples are entitled to participate in, contribute, and enjoy economic, social, cultural and political development, in which all human rights and fundamental freedoms can be fully realized. In 1997, UNDP research concluded that corruption has a pervasive and troubling impact on the poor, since it distorts public choices in favour of the wealthy and powerful, and reduces the state's ability to provide a social safety net. Such corruption would therefore interfere with the right to development, which is an inalienable right enjoyed by all people including the poor.

CORRUPTION AS A VIOLATION OF HUMAN RIGHTS

An analysis of corruption that draws on human rights will emphasize the harm to individuals that corruption causes. From this perspective, it is often taken for granted that corruption "violates" human rights. When people make this claim, they have a range of issues in mind. They mean that, when corruption is widespread, people do not have access to justice, are not secure and cannot protect their livelihoods. Court officials and the police pay more heed to bribes than to law. Hospitals do not heal people because the medical staff give better treatment to patients who pay backhanders or because clinics lack supplies due to corrupt public contracting procedures. Poor families cannot feed themselves because social security programmes are corrupt or distorted to support a patronage network. Schools cannot offer their students a sound education because the education budget has been looted and as a result teachers cannot be paid and books cannot be purchased. Farmers and market sellers cannot earn a living because police take a cut of their produce and sales. In numerous ways like these, corruption encourages discrimination, deprives vulnerable people of income, and prevents people from fulfilling their political, civil, social, cultural and economic rights.

UN treaty bodies and UN special procedures have concluded that, where corruption is widespread, states cannot comply with their human rights obligations. Some international documents have even considered corruption to be a "crime against humanity", a category of crimes that includes genocide and torture. However, these statements are generally framed in broad terms. The extent to which acts of corruption directly violate human rights, or lead to violations, is rarely defined or explained. Most existing work examines the causes of corruption, mechanisms and policies to prevent it, and forms of technical cooperation to assist developing countries and countries in economic transition. Little work has been done to describe in precise terms what the links are between acts of corruption and violations of human rights.

Every individual is entitled to be treated equally by public officials; and if a person bribes a public official, that person acquires a privileged status in relation to other similarly placed individuals who have not partaken in bribery. Similarly, when a person is asked for a bribe in order to obtain a service to which that person is entitled without payment, that person suffers discrimination in relation to other individuals in the same situation. There is a violation of the right in both examples because similar cases are treated in a different manner and the difference in treatment results from corruption which is not an objective or reasonable justification.

Corrupt practices commonly produce unequal and discriminatory outcomes with regard to human rights. If corruption restricts a person's access to adequate housing, for instance, it is discriminatory. Housing should be accessible to all, and disadvantaged groups in particular should be granted some degree of priority. After eviction, people are often promised alternative housing, but they may subsequently be denied effective access because the officials in charge require bribes. Well-intentioned low cost housing programmes, designed to benefit disadvantaged groups, may be exploited to the economic advantage of officials in the same way.

Corruption in the health sector often violates the right to equality and nondiscrimination.

As described below, when bribes are requested from patients, their access to health is severely restricted; in such cases, states have a duty to act at once to ensure that the right to health can be accessed without discrimination. An interesting link between bribes paid to health workers and the accessibility and quality requirements of health services may be noted here. Sometimes, when a payment or gift is made to a health worker, it is difficult to say whether the purpose of the payment was to obtain treatment, to save time, to ensure proper treatment by corrupt means, or to express gratitude. There is a fine line here that should be analysed carefully. First of all, if a bribe was extorted by the health worker, or given as a condition of receiving adequate healthcare, the right to health has been violated. By contrast, secondly, if the payment was made out of gratitude or to obtain a superior quality of treatment, what matters is whether the patient would have received care to a good standard whether or not she made the payment or gift. Third, the difficulty remains that, even in such a situation, the right to equality (the prohibition on discrimination) applies in all cases. As a result, even if the bribe or informal payment has no effect on the treatment received, or on access to treatment, corrupt acts may still technically violate the right to health.

Corrupt practices in the education sector harm the availability of education. Most notably, embezzlement removes resources required to equip educational institutions. *Accessibility* implies that education should be accessible to everyone without discrimination. It refers not only to physical but also economic access. In this context, all education should be affordable, and primary education should be free. *Acceptability* requires that the form and content of education programmes should be acceptable to students and parents (in terms of relevance, cultural appropriateness and quality). *Adaptability* implies that education should adapt to the needs of societies as they change.

Corruption is frequent in the education sector. In most countries, educational institutions occupy a large place in the public sector. This creates many opportunities and incentives for corruption. Frequent forms of abuse include: rigged tenders and bids; embezzlement of funds; illegal registration fees; absenteeism; and examination fraud.

Most corrupt practices in the education sector infringe one or more elements of the right to education. Corruption may restrict access to education in many ways. Children may be requested to make informal payments for services, for example, or required to pay a bribe on admission, or parents may be asked to pay the teacher fees for additional private lessons (covering material from the core curriculum that should be taught during the school day) or for correcting their child's work. In such cases, access to education is not based on equality but on ability to pay a bribe, which amounts to discrimination and puts vulnerable groups at particular disadvantage because they are least able to pay. All corrupt practices that entail the disbursement of money for primary education violate the right to education, because primary education should be free.

Corruption that harms the quality of education affects its acceptability. Corruption in procurement affects the acquisition of educational material, meals, buildings, and equipment, and usually lowers their quality. Corruption of recruitment procedures may result in the appointment of less qualified teachers, lowering the standard of education that pupils receive. These effects infringe the right to education. Corruption in the education system may discriminate against girl children and limit their opportunities. For example, when families living in poverty have to pay a bribe to send their children to school, many will prioritise the education of their male children at their daughters' expense, for religious, socio-cultural or economic reasons.

In a democracy like India, it is difficult to conceal corruption; instead, it is publicly debated, discussed, and examined. Opposition parties can cite the corruption of the previous government to gain political advantage, and this is the main reason for the government changing hands so frequently between so many political parties in India. It is evident from India's history that "corruption is a political problem that has far-reaching economic consequences: opportunities are lost, innovation is deferred, and entrepreneurialism and investment are aborted" (7).

In a large democracy like India, the people ultimately hold the power through their voting rights. When the people feel that the government is not committing to policies that increase economic growth, they express their disapproval for the government by voting for a new regime. Although India has had trouble reaching out and making the polls more accessible to voters in rural regions, there has recently been greater awareness of the problem, and many villages have agencies set up to relay feedback to the national government about the performance of the local governments to ensure accountability.

India's success at unifying a diverse secular state through democratic means is one of the great political achievements of the twentieth century. Information disclosure, an important component of any democracy, makes corruption difficult to hide and enhances economic performance. Corruption has plagued India for many years, causing successive governments to fail. However, these corruptions are ultimately exposed, and the voters will respond by making politicians pay when they have the chance.

REFERENCES

[1] Ades, Alberto and Rafael di Tella. "The Causes and Consequences of Corruption: A Review of Recent Empirical Contributions," IDS Bulletin, 27, No. 2, (1996).

[2] Alam, M. Shahid, "Some Economic Costs of Corruption in LDCs," *Journal of Development Studies* (1991).

[3] All India Reporter (AIR). SC 870 "State of Madhya Pradesh v. Shri Ram Singh", April 2000.

[4] Bardhan, Pranab. "Corruption and Development: A Review of Issues," *Journal of Economic Literature,* 35 (1997).

[5] Building a Global Coalition against Corruption: Transparency International Report 1995 (Berlin: Transparency International, 1995).

[6] Coolidge, Jacqueline and Susan Rose-Ackerman. High level Rent-seeking and Corruption in African Regimes: Theory and cases (Washington D.C.: World Bank, 1997).

[7] Doig, Alan, and Robin Theobold, Corruption and Democratisation (London: Frank Cass, 1999).

[8] Heidenheimer, Arnold J. Political Corruption: A Handbook (New Brunswick: Transaction Publishers, 1989).

[9] Elliot, Kimberly (Ed.). Corruption and Global Economy (Washington DC: Institute of International Economics, 1997).

[10] Gill, S.S., The Pathology of Corruption (New Delhi: Harper Collins, 1998).

[11] Girling, John. Corruption, Capitalism and Democracy (London: Routledge, 1997).

[12] Farooq, Omer. "India Corruption Row Halts Food Aid." 1 May 2003. <http://news.bbc.co.uk/1/hi/world/south_asia/2212217.stm>

[13] "India." 1 May 2003. <http://www.worldrover.com/history/india_history.html>

[14] "India: Organized Crime, Political Corruption and Underground Banking." 1 May 2003.

[15] <http://democracy.ru/english/library/international/eng_1999-6/page4.html>.

[16] Root, Hilton L. "India: Asia's Next Tiger?" 1 May 2003. <http://www-hoover.stanford.edu/publications/epp/82/b.html>.

[17] Roy, Bunker. "The Right to Information and India's Struggle against Grass-Roots Corruption." 1 May 2003. <http://www.un.org/Pubs/chronicle/2000/ issue1/0100p 86.htm>

Corruption and Human Rights in Indian Context: An Overview[1]

Janmejay Sahu

Project Officer in Keonjhar, Odisha - Magic Bus India Foundation
E-mail: janmejaysahu23@gmail.com

ABSTRACT

To examine the corruption and human rights in Indian context, it is very essential to look into the nature and behavior of the people of India as well as the people working under the governance system of the country having lack of the accountability as well as responsibility that creates a space for the corruption and violence of human right. Now, it is unfortunate that while a section of civil society are taking up the corruption issues and bringing remedies such as a Draft Jan Lok Pal Bill by Anna Hazare and others, many political parties including the ruling party in the Government of India are neither directly opposing nor indirectly giving a clear path for its actual mean that is a big concern/threat in India. So, it is clear that in India where on the one side, large of people are struggling to get a square of meal per a day and on the other side, a section people are enjoying with black money that really is an irony which affect the human rights of the larger section of the society. This paper critically examines scenario of corruption and its consequences that fingers towards the violation of human rights. It argues that the corruption has been affecting human rights of the people. The paper shall also highlights the various dimensions of the increasing corruption practices and violation of human rights in India.

INTRODUCTION

The motto of the National Human Rights Commission is "Sarve Bhavantu Sukhinah". Happiness and health for all is sought to be achieved through a rights-based regime

---

[1]The Full paper is submitted for the Two-Day National Seminar on Corruption and Human Rights", organised by Department of Political Science, Presidency College (Autonomous), Chennai, Tamilnadu-600005.

where respect for human beings and their dignity is cardinal. The Constitution of India provides the basic framework for this rights based regime. The constitutional framework is complemented by several legislations and institutional mechanisms that serve to respect, protect and promote human rights. The National Human Rights Commission of India was set up in 1993 for "better protection of human rights and for matters connected therewith or incidental thereto". It is a statutory and autonomous body, which works independently. It has full financial and functional autonomy and has a wide mandate.

Human rights are fundamental to the stability and development of countries all around the world. Great emphasis has been placed on international conventions and their implementation in order to ensure adherence to a universal standard of acceptability. Right to food or food security, Right to education, Right to health, hygiene and sanitation, Custodial justice, Human rights issues of Scheduled Castes (SCs) and Scheduled Tribes (STs), Right to culture and protection of Community Assets and right to life, living conditions and nature of responsibility of Government and Panchayat/logal Government are some of the fundamental right which should be ensured for its smooth implementation. Unfortunately, It is frequantly observed in India that particularly in these areas people are suffering a lot due to increasing of corruption practices in all levels of the governance.

With the advent of globalization and the introduction of new technology, these principles gain importance not only in protecting human beings from the ill-effects of change but also in ensuring that all are allowed a share of the benefits. However the efficacy of the mechanisms in place today has been questioned in the light of blatant human rights violations and disregard for basic human dignity in India in one or more forms.

HUMAN RIGHTS

Human rights are rights inherent to all human beings, whatever the nationality, place of residence, sex, national or ethnic origin, colour, religion, language, or any other status. The people are all equally entitled to human rights without discrimination. These rights are all interrelated, interdependent and indivisible. Human rights are "rights and freedoms to which all humans are entitled." Proponents of the concept usually assert that everyone is endowed with certain entitlements merely by reason of being human.[2]

The concept of human rights can be found as far back in time as the age of the Greek philosophers Socrates, Plato and Aristotle. Their writings on the idea of natural law

---

[2]Feldman, David (1993). *Civil liberties and human rights in England and Wales.* Oxford: Clarendon Press. p. 5.

contain many of the same principles that are associated with human rights. The Magna Carta (1215) is considered a milestone in the history of human rights and several great thinkers such as Grotius, Hobbes, Locke, Rousseau and Kant talk about the concept. Human rights approach is critically about empowering groups that are exposed to particular risks. The human rights framework emphasises explicitly that vulnerable and disadvantaged groups must be protected from abuse.

Universal human rights are often expressed and guaranteed by law, in the forms of treaties, customary international law, general principles and other sources of international law. International human rights law lays down obligations of Governments to act in certain ways or to refrain from certain acts, in order to promote and protect human rights and fundamental freedoms of individuals or groups.

"A human right is a universal moral right, something which all men, everywhere, at all times ought to have, something of which no one may be deprived without a grave affront to justice, something which is owing to every human simply because he is human."[3]

An alternative explanation was provided by the philosopher Kant. He said that human beings have an intrinsic value absent in inanimate objects. To violate a human right would therefore be a failure to recognize the worth of human life.[4] Any society that is to protect human rights must have the following characteristics:

- A *de jure* or free state in which the right to self-determination and rule of law exist.
- A legal system for the protection of human rights.
- Effective organized (existing within the framework of the state) or unorganized guarantees.[5]

CORRUPTION

It is not easy to define corruption. But in an Indian context, corruption is mostly concerned with bribery, scam and political blackmailing. From 'mantri' to 'santri' every individual is highly corrupt here. Nevertheless corruption is a global phenomenon and it is omnipresent. It has progressively increased, became high-tech and even a part of the professional world. Thus it is now rampant in most societies. Corruption in India has been a major concern since long. India became one of the most corrupt nations in South Asia in 2010, thanks to our politicians and law enforcement agencies. Criminalization of entire system along with manifold scams are the major obstacles and a serious problem for the development and security of the country. Be it a UPA or an

---

[3]S. Augender, "Questioning the Universality of Human Rights", 28(1&2) *Indian Socio Legal Journal* (2002) at 80.

[4]A.I. Melden, *Rights and Persons* (Berkeley: University of California Press, 1977) at 189.

[5]K. Vasak, *The International Dimensions of Human Rights Volume I* (P. Alston ed., Connecticut: Greenwood Press, 1982) at 4–8.

NDA government in the Centre or a State, corruption is a common virus from higher level to lower level.

The term "corruption" comes from the Latin word *corruptio* which means "moral decay, wicked behaviour, putridity or rottenness".[6] The concept may have a physical reference, as in "[t]he destruction or spoiling of anything, especially by disintegration or by decomposition with its attendant unwholesomeness and loathsomeness; putrefaction"; or moral significance, as in "moral deterioration or decay... [the] [p]erversion or destruction of integrity in the discharge of public duties by bribery or favour...".[7]

In China, the term corruption in general terms spells all types of irregularities and connotes bribery, extortion, expropriation of public money, favoritism, nepotism, and factionalism.[8] Heidenheimer (1970) categorised the nature of corruption into three groups: (i) market centred orientation, (ii) Public centred approach, and (iii) Public Office centred perspective.[9]

Michael Johnson, a Professor at Colgate University has stated: :in rapidly changing societies the limit between what is corruption what is not always clear and the term corruption may be applied broadly."[10] Most of the statutory definitions focus on bribery as corruption and mainly within the public sector. Whilst there is broad agreement that corruption is the "abuse of public office for private gain"[11]

India, like many emerging markets and democracies around the world, often faces the adulterated side of "righteous" path. It's therefore no surprise that Mahatma Gandhi's prophecy has come true. "Corruption and hypocrisy ought not to be inevitable products of democracy, as they undoubtedly are today," he had said much before India started calling herself as the most populated and vibrant democracy in the world. In late 1970s, Mrs Indira Gandhi, who was not related to Mahatma Gandhi, tried to console the victims of political corruption. Corruption, she declared, is global phenomena. She was right.

---

[6]Milovanovic, Milic, Endogenous Corruption in Privatised Companies. Collegiem, Budapest, 2001. www.cerge.cuni.cz/pdf/gdn/RRCI_17_paper_01.pdf

[7]Oxford English Dictionary, 1978, pp. 1024-1025.

[8]Lui, A.Y.C. Corruption in China During the Early Period: 1644 to 1660, University of Honk Kong, Centre of Asian Studies, hong Kong, 1979.

[9]Heidenheimer, A.T., ed. Political Corruption: readings in Comparative analysis, holt Rinebart and Winston, New York, 1970.

[10]Johnson, Michael. Syndromes of Corruption: Wealth, Power and Democracy, Cambridge, Cambridge University Press, 2005.

[11]Alhaji B.M. Marong, Toward a Normative Consensus Against Corruption: Legal Effects of the Principles to Combat Corruption in Africa." (2002) DENV J. INT'L l & poly Vol. 30: 23. (@ http://www.law. Dv.edvlilj/online-ssues-folder/marong.final 9.3.pdf. pp. 99-109.

RELEVANCE OF HUMAN RIGHS TO CORRUPTION

Corruption and human rights are interrelated to each because on the assumption that, if corruption occurs where there is inclination and opportunity, a human rights approach may help to minimise opportunities for corrupt behaviour and make it more likely that those who are corrupt are caught and appropriately sanctioned. A human rights approach also focuses attention on people who are particularly at risk and offers elements of guidance for the design and implementation of anti-corruption policies.

The rapid practicing of corruption violate human rights, which influences public attitudes. While corruption violates the rights of all those affected by it, it has a disproportionate impact on people that belong to groups that are exposed to particular risks (such as minorities, indigenous peoples, migrant workers, disabled people, those with HIV/AIDS, refugees, prisoners and those who are poor). It also disproportionately affects women and children. When people become more aware of the damage corruption does to public and individual interests, and the harm that even minor corruption can cause, they are more likely to support campaigns and programmes to prevent it. This is important because, despite strong rhetoric, the political impact of most anticorruption programmes has been low in India.

In India, the corruption starts from the birth of a person when a birth certificate has to be obtained and it extends up to death when bribe has to be given for cremation and for obtaining death certificate. It further extends even beyond death, if one would like to get legal heir certificate. Thus, corruption has become a total phenomenon that directly affecting the human rights of the people in their daily life in India today.A large section of people in the society are being affected due to rapid increasing of corruption practices in the country where the people are not able to raise their voice due to practice of the systematic corrupt mechanism where it hampers their human right as they are the human beings. Their rights are not given importance which is being captured by the corrupt practices.

PRESENT SCENARION IN INDIA: AN OVERVIEW

The National Huma Rights Commission has been stressing that health and education are two basic human rights and are part of our fundamental rights. In case of food security, It has consistently maintained that the Right to Food is inherent to living a life with dignity. The Commission has expressed the view that the Right to Food includes nutrition at an appropriate level. It also implies that the quantum of relief to those in distress must meet those levels in order to ensure that the Right to Food is actually secured and does not remain a theoretical concept. Unfortunately, in India the foodgrain is rotting while the large section of people are living with hunger. The age-old Indian philosophy of anna daan as the highest form of sacrifice best describes the human being's greatest want in life. No other act of giving away guarantees the citizen's basic need for survival. Yet in this land of ancient civilisation, at least one-third of its 1.2 billion citizens, or close to 400 million, do not get two square meals a day, up from just about 200 million who went hungry 50 years ago.

A recent World Bank report said nearly 50 per cent of food grains distributed to families below the poverty line under PDS scheme was lost due to leakage and wastage. The report, titled 'Social Protection for a Changing India', blamed the public distribution system for absorbing substantial public resources at almost one per cent of GDP. While it covered up to 25 per cent of households, its benefits for the poor have been limited. "Leakage and diversion of food grains from the PDS are high. Only 41 per cent of what is released by the government reaches households with some states doing much worse," the report said.[12] Here, it is clear that the mechanism of Public Distribution System in India has some lackings due to the corruption practices in various levels and stages of PDS in India that affects the basic rights of the poor of the country.

The Commission has constituted a Core Group on Right to Food with experts in the field. In last meeting of the Core Group, it was observed that Panchayats, being burdened with so many other responsibilities may not be in a position to pay focused attention to this aspect in all the areas in their jurisdiction. Hence a need for the constitution of watch committees at various levels in States was felt. The purpose of these independent committees is to see implementation of the related schemes, availability of food grains and their proper distribution and report to the concerned authorities in the State or to the SHRC/NHRC directly in some select cases, as the case may be. This is a good step to be implemented in the right way that will protect the rights of human being.

In regards to civil and political rights of the people, It is the duty of the National Human Rights Commission to monitor custodial deaths, rapes, deaths in alleged fake encounters etc. Besides the redressing individual complaints, the need for systemic reforms in the Police and Prisons is essential to avoid such problems in future. Over crowding in prisons, medical treatment of prisoners, sensitization of prison staff are main concerns which should be neatly looked into. Unless, it turns into violation. For example; Buddhadev Singh, a government doctor by profession was beaten to death Sunday (29th May, 2011) afternoon by the inmates in Gopalganj, some 125 km from Patna, when he went inside a ward to conduct a medical check-up of a prisoner serving sentence in a kidnapping case. According to a police officer, the prisoners wanted the doctor to issue them a certificate that they were ill, and needed to be shifted out of the jail. But Singh refused, after which he was thrashed.[13] Here, it clears

---

[12]http://www.worldbank.org.in
[13]The Economic Time, 30th May, 2011

two things, firstly the envirnoment of the Gopaljang jail was not to the par that may somehow irritate the prisioners and secondly the idea of corruption mean by which they wanted a fake medical certificate from that doctor that casued the death of him.

Corruption impacts men and women differently and reinforces and perpetuates existing gender inequalities. Women's lack of access to political and economic power excludes them from networks that permit access to decision-making bodies. Where institutions are controlled by men, women do not have enough power to challenge corruption or clientelism. Corruption in the legislative and executive branches can allow discriminatory laws to stand, while corruption in the judicial branch can discriminate against women who do not have the means to pay bribes to gain access to the justice system.

Women's rights include affording them resources and opportunities that they have previously been denied. One of the most important rights in this area is the right against sexual harassment which has been given greater importance due to the soaring rates of crimes against women. Women's access to justice is compromised in other ways. Trafficking, for example, often involves the corruption of border officials, police and members of the judiciary. As illegal immigrants, often without proof of identification and subject to (sexual) violence, trafficked women are obviously hindered in seeking protection from courts.

Many women also have fewer opportunities than men to achieve an education, or obtain land, credit and other productive assets. When they have access to work, they are often paid lower salaries. They tend to assume the domestic responsibilities of taking care of children and older adults, which means they are financially dependent, cannot work or are poorer. For all these reasons—but essentially because women are over-represented in the poorest social segments of society and under-represented in decision-making bodies—corruption and clientelism affect them in particular ways, often disproportionately. For example, corruption that diverts public resources from essential services or anti-poverty programmes will particularly harm the welfare of women and their dependents, who rely heavily on such services. In the same way, bribery that adds to the cost of public services will also disproportionately affect women, because they are on average less able to afford bribes, depend more on public services, and sometimes (for example during pregnancy) require services that men do not.

In India, though the Indian Constitution establishes righ to equality and prohibits discriminition based on caste, race, religion, sex or birth besides outlawing the age-old practice of untouchability, the ex-untouchabiles/SCs, Dalits have not been fully integrated into the social mainstream. Their rights are being violated every day. For example: On 7 November 2005, the State Level Scrutiny Committee declared as fake the ST certificate of Sri Pradyut Deb Barma, son of Late Durgadas Deb Barma of TP Road, Krishna Nagar, Agartala, West Tripura. The Committee after proper examination of all records found that Pradyut Deb Barma belongs to Laskar community, which is not recognized as ST in Tripura and therefore ordered for cancellation of his ST certificate bearing No. 62/DM/GL/W/74 dated 20/1/75 with immediate effect as per the Notification No. 38296–396/F.6–4(C-D)/TW/89 dated 31–3–90.[14] Here, it shows that the corruption is the only reason that had stoped the right of a tribal people to get employment who are genelly known as silent and innocent in nature for which they are being victimised by corrupt people, as per the right to equal opportunities to all in public services whereas it violatess here.

In many cases, those who are to blame cannot be brought to book because of political considerations, power equations etc. When such violations are allowed to go unchecked, they often increase in frequency and intensity usually because perpetrators feel that they enjoy immunity from punishment. So, the mechanism should be set up and realy work to check corruption as well as to protect human rights.

INSTRUMENTS TO PROTECT HUMAN RIGHTS AND CORRUPTION

UN Charter

The UN charter has been signed by 150 countries today. Though its obligatory status was in question, it is now the accepted view that Article 56 makes it necessary for all signatories to respect and promote human rights.[15]

Universal Declaration of Human Rights

Perhaps the most important document pertaining to human rights, it was adopted on 10th December, 1948 and the day is celebrated as Human Rights Day every Year. The Declaration specifies a common standard of achievement for all nations of the world and a number of UN bodies are responsible for implementing its contents.[16]

UN High Commission on Human Rights

This body created by the Economic and Social Council in 1947 makes recommendations on conventions, declarations and other issues like the status of women.[17]

---

[14]The National Commission for Scheduled Tribes: A Forum For Political Rehabilitation, Asian Indgenous and Tribal Peoples Network, New Delhi, August, 2008, p. 32.
[15]N. Singh, *Enforcement of Human Rights* (Calcutta: Eastern Law House Pvt. Ltd., 1986) at 15–18.
[16]*Human Rights in the Changing World* (E. S. Venkataramiah J. ed., New Delhi: International Law Association, 1988) at 12–16.
[17]D.J. Ravindran, *Human Rights Praxis: A Resource Book for Study, Action and Reflection* (Chennai: Earthworm Books, 1998) at 251–253.

UN High Commissioner for Human Rights

The High Commissioner's duties include investigating human rights violations, helping governments arrange mechanisms to protect human rights and submitting periodic reviews to the High Commission on Human Rights.[18]

The National Commission for Women

The National Commission for Women was set up as statutory body in January 1992 under the National Commission for Women Act, 1990 by the Governmentof India that aimed to review the Constitutional and Legal safeguards for women; to recommend remedial legislative measures; to facilitate redressal of grievances and to advise the Government on all policy matters affecting women. It is the mandate of the commission to protect the women from violation of human rights and corruption.[19]

The National Commission for Schedules Castes (SCs) and Scheduled Tribes (STs)

The National Commission for Schedules Cates (SCs)and Scheduled Tribes (STs) was constituted for the protection, welfare, socio-economic development and advancement of the Scheduled Castes and Scheduled tribes and to evaluate the working of such safeguards. It is empowered to enquir into specific complaints of deprivation of rights of this kinds of people. It has been protecting the rights of Scs and Sts who are being neglated due to violation of human rights and corrupt practice.[20]

Apart from this National Commission for Minorities and Backward Classes are also working for the upliftment of the minorities and backward class and their rights and to protect them from any kind of deprivation, violation of human rights in the society.

WAYS FORWARD

The corruption is the core issue behind the violation of human rights in many cases. So, It is emphasised here that curbing corruption will be able to protect violation of human right in some extend and It is rightly argued, 'corruption is an intractable problem. It is like diabetes, can only be controlled, but not totally eliminated' from the society. To be specific, it may not be possible to root out corruption completely at all levels but it is possible to contain it within tolerable limits. Keeping this in eye

---

[18] *The United Nations and Human Rights 18th Report of the Commission to Study the Organization of Peace* (New York: Oceana Publications Inc., 1968) at 8.
[19] http://ncw.nic.in/frmAboutUS.aspx, accessed on 24th May, 2011.
[20] Annual Report of NCSC&ST.

towards strenthening human rights and reduce corruption, some ways and means may be taken into account.

Thre are various ways to curb corruption as the followings:

- There is no want of legislative laws in India to curb corruption. But, the problem is that those responsible for implementing the laws are themselves often involved in corruption.
- A strong legislation with severe punishment like the ones against terrorists and anti-national elements must be enforced nation-wide.
- Honest and dedicated persons in public life be encouraged and rewarded by the civil society.
- Complete control over electoral expenses, vigorous screening of all candidates' profile by the election commission before granting nomination at any sort of election.
- The sure way to fight against corruption is to build revulsion in the minds of the students in the formative age group against corruption, by introducing corruption issue as a compulsory subject in curriculum for school students all over India.
- Efforts without aim such as some of those who claim to fight against corruption are now the senior citizens who have retired from jobs or taken voluntary retirement, who themselves have not done much to fight against corruption or might have remained as passive spectators, when they were working in government departments or elsewhere. Particularly, the All India Services Officers were picked up for criticism for speaking about the corruption issues only after safe superannuation.
- Unless there would be huge public pressure and pressure from media, the politicians would not improve their conduct and behaviour. While judiciary can help, unfortunately, judiciary itself is now being caught in several incidents of corruption, creating sort of doubts about the conduct of some judges themselves.
- While new laws and regulations can be introduced, this would not help by themselves. The battle against corruption should be ultimately fought in the minds and hearts of the people, particularly the youth. A concerted campaign against corrupt system should be launched just as the campaign against child labour, AIDS etc., now being launched. For this to happen, media must have less business orientation and should be more focused on building value system in the country.
- If media would not rise up to the occasion to carry out its responsibility to build pressure on the government machinery, politicians and public to refrain from corrupt practices, the situation could become hopeless with grave consequences for the national peace and progress. So, the time has arrived for media to take part active role to fight corruption.
- Right to Information (RTI) Act should be used by the civil society even in minor cases at block and panchayat levels. Right to information Act 2005 is a landmark achievement as through this corrupt politicians and bureaucracy would be exposed and there is hope to develop a clean public life.

- Public Interest litigation should be practiced and it is appropriate, anti-corruption organisations should consider using public interest litigation, for example to recover assets and to protect human rights.

NEED OF THE HOUR

The level of corruption practice and violation of human rights has been increasing which should be well tackled to protect human rights of the peopel by curbing corruption from the society The need of hour is all section of the society should come forward and raise voice against corruption and violation of human rights as well as at Indivisual level or collectively should fight against corruption. It is good sign that the issue like corruption is being raised in a mass movement by Yoga Guru Baba Ramdev and Anna Hazzare which is showing the democrating right of the peopel and at the same time it brings caution to the government to act towards the elimination of corruption. However, different section of the people, non-government organisations, civil society, intellectuals and common people should directly or indirectly unite their voice against the corruption practice that will help towards the protection of human rights of large section of the people in India.

CONCLUSION

The assumption of greater responsibility by Governance toward citizens; accountability in and transparency of the public sector operation; the idea that governments actions must be continuously monitored to ensure high efficiency, effectiveness, and better economic performance; and recognition that the government's power must depend principally on citizens' support, voice, and satisfaction with the services they receive which may create a different and more flexible model of governing that combines responsiveness, collaboration, and the ideal type of citizens' ownership that only can help in eliminating corruption and violation of the human rights from the soicety.

Although corruption is being addressed by financial institutions, government agencies, bilateral donors, international organisations, non-governmental organisations (NGOs) and development professionals. Combating corruption requires strong collective efforts from different sectors in society acting in co-ordinated ways. It should be practiced as a promise for everybody at all levels of the governance not to do corruption or to overlook the corrupt people while they are coming across the corruption practices. The people in real sense, have to unite or individually do their job with honest and sincerity that will put a reduction in the corruption practices and at the same time it will protect the human rights of the people in general. It is sure that a day will come where the level of the corruption will be seen at the very down in comparison to other countries aw well as the people of the country will enjoy their rights.

REFERENCES

[1] Melden, A.I., *Rights and Persons* (Berkeley: University of California Press, 1977) at 189.

[2] Alhaji, B.M. Marong, Toward a Normative Consensus Against Corruption: Legal Effects of the Principles to Combat Corruption in Africa." (2002) Denv J. Int'l l & poly Vol. 30, 23. (@ http://www.law. Dv.edvlilj/online-ssues-folder/marong.final 9.3.pdf. pp. 99–109.

[3] Annual Report of NCSC&ST.

[4] Ravindran, D.J., *Human Rights Praxis: A Resource Book for Study, Action and Reflection* (Chennai: Earthworm Books, 1998) at 251–253.

[5] Feldman, David (1993), Civil liberties and human rights in England and Wales. Oxford: Clarendon Press, p. 5.

[6] *Human Rights in the Changing World* (E.S. Venkataramiah J. ed., New Delhi: International Law Association, 1988) at 12–16.

[7] Heidenheimer, A.T., ed. Political Corruption: readings in Comparative analysis, holt Rinebart and Winston, New York, 1970.

[8] Johnson, Michael., Syndromes of Corruption: Wealth, Power and Democracy, Cambridge, Cambridge University Press, 2005.

[9] Vasak, K., *The International Dimensions of Human Rights Vol. I* (P. Alston ed., Connecticut: Greenwood Press, 1982) at 4–8.

[10] Lui, A.Y.C., Corruption in China During the Early Period: 1644 to 1660, University of Honk Kong, Centre of Asian Studies, hong Kong, 1979.

[11] Milovanovic, Milic., Endogenous Corruption in Privatised Companies. Collegiem, Budapest, 2001. www.cerge.cuni.cz/pdf/gdn/RRCI_17_paper_01.pdf

[12] Augender, S., "Questioning the Universality of Human Rights", 28(1&2) *Indian Socio Legal Journal* (2002) at 80.

[13] Singh, N., *Enforcement of Human Rights* (Calcutta: Eastern Law House Pvt. Ltd., 1986) at 15–18.

[14] *The United Nations and Human Rights 18th Report of the Commission to Study the Organization of Peace* (New York: Oceana Publications Inc., 1968) at 8.

[15] The National Commission for Scheduled Tribes: A Forum For Political Rehabilitation, Asian Indgenous and Tribal Peoples Network, New Delhi, August, 2008, p. 32.

[16] Oxford English Dictionary, 1978, pp. 1024–1025.

[17] http://ncw.nic.in/frmAboutUS.aspx, accessed on 24th May, 2011.

[18] http://www.worldbank.org.in

[19] The Economic Time, 30th May, 2011.

Combating Corruption in India: Major Threats

Syed Umarhathab

Department of Criminology, Manonmaniyam Sundranan University, Tirunellveli

INTRODUCTION

India has the most multi-cultured and linguistic people in the world, also it is an emerging super economy with population of more than 1.2 billion, 3287263 Sq. Km. of land and second fastest growing economy in the world despite the global economic slow down (Goenka, 2009). In India, corruption is something we all learn to live with. But, we need not be resigned to it or cynical. Instead of breast-breathing over the sorrow of the state of affairs, let's explore the solutions. May be there are no satisfactory answers to our questions (Chopra, 2009 para 1). Corruption is all around us, almost like a distorted and omnipresent. The epidemic proportion of corruption has acquired in India. It is literally under every stone you turn. It is also in every alley you turn into, every nook and cranny you might care to peep into. It happens as much in the broad daylight as it does behind closed doors. Corruption in public services is concerned; various factors have been responsible for the widespread of it among the government servants.

Long ago Gibbon, (1993) wrote *"Corruption, the most infallible syndrome of constitutional liberty"*. We had a corrupt administration even when we did not have constitutional liberty. Our Administration was even corrupt during the Colonial days and earlier and still continues (Umarhathab, 2007). A sensitive Shastri former Prime Minister of India took serious note and appointed a "Commission of Inquiry" in 1962 under late Santhanam. This committee came out with its report in the year 1964. Some of its recommendations in the after light of events appear naive and laughable. The Committee felt bulk of elected representatives, most of the Ministers (both Central and State) and Senior Servants, most of the Chief Ministers of the state were above board and corruption was absent in the higher reaches of the judiciary and slight at lower levels, but today it has reached even beyond.

Recommendations of the Commission's were very mild, merely cosmetic and nothing beyond. A Central Vigilance Commission (CVC) was announced with loud trumpets and the Central Bureau of Investigation (CBI) was the new name for the old Delhi based special police establishment, but as events would prove these measures turned to be a mere eye-wash. The CVC was a mere shadow of the vigorous ombudsman that Santhanam dreamt. Government is still unwilling to give operational autonomy to the police, state vigilance and anti-corruption agency and CBI. We have achieved results by clumsily liquidating the freedom of action of the CBI and rendering the CVC an irrelevance except for name. There was another observation in the report that the integrity of Members of Parliament (MP) and of the Member of Legislatives Assembly (MLA) in the states will be a great factor in creating a favorable social climate against corruption. Political parties to publish annual audited accounts, and judiciary should have an effective machinery to deal with complaints of corruption. Though this is in practice, reality of proportionate wealth of the party or its member is disclosed only as of night lamp in a dark room.

Corruption is a difficult thing to measure or compare, it is both a major cause and a result of poverty around the world. It occurs at all levels of society, from local and national governments, civil society, judiciary, functions, large and small businesses, military and other services and so on. Corruption affects the poorest the most, whether in rich or poor nations (Shah, 2009). Another committee on corruption was headed by Vohra has many carping things and found that it is the Criminal-Politician nexus that defeats anti-corruption measures. Most of the recommendations of Santhanam committee were accepted by this commission, but in actual practice none of them was implemented. To be truthful, we are making headway backwards, the investigation agency is not really strengthened, and its operational independence is progressively abridged. All investigative outfits, Central and State are subjected to political manipulations. It has been so, from the beginning, except that earlier, our leaders both Political and in Civil service (including Police), had respect for Rule of Law and Conflicts. Political unscrupulously, combined with hypocrisy and a certain spinal deficiency in the Civil Services and lubricating lucre has undermined all our institutions.

MAJOR THREATS IN COMBATING CORRUPTION IN PUBLIC SERVICES OF INDIA

The list of Santhanam Committee report is long; a principle based on the report is that a *tradition of integrity* can be established if example is set by those who have the ultimate responsibility for the governance of the country and this is said to be the first *biggest threat*. Similar views has been expressed by some of the researcher (Hanlon, and Pettifor, 2000; Neild, 2002; Chopra, 2009a). This view is witnessed in year 2011 with the appoint of a post that is said to be more authoritarian i.e., appoint of the chief vigilance commissioner in central vigilance commission of the worlds largest democracy was questioned by the supreme court of India ended with lack of integrity.

The second biggest issue is that *absence of autonomy and accountability of criminal justice official and their social responsibility*, to be practical there are very few who come out to join criminal justice profession with passion much of the best brain join medical or engineering or any other professional course expect for those who come with family history of working with the criminal justice agencies. Invariably in most prosecutions the police come off second best delay in courts kill cases. Venkatesan (2009) were Verrappa Moily, Ministry of law, Government of India commented about 9310 CBI cases are pending before various courts and more than 2000 cases have been pending for more than 10 years. A large number of these cases are against dishonest and corrupt public servants and the associates. An agency dedicated for fight corruption has so many cases pending; it portrays the lack of autonomy of this organization. The another biggest issue with reference to accountability is *promptness,* India's largest scan in telecommunication ministry came to light after 1000 days with the first report only from comptroller of audit, government of India. The question on autonomy is answer for such delay in the criminal justice system.

The third biggest issue being *slow motion justice* as approximately 20 million cases are pending in Indian courts (Menon, 2009), the people can be taught to believe in one court of appeal; but when there are two they cannot be blamed if they believe in neither. More than this, we have *Appeal, Revisions, Writs and Reviews*; finality is unknown in the terms of law, though law is supreme. People want to see justice done un-delayed because "*Justice delayed is justice denied*". When cases drag on for years, witnesses vanish; when judgments take months to write and deliver, you can't blame the public who take note of our emerging culture of not trusting public institutions this task is daunting but can be done. When public believe court as apathy to corruption on the other hands state is unwilling to correct the road blocks.

The fourth biggest issue is in connection with the third, is that *disparities in verdict, judgment, and sentencing*, one case many verdict is something unbearable for most of the Indian's. In India, especially corruption cases or any other cases end up with acquittal, while the case is heard in higher court it end up either in conviction or acquittal and vice-versa. How is it acceptable, the same law, witness/evidence, investigating officer and mere change in magistrate/judge/justice finalize the cases with change in verdict, judgment, and sentencing. When it is un-interesting to note sea change in the system but nothing has changed over the years. Over the years complainant feel bad of complaining the case corruption to the authority as it involves more formalities and physical stress and strain with financial commitment to fight the case corruption is unbearable for many of the complainant.

The fifth biggest issue is that we suffer from *lack of agency(s)* to which the Ministers and High Dignitaries are accountable. Not one single authority perched in distant Delhi, but available in every state and to whom all public officials are responsible.

The law must be made to swiftly nip the troubles in the bud. In cases involving White Collar Crimes the *accused must be made to give his/her pull version as in civil cases*. Sitting back and enjoying the unequal contest between an outstanding expensive counsel and an ill-paid with heavy-work loaded prosecutor is not fair. When it comes to the governance in India, it is absolute unthrift, because a responsible central minister of information technology involved in the country' s largest ever scam involving 1,74,00,000 Crores arrested and prosecuted for the same. Another learned minister from the same portfolio involving in another huge scam made him to resign the ministry are live example of the biggest threat of integrity.

The sixth biggest issue is that use of *technology and scientific approach* Gupta, (2001) in fighting crime in order to dispose the cases which require technology support while delivering the justice. Using technology would speed up the process of justice in prompt and appropriate manner.

Lastly, *the seventh biggest threat* is *lack of researches, awareness and transparency* similar views has been expressed by some of the researcher (Hanlon, and Pettifor, A., 2000a; Neild, 2002a; Chopra, 2009b; Sreevatsan, 2009). The level of awareness on the issues and governance is less among Indian, compared to people living in western world. We have imported almost all the culture and way of life from west but lack of tendency to question the government on most of the aspects. In fact, today Indian's are changing to that extent we are even unaware of what is happening in own neighborhood. Other wise it is well known fact that lack of transparency is one of the major cause of corruption. Researches should be conducted on a continuous basis and situation should be published for public opinion else all the efforts and reports of the researchers go waste with financial commitment from the government or the funding agencies. For the research on a corruption the outputs from the students of criminology, public administration and political science would be appropriate and government shall form a team with such combination for understanding the social impact of legislations.

CONCLUSION

Corruption is aged as society, which has rooted from the beginning; on the other hands it is unrealistic to expect a corruption free country. There is growing culture that corruption is inevitable because it is experienced from birth to death in India. Types of corruption include in its preview Bribery, Graft, Patronage, Nepotism and cronyism, Embezzlement, Kickbacks, Unholy alliance, Involvement in organized crime and misappropriation of government properties including tax evaders shall also be included as one of the corruption. Venkatesan, (2009a) writes Verrappa, Minister for Law and Justice, Government of India during an interview commented that there is need for change or amendment to the article 309, 310 and 311 of the constitution of India. These articles empower state and central government to prosecute against any public servant (both central and state) charged with corruption. In order to make it possible to fight corruption, the task of fighting corruption shall be outsourced to non-profit and professional organization such as transparency international, to directorate of vigilance and anticorruption and central bureau of investigation, any government agency established with a mission to fight corruption, shall achieve its mission, only when the organization are made autonomous as election commission of India. Government of India shall concentrate on the implementation rather than new laws.

Transparency International is a global organization that seeks to empower civil society to participate in efforts to fight corruption. Here are some ways advocated (and implemented) by this nonprofit organization with which can make a difference: To make system workable and fight the threats it good to organize the following matter and act according to the recommendation of the *(i) Public debate on contemporary issues in combating corruption, (ii) transparency in government, (iii) protecting the whistle blower, (iv) from an integrity circle, (v) remove temptations of the contemporary corruptions in the country and finally, (vi) a macro level research at state or district level to understand the situation on regular interval.*

REFERENCES

[1] Chopra, S. (4 August 2009), Ethics—Corruption-You can say no to it. Retrieved on September 25, 2009 from http://www.lifepositive.com/Mind/ethics-and-values/ethics/corruption.asp

[2] Gibbon, E., The Decline and Fall of Roman Empire in Peter, D. (1993). Thinking about Political Corruption, NYC, ME Sharp, p. 207.

[3] Goenka S.P. (06 September, 2009), Look East for Food and Energy Security, The Hindu (Daily), p. 14.

[4] Hanlon, J. and Pettifor, A. (2000), Kicking the Habit, Finding a Lasting Solution to Addictive Lending and Borrowing-and its Corrupting Side-effects, Jubilee Research.

[5] Neild, R. (2002), Public Corruption; The Dark Side of Social Evolution, London: Anthem Press.

[6] Shah, A. (29 December, 2008), Corruption. Retrieved on September 12, 2009 from http://www.globalissues.org/article/590/corruption

[7] Sreevatsan, A. (10 September, 2009), The Hindu (Daily).

[8] Umarhathab, S. (2007), Public Rating of Corruption, The Indian Police Journal, April–June, Vol. LIV, No. 2, p. 82.

[9] Venkatesan, J. (28 August, 2009), First Step Towards Judges Accountability, The Hindu (Daily).

[10] Vir, J.R. (2006), Crime and Corruption in India, New Delhi, Friends Publishing House.

[11] Menon, M. (2009), Special address, All India conference of the Indian society of Criminology, Bangalore.

[12] Gupta, K.N. (2001), Corruption in India, New Delhi, India, Anmol Publications Pvt. Ltd., 98, p. 107.

Corruption Free Service as a Fundamental Right

N.M. Nilofer Nisha

Department of Political Science, J.B.S.A. College for Women, Chennai

"I have derived my politics from ethics… It is because I swear by ethics that I find myself in Politics".

—M.K. Gandhi

Corruption is an abuse of power for public or private gain keeping the formal rules aside. One of the definitions of the term corruption is "giving something to someone with power so that he will abuse his power and act favouring the giver". Another definition is "the offering, giving, soliciting or acceptance of an inducement or reward, which may influence the action of any person".

It includes bribery and extortion which involve at least two parties, and other types of malfeasance that a public official can commit alone, including fraud and embezzlement. The appropriation of public assets for private use and the embezzlement of public funds by politicians and bureaucrats have such clear and direct adverse impact on India's economic development that their costs do not warrant any complex economic analysis.

This paper is to understand that the corruption free service is our fundamental rights. The problem of corruption in India needs to be analyzed in the context of its potential implications for human rights. There are numerous connections between corruption discourse and human rights discourse. Corruption dilutes human rights in a significant way.

CORRUPTION FREE SERVICE AND FUNDAMENTAL RIGHTS

In India, Corruption attacks the fundamental values of human dignity and political equality of the people and hence there is a pressing need to formulate a fundamental human right to corruption-free service.

The development of a fundamental human right to a corruption-free society will be observed initially from an international perspective so as to elevate the violation of this right to the status of an international crime. This would provide the comparative basis to elevate the right to corruption-free service to the status of a fundamental right within the framework of the Indian Constitution.

The Constitution of India, which is famous for its progressive provisions and for its liberal interpretations by courts that have judicially expanded the rights set forth in it, should recognize this right. The fact that corruption remains an important problem even after fifty-five years of independence in India and continues to eat away the precious resources of the country, and that all forms of victimization result from civil, political, economic and social rights violations, is enough justification for formulating new strategies to address corruption.

Human rights offers powerful resistance to violations of various rights, and the problem of corruption can be addressed by framing it as a human rights violation. The benefit of regarding corruption as a human rights issue will enhance efforts to contain corruption, due to the development of international human rights law as an important aspect of international law, as well as national developments in constitutional, legal, and judicially recognized rights. The corruption problem, when framed as a human rights issue, can empower the judiciary to enforce certain rights for the citizenry, demand a transparent, accountable and corruption-free system of governance in India, and help establish a basis to monitor this process. The right to information for promoting transparency and accountability is one instance in which the corruption issue has been elevated from a public policy matter to a higher level of political discourse by invoking the right to freedom of information of the Indian citizenry.

TOWARDS RECOGNISING A FUNDAMENTAL RIGHT TO CORRUPTION-FREE SERVICE

As early as 1964, the Santhanam Committee, which was set up to examine the increasing menace of corruption in the administration, observed that the "tendency to subvert integrity in the public services instead of being isolated... is growing into an organised, well-planned racket". If anything, it has grown much larger and become even better organised since this report was prepared. Granville Austin has said that the Indian Constitution is first and foremost a social document. Thus, when those who drafted the Constitution included the chapters on fundamental rights and directive principles of state policy, they hoped and expected that these would give strength to the pursuit of the social revolution in India. Fundamental rights of the Constitution are in general those rights of citizens, or those negative obligations of the state not to encroach on individual liberty.

Although the fundamental rights primarily protect individuals and minority groups from capricious, prejudicial, state action, three of the articles are designed to protect the individual against the actions of other private citizens. Article 17 abolishes untouchability; Article 15(2) lays down that no citizen shall suffer any disability in the use of shops, restaurants, wells, roads and other public places on account of his religion, race, caste, sex or place of birth; Article 23 prohibits forced labour, which, although it had been practised by the state, was more commonly a case of landowner versus peasant struggle.

Thus the state, in addition to obeying the Constitution's (negative) injunctions against interfering with certain of the citizen's liberties, must fulfil its positive obligation to protect the citizen's rights from encroachment by society (Granville Austin, 1966). It is this negative injunction and positive obligation within the scheme of fundamental rights that needs to be built upon while evaluating the impact of corruption on governance administration in India. In India, corruption has scuttled the realisation of fundamental rights, discouraged any scope for the development of egalitarianism, and thereby significantly hindered the process of achieving a social revolution. This has resulted in liberty becoming the privilege of a few who happen to hold economic, bureaucratic, judicial or political power. "The struggle for career advancement," said former Secretary to the Government of India R.C. Dutt, "is greatly influenced by the surrounding moral atmosphere of the struggle for existence of different classes and groups in society... (This) has provided ample opportunities for corruption, and indeed for collective self-aggrandisement at the expense of the poor". P.N. Haksar thought "our civil services... are committed first of all to themselves and their nuclear family... (and beyond this to) making secure the future of our sons, daughters...and if possible... the members of our sub-caste, caste, community and region".

The concept of identifying corruption as a cause and an effect of poor governance and the resultant violation of human rights is a recent phenomenon. Its massive impact on the legitimacy of all institutions in India needs to be examined thoroughly. This observation rests on the argument that when the government of a country fails or neglects to curb or contain corruption, that government fails to fulfill its obligation to promote and protect fundamental human rights in the country.

In the Indian context corruption distorts the principle of equality before the law and equal protection of law, which is enshrined in the Constitution. It is clearly understood both from a legal and constitutional interpretation and from the plethora of judicial decisions in India that the principle of equality and non-arbitrariness is the "brooding omnipresence" (Justice P.N. Bhagwati in *Maneka Gandhi vs. Union of India*) of the Indian Constitution. Corruption not only perpetrates injustice, resulting in the breakdown of the governance machinery, but also violates the fundamental rights that are guaranteed to citizens. Conversely, it may be argued that the present proposal to include the right to corruption-free service as a part of the scheme of fundamental rights might strengthen the other rights, including the right to equality and the freedoms that are enshrined in other portions of Chapters III and IV of the Constitution.

Article 11(2) of the Constitution of Eritrea provides that "all administrative institutions shall be free from corruption, discrimination and delay in the delivery of efficient and equitable public services". Even though this provision hardly guarantees a fundamental right to corruption-free service, the fact that "corruption" in administration has been constitutionally proscribed sets the right tone for the corruption discourse. However, developing countries like India need to think hard as to how to tackle corruption legally and, in this case, constitutionally. The Indian judiciary has progressively developed and expanded the scope of fundamental rights to include a plethora of rights, mostly, within the ambit of the "right to life" provision in Article 21 of the Constitution. A classic case in point is the initial judicial recognition of a fundamental right to education, through a creative interpretation that the right to life includes the right to education. It brought home the most valuable argument that life without education indeed amounts to vegetative existence.

The role the Indian judiciary has played in expanding the 'right to life' concept to include numerous economic and social rights, which were hitherto considered merely policy guidelines in the form of the directive principles of state policy, is amazing. The judiciary was able to justify all the rights that we claim today to be part and parcel of fundamental rights. It has resulted in the legislature bringing a constitutional amendment making the right to education a fundamental right.

But when it comes to corruption, the judiciary in India has not been able to develop in clear terms any fundamental right to corruption-free service for the citizens. Article 14 of the Constitution guarantees equality before the law and equal protection of laws to all Indian citizens. Further, it may be argued that corruption directly violates the protection guaranteed under the equality clause, because a corrupt public servant discriminates against a person who does not bribe him as opposed to a person who bribes him. This isolated incident of discrimination gets institutionalised into an all-pervasive phenomenon, thereby violating the equality clause. Similarly, Article 19 gives Indian citizens the fundamental right to practise any business or profession. In India, public servants who hold positions of power and authority use their discretion to grant or deny permission to start business enterprises. The corrupt public servant often justifies such action by arguing (to himself) that he has the right to a share in the profit of the professional or the businessperson (N. Vittal, Central Vigilance Commissioner of India, 2000). Thus, the equality clause in Article 14 and the freedoms provided in Article 19 lose their meaning and relevance owing to the institutionalisation of corruption at every level of the citizens' interaction with the government.

CORRUPTION AND ITS RELEVANCE FOR HUMAN RIGHTS AND HUMAN DEVELOPMENT

Human rights have indeed acquired a special position in the contemporary world because of the increasing tendency of national governments to include these rights in their respective constitutions as well as laws. This has resulted in several judiciaries around the world interpreting different human rights as a part of their own national laws or for that matter as a part of the International Law, which their respective country has been a signatory to, through treaties and other conventions. Thus the Universal Declaration of Human Rights (UDHR), the International Covenant on Civil and Political Rights (ICPR) and the International Covenant on Economic, Social and Cultural Rights (ICESCR) have acquired greater legitimacy in the last few decades as more and more nations have realised the importance of these human rights as instruments for better governance. Probity in governance is a sine qua non for an efficient system of governance and for socio-economic development. An important requirement for ensuring probity in governance is the absence of corruption. The other requirements may be effective laws, rules and regulations that govern every aspect of public life coupled with effective law enforcement and criminal justice systems.

The right to a society free of corruption is inherently a basic human right because the right to life, dignity, equality and other important human rights and values depend significantly upon this right. That is, it is a right without which these essential rights lose their meaning, let alone be realised. As a fundamental right, the right to a corruption-free society cannot be discarded easily "even for the good of the greatest number, even for the greatest good of all" (Louis Henkin, The Age of Rights, 1990). It may be argued that the right to a corruption-free society originates and flows from the right of a people to exercise permanent sovereignty over their natural resources and wealth, that is, their right to economic self-determination, recognised in the common article of the ICPR and the ICESCR (Ndiva Kofele-Kale, 2000). Hence it may be argued that the state is in violation of the right to economic self-determination if it transfers in a corrupt manner the ownership of national wealth to select power-holders who happen to be influential in a society at a particular point of time. This violation by the state also results in a situation where people are denied individually and collectively their right to use freely exploit and dispose of their national wealth in a manner that advances their development.

The Declaration on the Right to Development, which stated unequivocally that the right to development is a human right, was adopted by the U.N. in 1986 by an overwhelming majority, with the United States casting the single dissenting vote. The Declaration has four main propositions: 1. The right to development is a human right; 2. The human right to development is a right to a particular process of development in which all human rights and fundamental freedoms can be fully realised, which means that the right to development combines all the rights enshrined in both the covenants and that each of the rights has to be exercised with freedom; 3. The meaning of exercising these rights consistently with freedom implies free, effective, and full participation of all the individuals concerned in decision-making and in the implementation of the process, and therefore the process must be transparent and accountable, and individuals must have equal opportunity of access to the resources for development and receive a fair distribution of the benefits of development (and income); and finally, 4. The right confers an unequivocal obligation on duty-holders - individuals within the community, states at the national level, and states at the international level. Nation states have the responsibility to help realise the process of development by initiating appropriate development policies. Other states and international agencies have the obligation to cooperate with the nation states to facilitate the realisation of the process of development. It is in this context that the fundamental right to a corruption-free society adds a new and necessary dimension to the right to development. No development process will have any meaning and relevance if corruption as an institutionalised process interferes with people's struggles to realise their right to development.

HUMAN RIGHT TO A CORRUPTION-FREE SOCIETY UNDER INTERNATIONAL LAW

It has been argued that the struggle to promote human rights and the campaign against corruption share a great deal of common ground. A corrupt government that rejects both transparency and accountability is not likely to respect human rights. Therefore, the campaign to contain corruption and the movement to protect and promote human rights are not disparate processes. They are inextricably linked and interdependent and both the elimination of corruption and the strengthening of human rights require a strong integrity system (Laurence Cockcroft, TI Working Paper, 1998).

Having said that, it needs to be borne in mind that this generalized system of linkage need not be applicable in all situations. Hence it should not be presumed that the fight against corruption is synonymous with the struggle to enforce human rights. For example, in the Corruption Perception Index for the year 2000, Singapore was considered to be the eighth least corrupt country. This was largely the result of systematic anti-corruption measures initiated from the top tier of the administration. At the same time, Singapore is hardly known for its progressive position on human rights. On the other hand, there is evidence to suggest that whilst the human rights situation in Central America and many parts of Latin America and certainly India has been improving steadily, the incidence of corruption has also been increasing.

It may be argued that there is sufficient state practice to support a claim for an international customary law to prohibit corruption in all societies. That is, a case can be made for the right to a corruption-free society as a fundamental human right; a right that should be recognized as a component part of the right to economic self-determination and the right to development (Neiva Kofele-Kale, 2000).

CONCLUSION

In the Indian context, corruption distorts the principle of equality before the law and equal protection of the law, which is enshrined in the Constitution. There is an urgent need for a constitutional reform in the form of an amendment to the Constitution to include the fundamental right to corruption-free service. This is not to suggest that the mere inclusion of a fundamental right would result in an immediate success in the struggle to prevent corruption; it would, however, be a significant step in the right direction. It would open up several avenues for lawyers, judges, non-governmental organisations and parliamentarians to mobilise public opinion on the subject. The importance of the subject should not be underestimated as all our goals, ideals and aspirations of constitutional democracy rests on the legitimacy of the state as an institution to deliver the goods. The kind of corruption that is prevalent in India and other developing countries fundamentally threatens this structure. One hopes that the legislature will take the lead in this matter. I guess we are not far from the day when the Supreme Court of India would read Articles 14 (equality), 19 (freedoms) and even 21 (life) coupled with the directive principles of state policy that relate to good governance and sound public administration and conclude that Indian citizens indeed have a fundamental right to corruption-free service.

This is not to suggest that the lawmakers should actually wait to bring a constitutional amendment so as to include corruption-free service as a fundamental right. But experience has shown that in the area of law reform in India, the judiciary has indeed taken the lead. By way of constructive judgments, it has instructed as to what the law is or rather what the law ought to be. The parliamentarians have followed it up after adequate pressure from the civil society and the populace. Vittal supports the view that corruption-free service should be made a fundamental right by including such a provision in the Indian Constitution. His arguments are based on the fact that corruption-free service must become a fundamental right of every citizen in India, as that is a basic necessity for good governance. He supports the view of the United Nations Development Programme (UNDP) that good governance is indeed a universal human right and that the right to good governance should be part of fundamental rights.

Thus, the inclusion of the right to corruption-free service as a fundamental right would result in not only our recognising that corruption affects good governance, but also delineating the principle that the citizenry have a right to demand governance without corruption and if it is not given to them, they will be able to approach a court of law through the use of writ jurisdiction.

The possible objections to the inclusion of such a right would mostly come from those who are against the judiciary taking up the role of governance in India. It is worth noting that in so many ways the right to corruption-free service in so many ways is not very different from other fundamental rights that the judiciary has evolved through creative and progressive interpretation.

Subodh Mohite, Member of Lok Sabha, introduced a private Bill in the winter session of Parliament in 2000 for the inclusion of a new Article 17A in the fundamental rights chapter by which the citizen will be entitled to get corruption-free service from the state. It is anybody's guess as to what happened to the proposal. I would have liked the National Commission to Review the Working of the Constitution, which recently submitted a good report, to have proposed such an inclusion in the chapter on fundamental rights. Despite the recommendations of the Commission to deepen and expand the scope of fundamental rights within the Constitution, corruption-free service ought to have been made a fundamental right, and this would have added practical meaning and increased the relevance of the recommendations.

Thus, the constitutional quest to develop human rights against corruption goes beyond demanding that the government respect the rule of law. Even where the rule of law may be respected, the humanitarianism of human rights under the Indian Constitution cannot fall short of a tireless search to increase the level of constitutional protection beyond the negative requirement of disciplining the state to achieve equality, promote egalitarianism and uphold dignity. The fundamental human right to corruption-free service would be justified even within the Dworkinian scheme of taking rights seriously, if we are able to develop a theoretical argument that corruption affects equality and dignity. And hence the right to corruption-free service is part of the human rights jurisprudence that struggles to protect the dignity of Indians, who are entitled to equal treatment, concern and respect.

Police Corruption: A Debauchment to Human Dignity

Shan Eugene

Department of History and Tourism, Stella Maris College (Autonomous), Chennai-86

"The wealth earned through pious means flourishes; those who earn through dishonest means are destroyed"

—Atharva Veda

CONCEPT

Corruption in simple terms may be described as 'an act of Bribery'. The dictionary meaning of corruption is 'decomposition, moral deterioration'. The Encyclopaedia Americana gives a very broad definition of corruption as 'the unsanctioned use of public/political resources and/or goods for non-public ends'. It has also been described as 'the use of public power for private profits in a way that constitutes a breach of law or a deviation from the norms of society'. Thus according to the Santhanam Committee[1] the term includes all 'improper or selfish exercise of power and influence attached to a public office or to a special position one occupies in public life'. The temptations of corruption are universal. 'Corruption is the most infallible symptom of constitutional liberty' is the striking remark made by Gibbon in his classical work *Decline and Fall of the Roman Empire* (Chapter 21). But the statement of Gibbon is true only partially. There is widespread corruption even in countries where individual liberty is nothing much to speak of.

Corruption is spread over in the society in several forms[2]:

1. Bribe (money offered in cash or kind of gift as inducement to procure illegal or dishonest action in favour of the giver)

---

[1] Report of the Committee on Prevention of Corruption (New Delhi: Government of India, Ministry of Home Affairs, 1964) 5.

[2] David P Forsythe, Human Rights in International Relations (Cambridge: Cambridge University Press, 2000) 20.

2. Nepotism (undue favour from holder of patronage to relatives)
3. Misappropriation (using other's money for one's own use)
4. Patronage (wrong support given by patron and thus misusing the position)
5. Favouritism (unduly preferring one to another).[3]

Corruption in any system or society depends on 3 factors: (1) the set of individual's sense of values (2) the set of social values which are accepted by the society as a whole (3) the system of governance or administration. This organisation of our society based on caste and kinship and the differences in the state of development between the states provides a very strong rationale for corruption. The specific types of corruption include:[4]

1. *Political corruption*, corruption of a political system where public officials seek illegitimate personal gains through actions such as bribery, extortion, cronyism.
2. *Police corruption*, a form of police misconduct sometimes involving political corruption and generally designed to gain a financial or political benefit for a police officer or officers in exchange for not pursuing an investigation or arrest.
3. *Data corruption*, the receiving of data which is different from that which was transmitted or otherwise intended.

Police corruption is defined as 'abuse of police authority for personal or organisational gain by a police officer acting officially'.[5] Corruption can be broken down into two sections, Internal and External corruption. With reference to the Police department, Internal corruption is the illegal acts and agreements within a police department by more than one of the officers and External corruption is the illegal acts and agreements with the public by one or more officers in a department.

The most important elements of police corruption are misuse of authority and misuse of personal attainment. Widespread corruption at every level of the administrative department poses as a great obstacle in its working, efficiently and effectively. It inverts the goals of the organisation, that is, it may encourage and create crime rather than deter it. One of the main causes for this is that the police officials have ceased to act as professionals and are politicized to a great extent.[6] They are manipulated by political leaders, who have misused the power of appointments and transfers to patronize weak or corrupt officers for their own selfish purposes at the cost of public interest. These leaders appoint wrong persons for the top jobs as they are willing to carry out the dictates and wishes of their political masters for their own survival. The main areas for their

---

[3]Ram Ahuja, Society in India—Concept, Theories and Changing Trends (New Delhi: Rawat Publications, 2002) 403.
[4]David P Forsythe, Human Rights in International Relations, 45.
[5]As defined by International Encyclopaedia of Justice Studies (IEJS).
[6]Glaeser L Edward and Claudia Goldin (Eds.), Corruption and Reform: Lessons from America's Economic History (University of Chicago Press, 2006) 380.

interference are appointments, transfers, rewards, and punishments. General police corruption includes bribery or exchange of money or something of value between the police and the wrong doer.[7] Other police crimes may range from brutality, fake encounters, sexual harassment, custodial crimes, to illicit use of weapons.

Unfortunately, corruption has occupied a permanent place in Indian society and continues to loom large over the police. The Police Department is said to be the most corrupt department where bribes are taken by constables upwards to high status officers. What is surprising is that the police take money both from the accused and the complainants.[8] One common form of police corruption is soliciting or accepting bribes in exchange for not reporting organized drug or prostitution rings or other illegal activities.

HISTORICAL ASPECT

In the olden days the media was not so open and there was a fear of authority which kept the extent of corruption effectively concealed from public knowledge. Corruption in the police department was widespread in western countries since time immemorial. Those who were serving the kings and barons became the instruments for the collection of tainted money. The growth of corruption in ancient period could be attributed to the increase in economic activity and the growth of political apathy.[9] Then came the period of exploration and colonisation and corruption took the same form. England was described a 'sink-hole' of corruption in the 17th and 18th centuries.

In ancient India, the policemen were responsible to the king and if anything were wrong or did not please the king, the policemen were held responsible. From the works of Kalidas, it appears that the administration of urban police department was not always satisfactory and the integrity of the officials was questionable. They were experts in accepting bribes.[10] But the extent of this evil seems to have been less than what it is at present. Corruption and bribery during Ashoka's reign was to an extent very less.

Policing under the Mughals suffered from inherent infirmities as they had no established hierarchy, no effective command no criminal or civil code existed. The *Kotwals* (chief officer of police and a magistrate for a city or town) and *Kazis* were notoriously corrupt.[11] 'Torture' to extort confessions was widespread and could only be avoided by bribing the

---

[7]Sumesh Kohli, Corruption in India (New Delhi: Chetan Publications, 2000) 30.

[8]Sumesh Kohli, Corruption in India, 57.

[9]M. Halayya, Emergency: A war on Corruption (New Delhi: S Chand and Co., 1975) 6.

[10]Sukla Das, Crime and Punishment in Ancient India (c AD 300-AD1100) (New Delhi: Abhinav Publications, 1999) 34.

[11]Sir Jadunath Sarkar, A Short History of Auangzeb (1618-1707) (Calcutta: M.C. Sarkar and Sons Ltd., 1962) 36.

Kotwal or *Kazi*. There was a good deal of corruption and it was a familiar saying that 'to know the *Kazi* is to court misfortune'. Later the disintegration of the central authority not only resulted in political disorder but also relaxed control from above and the police officers started exploiting the situation to their advantage and became notoriously corrupt and oppressive. Besides, the *Kotwal*, his subordinates, supplemented his stipend authorised exactions from the inhabitants, whose interests he was supposed to protect.

With the disintegration of the imperial authority of the Mughals, there was complete breakdown of the police system and it was to this legacy that the EIC succeeded as *Diwans* in Bengal, Madras and Bombay. Crime was continuously on the increase in all Presidencies. By the Regulation of 7 December 1782, the EIC took the police of the country into their own hands and it was during this time that the *Darogas* (police superintendent) ruled the territories like little kings. This period was also noteworthy for the systematic division of the city for purposes of police administration. Their misdeeds were legion and being low paid and unable to maintain the dignity of their office, they indulged in malpractices and corruption. By 1812, the administration of Criminal Justice in all the Presidencies had deteriorated to such an extent that the Directors of the EIC could no longer follow a policy of drift. But by Regulation XI of 13 September 1816, Regulations XXXV of 1802 was rescinded and the police duties were vested in the hands of villages aided by *Talliaries*. The British attitudes towards the *Kavalkars* were coloured by a conviction that they had become a corrupt and predatory 'robber police' and that they constituted a rival system inimical to European control. The period 1844AD marked the beginning of the administration of Lord William Bentinck as Governor General of India, marked by no warlike demonstrations. Bribery and corruption by the officials were pointed out as grave crimes and were accordingly punished. One of their ordinary modes of extorting money is, meeting of a party of respectably Hindus travelling in any remote part of the country, to seize them and lock them up in the nearest *chowkey* or failing that, in any cottage at hand. Nothing but a bribe releases them; and the police scoundrels feel pretty safe, for the magistrate used to be far away in the city.[12] Even if such complaints reach the magistrate's ear, the bribe is denied and as to the imprisonment, the police had warrants for the apprehension of certain parties, for whom they mistook the complainants; and therefore they were not at fault. Thus the parties aggrieved get no redress, but leave their oppressors triumphant.

The conditions of law and order deteriorated and corruption was growing among the police. This period marked a distinct deviation from the traditional course of British administration.[13] In Bengal, however due to the permanent revenue settlement and absence of a separate revenue department, there could be no marked improvement in the

---

[12]John Capper, The Three Presidencies of India (London: Ingram, Cooke & Co., 1853) 462.
[13]M.B. Chande, The Police in India (New Delhi: Atlantic Publications, 1997) 73.

organisation of the police system. The Government of Madras, in order to inquire into the allegations of torture by the police officials, appointed the Torture commission on 9 September 1854 and then submitted their report on16 April 1855 which quoted at length from the Court's letter to Madras of the 11ᵗʰ April 1826 and some observations of Colonel Munro dating back to 1802. They observed that the whole of police was under paid, notoriously corrupt and without any of the moral restraint and self respect which education ordinarily engenders, and required 'either thorough replacement or reorganization' and that there was 'but too good reason to support the existence of a league in which the native officials, with some bright expectations, are banded together from the highest to the lowest, for the common purpose of extorting illicit gains, and for mutual protection from discovery' which led to 'the universal and systematic practice of personal violence'.[14] They suggested therefore that, to render the police efficient, it must be places 'under independent European authority'. The Commission observed that torture, oppression, harassment continued till such time the victims of torture who made complaints and their family had their ruin or consummation. Then the British government made a distinct change in its perception of a reformed police with a view to increase its efficiency and their acceptability to the police in general and nearer to the base of the British police. Thus upto 1860, the Indian police had not enjoyed uniformity either in its organization, discipline or control. It had a very general character for corruption and oppression. The recognized defects of the system were: 'low rate of pay, consequent inferiority of the class of men who enter the police and also the disproportion of the strength of the force to the density of the population and to their charge'.[15] The Indian Police Commission of 1902–03 recorded extensive evidences of oppression and corruption of the police. On the threshold of freedom, the police in India found themselves engaged in a grim struggle with the evil forces let loose by the communal carnage that followed in the wake of partition. Various measures were taken including compulsory retirement of corrupt officers but the results have not been rewarding.

The Madras Presidency at this time comprised the whole of the East and south of the peninsula; yet the duties of its government may be said to be limited, as they were by no means numerous or complex. Most of the native establishments were poorly paid

---

[14]The commission quoted 2 opinions as to the character of the native police. Mr McKenzie said that 'the so called police' of the mofussil was 'little better than delusion', that it was 'a terror to well disposed and peaceable people, none whatever to thieves and rogues'. Mr Seafelt described police as 'the bane and pest of the society, the terror of the community, and the origin of half the misery and discontent', that existed among the subjects of the government. He said 'corruption and bribery reign paramount throughout the whole establishment, violence, torture and cruelty are their chief instruments for detecting crime, implicating innocence, or extorting money. 'The torture enquiry in Madras', Parliamentary paper 420 of 1855, pp. 3–47

[15]A Brief summary of facts and findings collected from *The Torture Commission Report 1855*, compiled by The Deputy Superintendent of Police, Police Research Centre, TN, Madras (1978), pp. 5–15

and with no hope of rising by integrity and energy. The lower grades of police officials were composed entirely of natives generally the poorest and most unprincipled, who took to the peculation and bribery of such places as sure means of fortune. When it is found that the pay of some of these sub-officials did not amount to more than a few shillings a month and that every means of adding to their emolument was considered as a legitimate consequence of their position, we can scarcely wonder that extortion, oppression & brutalities on the public were the universal rules among them.[16] The reins of the government were soon relaxed and misrule began to produce its neutral results. Public duty was neglected for festivals, the police and court grew corrupt, character of many of the high police officials was bad and monstrous. The state of affairs became increasingly worse, until the Madras government was compelled again to interfere and urge reforms. The new offices were created for men who were grossly, notoriously incompetent, unqualified and were also posted to higher grades. The extraordinary state of crime and prevalence of anti-social practices in the first half of the 19th century have been touched upon to show how the straggling police forced in the process of their inception and early growth were totally inadequate to deal with matters of law and orders.

The state police represent a mixed bag-it has some of the finest investigators in the country and many good officers and personnel. But it also has a fair sprinkling of the corrupt and the heartless, who take the sheen off the good work done by others, leaving behind an image of a corrupt force, which cares little for human rights and takes pleasure in the woes of many, mostly from the underprivileged sections of the society.

POLICE CORRUPTION AND HUMAN RIGHTS

It is a timely coincidence that 9th December, International Anti-Corruption day is followed on 10th December by International Human Rights day, because corruption is a human rights issue. Police Corruption is also violation of human rights as it denies some very basic rights to the citizens. The fundamental right of being protected by a law enforcing agency, mainly constituted for this purpose is being denied by the prevailing corruption.[17] The right to self-defence is under a threat with more and more cases of custodial crimes and wrongful persecution and prosecution being reported. With the present day situation worsening, the basic Right to life granted under Article 21 of

---

[16]Letter from Charles Mead dated Neyyur, January 1842, Missionary Magazine and Chronicle, Vol. VI, April 1842, p. 56.

[17]J.T. Panachakel and P.G. Thomaskutty, Economics of Corruption, Paper presented in international Conference on 'A decade of Decentralization in Kerala: Issues, Options and Lessons", 7–9 October 2005, Trivandrum, India.

the Constitution is being denied[18]. Cases of fake encounters, rising death toll in the prisons, and unnecessary delay in investigation makes one feel insecure and vulnerable.

Despite an attempt to eliminate corruption by ways like increased salaries, upgraded training, incentive for education, and developing policies that focus directly on factors leading to corruption, it still exists. Many factors converge to produce this unhappy state of affairs. By the same token, no single reform is likely to prove sufficient to the need. Among the reasons most persistently authoritively advanced to explain corruptions in the police force are the following:

1. Economic causes include craze for higher living standards, profiteering tendencies.
2. Social causes include materialistic outlook of life, erosion in social values, illiteracy, acquisitive cultural traits and exploitive social structure.[19]
3. Legislative factors include inadequate legislation, loopholes in law, callousness in implementation of laws.
4. Corruption can be traced to ineffective administrative organisation. Lack of proper vigilance, unaccountability, etc., give scope to officials not only to be corrupt but also remain unaffected even after following corrupt practices. Access is rigidly rationed through a system of intermediaries. Every multiplication of steps in the process of decision-making or implementation increases the opportunities for corruption.[20]

Given causes such as these, it is apparent that corruption will not yield to a single and simple solution and it will be a long time giving way, whatever reforms are enacted. In the past, the perception was that a citizen will have to bribe a public servant if he wants to get a benefit which was illegal. But today we have reached a stage when even for getting the legitimate demand satisfied, the citizens have to bribe the public servant. Some factors promoting corruption could be described as: (1.) attitude of the public of unquestioning subjugation to power, bred by colonial and feudal forces;[21] (2.) the clumsy handling of corruption cases; (3.) lack of public outcry and lack of strong public forum to oppose corruption also promote it.

Transfers, postings, favours, promotions and contracts normally constitute the basis for corruption. Everywhere the rule of law may be respected, the humanitarianism of human rights under the Constitution must also provide positive rights as well as negative rights, which it serves, to provide equality, concern and dignity for the citizens. A corruption free service offered is meant to provide all the human rights.

---

[18]Dr. D.D. Basu, Introduction to the Constitution of India (New Delhi: Prentice Hall of India Pvt. Ltd., 2000) 15.

[19]Jack Donnelly, Universal Human Rights in Theory and Practice (London: Cornell University Press, 2003) 150.

[20]Jack Donnelly, Universal Human Rights in Theory and Practice, 145.

[21]M. Halayya, Emergency: A War on Corruption, p. 6.

IMPACT OF POLICE CORRUPTION

Corruption comes in only when the price is paid but for which no service has been done. The existence of even a small amount of corruption in the police force is of special significance and concern, as the misuse of tremendous powers wielded by the police pose complex problems. We should not forget that corruption has affected our society in many ways:

1. It has diminished morality and destroyed individual character.
2. It has heightened inefficiency, nepotism and lethargy and has created indiscipline in Police department, making the life of the common man miserable.[22]
3. It has reduced credibility of officials in the eyes of the masses. Corruption's pernicious claws hurt more than just individuals and families—they hurt economy as well.

Some have argued that corruption is necessary for smooth functioning of societies, others even that it is beneficial to all involved. Fortunately, neither is even remotely true. Corruption harms the victim on whom it is perpetrated needs no elaboration. But that it also surely harms the perpetrator does. Perpetrators often need the collusion of their peers and connivance of their superiors (to whom they owe their power and its attendant benefits). As a result, they are forced to share their spoils with these peers and superiors. Worse, they also live in constant fear, of being betrayed or exposed.[23] This constant fear they live in as well as the easy money they have access to force them to lead sub-optimal lives, inhibiting them from fully using their potential. Corruption is also an obstacle to development. Over the years the powerful institutions of law and order have been bent to conform to executive's will and convenience. The task of improving the existing situation cannot be left to the police department alone. Political authorities and the Union Home Ministry have to step in for stopping the situation from deteriorating further and also for its betterment. One reason why we cannot check corruption is because the corrupt, with the financial clout of their ill gotten wealth, are able to engage the best brains and quibble their way through the legal system and laugh all the way to the bank.

CRUSADE AGAINST CORRUPTION

Most of the human rights violation scenarios are resulted from corrupted environment and it is obviously contradicting human rights. A genuine attempt has been made by the government to make the Central Vigilance Commissioner (set up in 1964) into an effective instrument to check corruption. There is a need for explicitly articulating the

---

[22]Robin Hoddes, Victoria Jennett and Diane Mak, Global Corruption Report–2007 (New York: Cambridge University Press) 245.
[23]Robin Hoddes, Victoria Jennett and Diane Mak, Global Corruption Report–2007, 267

corruption-free service as a patent fundamental right of the Indian citizen so that what is latent and lying hidden in the other provisions of the Constitution can be made explicit. Making this explicit has the advantage of sending a signal throughout the country about the commitment of the state for improving the quality of life of the citizens of this country. Article 19 gives fundamental right to business or profession. If a corrupt police official uses his power of office to restrict a citizen because he has not bribed him, he is indirectly preventing the exercise of the fundamental right of the citizen by his act of corruption.

A committee to draft an Act for making the working of the police department transparent and accountable was constituted on 20th September 2005. It is called The Police Act Drafting Committee (PADC).[24] The Supreme Court had set the deadline as 31st December 2006 for the Central and State governments to implement the reforms so as to keep country's police administration above political interference and corruption. These reforms mainly include:

1. A minimum tenure for DGP's and other senior officers[25]
2. Setting up of State Security Commissions
3. Separation of investigation from law and order, and
4. Establishment of a police panel to decide transfers and promotions.

Society members should be educated about the negative affects of corruption within the police force and its long term disadvantages. For controlling corruption the police department requires an organisation lead by people of strong character and who have good leadership qualities.[26] The departmental goal should be well defined and should be pursued earnestly. But the task of eliminating or at least reducing corruption among the police is handicapped by two factors:

(a) lack of information about instances of corruption and
(b) cumbersome procedures for assessing guilt and awarding punishment.

Moreover many officers feel they must tread softly in the handling of complaints about corruption because they are aware that morale in a force may be destroyed if subordinates are not defended by superiors from malicious charges. An unusual amount of courage is required to use the full resources of one's office to eliminate widespread and customary abuses.

Various other measures to combat police corruption could be:

1. Set up watchdog groups and special investigations. Use external and politically independent commissions to investigate corruption. Because they are not part of the department, hopefully they will be unbiased and not influenced by corruption

---

[24]The Hindu, October 10, 2005.
[25]Police Act Drafting Committee 2006, New Delhi: Government of India, Ministry of Home Affairs, p. 3.
[26]The Indian Express, September 25, 2006.

in the dept. The problem with this, is that because the members of the commission are not police officers, they may not understand how policing really works.

2. Use the mass media to expose corruption, mobilize public opinion, and provide chief with support for anti-corruption policy which may be unpopular with officers

3. In the Police department, frequent transfers at the lower level should be avoided. For promotions both seniority with 10 years service and academic merit with graduation along with Diploma in Human rights should be insisted. There should be more emphasis on corruption control at the selection and training phase of policing. This would include greater focus on each applicant's integrity recruitment phase (background checks, integrity tests, polygraph tests) as well as providing more anti-corruption and ethics training at the academy

4. Artificial shortages and scarcities which facilitate illegal gratification have to be controlled

5. Vigilance should be increased. Surprise checks should be carried out at vulnerable points of corruption

6. Cooperation of the people has to be obtained for successfully controlling corruption. Increase citizen involvement. Some departments have civilian review boards or oversight committees who monitor the dept and review allegations of police misconduct.

Corruption is a hydra-headed monster which can be vanquished only by the collective efforts of the public. There is a clamour for the establishment of an all-powerful ombudsman as a custodian of police conscience, but this still seems to be a distant dream. It is necessary that problems of corruption at different levels be tackled with a sense of priority. Parents and teachers have a vital role in imparting values to children, especially against the canker of corruption. It is high time that everyone in the family try to be blemishless so that the children follow the footsteps of the elders.

Let us begin to reject the 'bad apple' theory—that corrupt officers are only a few rotten apples in the barrel. Instead, begin to examine the 'barrel'—the individual police department—for signs that corruption is allowed, encouraged, or ignored. It is no surprise therefore that when Anna Hazare began his 'fast-unto-death' at Jantar Mantar in Delhi on April 6, 2011,[27] thousands of social activists descended on the venue to express their solidarity with the crusader against corruption and back his demand for putting in place a Jan Lokpal Bill, drafted through a civil society initiative.

---

[27]The Hindu, April 22, 2011.

REFERENCES

[1] Forsythe, David P., Human Rights in International Relations, Cambridge: Cambridge University Press, 2000.

[2] Basu, D.D., Introduction to the Constitution of India, New Delhi: Prentice Hall of India Pvt. Ltd., 2000.

[3] Edward, Glaeser L. and Goldin, Claudia (Eds.), Corruption and Reform: Lessons from America's Economic History, University of Chicago Press, 2006.

[4] Donnelly, Jack, Universal Human Rights in Theory and Practice, London: Cornell University Press, 2003.

[5] Capper, John, The Three Presidencies of India, London: Ingram, Cooke & Co., 1853.

[6] Chande, M.B., The Police in India, New Delhi: Atlantic Publications, 1997.

[7] Halayya, M., Emergency: A war on Corruption, New Delhi: S. Chand and Co., 1975.

[8] Ahuja, Ram, Society in India—Concept, Theories and Changing Trends, New Delhi: Rawat Publications, 2002.

[9] Sarkar, Jadunath, A Short History of Auangzeb (1618–1707), Calcutta: M.C. Sarkar and Sons Ltd., 1962.

[10] Kohli, Sumesh, Corruption in India, New Delhi: Chetan Publications, 2000.

[11] Das, Sukla, Crime and Punishment in Ancient India (c AD 300-AD1100), New Delhi: Abhinav Publications, 1999.

[12] Hoddes, Robin; Jennett, Victoria and Mak, Diane, Global Corruption Report 2007, New York: Cambridge University Press.

[13] 'The Torture Enquiry in Madras', Parliamentary paper 420 of 1855.

[14] 'The Torture Commission Report 1855', compiled by The Deputy Superintendent of Police, Police Research Centre, TN, Madras (1978).

[15] Report of the Committee on Prevention of Corruption, New Delhi: Government of India, Ministry of Home Affairs, 1964.

[16] Police Act Drafting Committee 2006, New Delhi: Government of India, Ministry of Home Affairs.

[17] Missionary Magazine and Chronicle, Vol. VI, April 1842.

[18] Panachakel, J.T. and Thomaskutty, P.G., Economics of Corruption, Paper presented in international Conference on 'A decade of Decentralization in Kerala: Issues, Options and Lessons", 7–9 October 2005, Trivandrum, India.

[19] The Hindu, October 10, 2005.

[20] The Indian Express, September 25, 2006.

[21] The Hindu, April 22, 2011.

[22] International Encyclopaedia of Justice Studies (IEJS).

Indian Political Corruption— A Sociological Analysis

G. Venkatesan[1] and M. Thamilarasan[2]
Department of Sociology, University of Madras, Chennai-600 005
E-mail: [1]sivamvenkat@live.com; [2]mahathamil@yahoo.co.in

INTRODUCTION

Corruption is a disease, a cancer that eats into the cultural, political and economic fabric of society, and destroys the functioning of vital organs. In the words of Transparency International, "Corruption is one of the greatest challenges of the contemporary world. It undermines good government, fundamentally distorts public policy, leads to the misallocation of resources, harms the private sector and private sector development and particularly hurts the poor."

Political Corruption

Political corruption is defined as the legislative powers of government employees through which they misuse the services provided to them for their own profits. The basic reason of political corruption is to make their own gains from the finance which is meant for the general public. The leaders and government officials uses the unfair means according to which they do not do their tasks with honesty and uses the public finance for their own gains. For example—If you want to register some land to your own name, for this purpose you have to go to court for registration and this registration process requires so much interaction with government officials and employees which is so time consuming process because the employees and officials neglect their duties and uses the unfair means according to which they demand some finance from the customer (who want to register his land with his/her own name) and due to this reason only, they neglect their work and if all requirements of government officials are fulfilled by the customer then only it will be provided with complete register documents otherwise the customer has to wait for the approval of documents, Not only this if any unfair means is adopted by the government officials after neglecting their duty then it is referred as Corruption.

Corruption has been the subject of a substantial amount of theorizing and empirical research over the last 30 years, and this has produced a bewildering array of alternative explanations, typologies and remedies. However, as an extensively applied notion in both politics and social sciences, corruption is being used rather haphazardly. Corruption is understood as everything from the paying of bribes to civil servants in return for some favour and the theft of public purses, to a wide range of dubious economic and political practices in which politicians and bureaucrats enrich themselves and any abusive use of public power to a personal end.

Besides, corruption is in itself a many-faceted phenomenon and the concept of corruption contains too many connotations to be analytically functional without a closer definition. The forms of corruption are diverse in terms of who are the actors, initiators and profiteers, how it is done, and to what extent it is practiced. Also the causes and the consequences of corruption are complex and diverse, and have been sought in both individual ethics and civic cultures, in history and tradition, in the economic system, in the institutional arrangements, and in the political system.

Effects on Politics, Administration and Institutions

Detail from Corrupt Legislation (1896) by Elihu vedder Library of Congress Thomas Jefferson Building Washington, D.C. Corruption poses a serious development challenge. In the political realm, it undermines democracy and good governance flouting or even subverting formal processes. Corruption in elections and in legislative bodies reduces accountability and distorts representation in policymaking; corruption in the judiciary compromises the rule of law; and corruption in public administration results in the inefficient provision of services. It violates a basic principle of republicanism regarding the centrality of civic virtue. More generally, corruption erodes the institutional capacity of government as procedures are disregarded, resources are siphoned off, and public offices are bought and sold. At the same time, corruption undermines the legitimacy of government and such democratic values as trust and tolerance.

Economic Effects

Corruption undermines economic development by generating considerable distortions and inefficiency. In the private sector, corruption increases the cost of business through the price of illicit payments themselves, the management cost of negotiating with officials, and the risk of breached agreements or detection. Although some claim corruption reduces costs by cutting red tape, the availability of bribes can also induce officials to contrive new rules and delays. Openly removing costly and lengthy regulations are better than covertly allowing them to be bypassed by using bribes, where corruption inflates the cost of business, it also distorts the playing field, shielding firms with connections from competition and thereby sustaining inefficient firms.

Corruption also generates economic distortions in the public sector by diverting public investment into capital projects where bribes and kickbacks are more plentiful. Officials may increase the technical complexity of public sector projects to conceal or pave the way for such dealings, thus further distorting investment. Corruption also lowers compliance with construction, environmental, or other regulations, reduces the quality of government services and infrastructure, and increases budgetary pressures on government.

Environmental and Social Effects

Corruption facilitates environmental destruction. Corrupt countries may formally have legislation to protect the environment; it cannot be enforced if officials can easily be bribed. The same applies to social rights worker protection, unionization prevention, and child labour. Violation of these laws rights enables corrupt countries to gain illegitimate economic advantage in the international market.

The Nobel Prize-winning economist amartya sen has observed that "there is no such thing as an apolitical food problem." While drought and other naturally occurring events may trigger famine conditions, it is government action or inaction that determines its severity, and often even whether or not a famine will occur. Governments with strong tendencies towards kleptocracy can undermine food security even when harvests are good. Officials often steal state property. In Bihar India, more than 80% of the subsidized food aid to poor is stolen by corrupt officials. Similarly, food aid is often robbed at gunpoint by governments, criminals, and warlords alike, and sold for a profit. The 20th century is full of many examples of governments undermining the food security of their own nations—sometimes intentionally.

Effects on Humanitarian Aid

The scale of humanitarian aid to the poor and unstable regions of the world grows, but it is highly vulnerable to corruption, with food aid, construction and other highly valued assistance as the most at risk. Food aid can be directly and physically diverted from its intended destination, or indirectly through the manipulation of assessments, targeting, registration and distributions to favour certain groups or individuals. Elsewhere, in construction and shelter, there are numerous opportunities for diversion and profit through substandard workmanship, kickbacks for contracts and favouritism in the provision of valuable shelter material. Thus while humanitarian aid agencies are usually most concerned about aid being diverted by including too many; recipients themselves are most concerned about exclusion. Access to aid may be limited to those with connections, to those who pay bribes or are forced to give sexual favours. Equally, those able to do so may manipulate statistics to inflate the number beneficiaries and syphon of the additional assistance.

OTHER AREAS: HEALTH, PUBLIC SAFETY, EDUCATION, TRADE UNIONS, ETC.

Relation of India with Corruption

The India is the vast country which consists of so many cultures and languages, every culture has its own significance. So, India as a whole is united as the single country but only thing which India wants to improve is to become the developed country. Many reasons are responsible which has resisted India to become the developed country such as poverty, employment, women inequality, corruption, economic crisis, Instability in stock market, gap between the rich and poor etc. In this article, we have only concerned with the corruption because recently we have seen so many cases of corruption in India on the large scale which has made a huge impact on the National image of India. Moreover, the Relation of India with corruption for last one year is explained with the help of recently happened examples which is discussed below.

2G Spectrum Spam Corruption in India

The people still have the live memories of above mentioned corruption acts, many of them still not able to forget the Corruption acts. At the same time phase, The Government of India has undergone through the big Corruption act which leads to the large loss of finance for the Indian government such that the Telecom Ministry of the India has distributed so many licenses to the telecom companies without verifying their personal report card, these companies which is not fully ready for the memberships are provided with the rights to use the 2G technology, even though some companies do not have that much power to afford the finance requirement but still they are provided with 2G technology because most of these companies are relational known for the telecom minister. Finally at the end, the telecom minister was send to the jail for the trail because of the large Corruption he has done, this corruption has made a huge loss for the telecom sector and also the share and stock market too which indirectly a bad news for the investors whom had invested their amount in the market.

The Fuel of Corruption

But the situation is much more alarming than this. On a purely theoretical level, assuming that a candidate does not get the financial support of any party, organization, or other individual, as in the case of some independents, and actually spends the Rs.15 lakhs prescribed by the Election Commission, what would he actually receive at the end of the process, if successful? An MP in India receives approximately Rs.10, 000 per month excluding perquisites. It is trivial to demonstrate that it is impossible to recover the admissible expenses of elections from the salary officially received by MPs. Thus we have the strange phenomenon that at least some of our representatives are happily losing big money by representing us. Apart from a few charitable folk who might thus find spiritual bliss in 'serving' the society, I find it very difficult to believe that people in general would voluntarily give up their time and money merely to have the thankless and often dangerous and dubious pleasure of representing us.

CONCLUSION

Among the working people of India, 94 per cent are in the unorganized sector. It is this section that urgently needs social security, since they are the most exploited. Only one lakh crore is needed as seed money to start social security to them. Our villages need roads, our children need schools and teachers. Villagers need primary health Centres with doctors and equipment. We want clean hygienic drinking water; we need energy, irrigation, water, and houses for poor. Our downtrodden need nutritious food to keep them healthy. All these minimum facilities can be provided with less than 25 lakh crores of rupees. It is not only in Swiss banks but in many other countries that the black money is deposited. There should be an international agreement to put an end to deposit of unaccounted money.

The corruption can be fought successfully by unearthing the unaccounted money. The Supreme Court said that keeping black money out of the country is an act of keeping the loot of the nation. It further said that a part of black money might find its way to terrorist activities. Hence there is urgency in this regard. After 26 names of Swiss Bank depositors were given in a sealed cover by the Solicitor General, the Supreme Court made the above observations.

REFERENCES

[1] Madan, G.R., Casteism, Corruption and Social Development in India, Radha publication, New Dehli-110 002.

[2] Vittal, N. (2003), Corruption in India, The Rood block to National Prosperity, Academic Foundation.

[3] Corruption in India: Gupta, K.N. (2001), Anmol Publication Pvt. Ltd.

[4] Gupta, R.K., Corruption in India: Origin cause and solutions: Anamika publication Pvt. Ltd.

Election and Political Corruption in India— A Human Rights Perspective

T. Arumugam

Department of Political Science, Presidency College, Chennai-600 005

"Rights are those essential conditions of social life without which no man can seek himself to be at his best."

—*Prof. Laski*

Rights are essential for every individual to attain fullest development in life. Human Rights are those rights one he entails to posses, enjoy and to have protected irrespective of his nationality political view citizenship or the form of government under which he lives.

According to ancient Indian political intellectual Kautilya, 'just as it is impossible not to taste that honey the finds itself at the top of the tongue, so it is impossible for government servants not to eat up atleast a bit of kings revenue'. Just as fish moving in water cannot possibly found out either as drinking or not drinking water. So government servants employed cannot be found out taking money for themselves.'

Shakespeare pointed out in Measure for Measure that laws are like scare crows, set up to scare birds, once birds realise that the scare crow is lifeless, they build their nests on it. Thus corruption is in form of bribes, special treatment, nepotism, non-performance and under performance. Justice Chawhan observed, corruption is the worst form of human rights violation.

Soundness of a democracy depends upon the quality of representatives elected by the people. The democratic electoral system plays a fundamental key role in the formulation of the government and also to the quality of any form of governance.

This paper is a modest attempt in focussing the prevailing role of corruption in various stages of electoral process in electing the peoples representative to the democratic institutions and thereafter in the exploring political corruption.

According to the 2006 Transparency International global corruption survey reported India is ranking 87th among 178 countries and among 15 Asian countries ranks 9th with low transparency score of 2.9 out of 10 as per corruption perception. This figure shows the breadth and depth of corruption that has routed in the day today life of Indian society. The pervasive corruption not only affects every citizen of the country but also damage the cultured Indian society.

Even the poor have nots are compelled to pay bribe to exercise their rights guaranteed in the constitution. They have to pay bribe forgetting their wages under MGNRES and other welfare schemes intended for them. In fact it is very difficult to lead life for common poor due to the low level corruption in the every level of the administration. Corruption in high level is looting our public exchequer, damage so heavily public government policy and make way for creating a mafia group who dominate the directly or indirectly the power and administration. Cancer in human body if not timely treatment is given, it will certainly invade and destroy the entire body and make our end of the breath, so as administrative and political corruption are the two major hindrances to the development of the country. A concert effort on all fronts is required to combat the evil growth.

The representative government is the foundation of principle of popular sovereignty. The popular sovereignty can exists only with popular government. The most important basic means by which the people exercise their sovereignty is by voting. These people who are qualified by the law of the land form their electorate to elect the representatives.

ELECTION PROCESS

Election is a continuous process. In delimitation of constituency the Gerry meandering concept is followed by political party in power with the collusion of the bureaucracy. The polling stations are not provided as per norms prescribed. The previous polling station is authorised without due verification. There may be some changes in the buildings that may lead polling congestion while exercising vote pay way for impersonization, booth capturing and other illegal election oriented offences.

The rule provides that the candidate contesting for election needs to furnish his movable and immovable asset, educational qualification and his criminal antecedents. No provision to verify the facts at the time of scrutiny if otherwise the information is objected by the opposition candidate submission of false and incorrect information of the individual itself is a kind of corrupt act. Withdrawal of nomination is being done with forgery signature.

Muscle and Money Power

Theses play an important unhealthy role which appeals to the narrow interest of the caste, community, religion and language. Candidates who are capable of winning by fair means are defeated and fouled are selected. Even criminals with associated of murder, decoy and rape get elected only with the help of the black money.

Criminals in Democratic Institution

Indian democracy institutions namely parliamentary, state assembly, local bodies have an overwhelming graded percentage of criminals. In the 2004 Lok Sabha 120 MPS had criminal cases pending on them out of 543 or 22.1 % were from criminal background. Among the major parties BJP 20, INC 24, SP 11, RJD 8, CPM 7, BSP 7, NCP 5, CPI 2 had criminal background.

> *I cannot accept your cannon that we are to judge pope and king unlike other man, with the favourable presumption that they did no wrong. There is one provision it is the other way against the holders of the power increasing as the power increases. Historic responsibility has to make up for the want of legal responsibility. Power tends to corrupts and absolute power corrupts absolutely,*
>
> *—Lord Acton in a letter to the bishop of England in 1857*

Challenges to Indian Democracy

What the past six decade of independence proved to the world is that rich are becoming rich and poor are becoming poor. The gap between the have and have nots have been widened the development we perceived is not a healthy one. Indian democracy is only partial success in holding the election and ensuring the right of the citizen, but the functioning of the politicians and institutions is not in the right path of performance that leads to corruption and human right violation. Certain shortfalls are there in our electoral system that can be experienced from the governance of elected bodies. Infirmity and weakness of electoral system coupled together with corrupt politician have made our democracy chaotic and rust. Illiteracy and poverty and caste based society among majority tend to have corrupt and cumbersome bureaucracy also cause for the decay of the system.

India the biggest democratic in the world having largest technical manpower in the world and blooming software industries have achieved in 9% growth. Though it is in the front line in the racing, in the race of developing countries yet the grave facts reminds that 26% of people are still below poverty line. Prevailing of unemployment among the youth, need of health care even safe drinking water and basic shelter are still scarce. These results in what we perceive are not real development or achievement but are pseudo. Than what is the purpose of existing of good governance? The CAG of India reports on major scams about the political corruption in India and administration.

Good Governance and Corruption

The root cause of corruption can be traced from many factors among which the most important is lack of good governance. Shakespeare pointed out in "Measure for Measure", that laws are like scarecrows set up to scare birds once birds realize that scarecrow is life less, they build their nest on it. They Good governance is a combination of appropriate institutional mechanism and a process for effectiveness without loophole for any irregularity or corruption in administration within a democratic constitutional set up, which may lead to development and equal distribution of wealth.

According to Gandhi, corruption lay not only in those who are in power and misuse it, but also in the weak who submitted to it. Of universal values and morality the 20th centuries has already proclaimed human rights as a cherished ideal that must develop in the mind and heart. Through politician the future world must conduct good governance through respecting human rights of all people.

"The supreme court of India on 3rd February 2000 stated that if corruption has not checked effectively at the earliest the socio economic system might collapse." Corruption is against democracy and opposed to the human rights.

Political Corruption

> *"I would go the length of giving the whole congress a decent burial rather than put up with the corruption what is rampant."*
>
> *—Gandhi 1937 May*

These are the word of the father of the nation in the year 1937 against large scale corruption in congress ministry in six states constituted under 1935 act. More than three decade of democracy corruption had made the poor citizen of India to such an extent to learn how to live with corruptive system. Even they know that corruption is cancer its growth will finally destroy them but they have no other go.

> *"History has thought us that corruption and nepotism are the major cause of French revolution, Russian revolution, the long march of Chinese revolution yet we have learnt how to live with tolerance with non violence. There is corruption and Human rights the violence which is silently destroying our. Society like King Nero playing piddle while Rome was burning."*

Economic System and Corruption

The present economic system is vulnerable to cronyism and criminality which provide opportunities to corruptive politicians in power to misuse authority to earn in an illegal way. Further criminals make use of the elections as base and get elected to the democratic institutions in order to safe guard themselves and black money. There is no effective mechanism to curb corruption, and also no political will to combat corrupttion. The society itself has learned to survive and emerge into it unwillingly.

According to Prakash Karat, General Secretary, Communist Party (Marxist) gravity in corruption is the result of neo-liberal policies followed by the successive governments. There must be systematic reforms to curb the nexus between politicians, bureaucracy and big corporate deal with corruption. On corruption in judiciary, a judicial commission needs to be setup to deal with the appointment and conduct of the judiciary.

Election and Corruption

According to Chief Election Commissioner of India, Qurashi, India must ban politicians accused of serious crimes from contesting elections if it wants to eradicate the root cause of official corruptions.

Party spending money should be made more transparent in order to make a stop to the practice of giving money in return of vote. Under the existing system politicians on trail or who have appealed against their conviction are free to contest in elections. Where as the most criminal cases last for more than a 10 years. There is a black dot on the quality of Indian democracy. The person responsible for this shameful cause need to be identified and remove from the public life.

During the recent election to the five state legislative and estimated of 750 dollars millions were paid to the voters as bribes out of which only a small amount of money was recovered and in Tamil Nadu nearly rupees 60 crores had been seized. Further it is repotted by the election commissioner of India Mr. Quraishi that the commission could not able to check black money used to influence voting and that the election commission believes on self discipline by political parties and transparency in them in spending money to reduce payment of black money.

In Raj Narain *vs.* Smt. Gandhi, justice Sinha of Allahabad high court delivered his judgment disqualifying Gandhi for misuse of official power to be elected to Member of Parliament. In the recently concluded by election to ward 5 of Madurai corporation nomination was rejected on the ground that the applicant did not fill the nomination properly, name in the voter list did not tally with ID card, property details in the application did not match the corporation records. Later the nominations were accepted following a direction of the state election commission. The election officials responsible for rejecting the nomination were relieved from the duties. This is an example only were the bureaucrat collides with politician and indulge in corrupt activities.

License to govern does not mean license to corrupt. M.K. Gandhi believed in creating a society with self sufficient itself with dignity of human rights in which corruption would not grow. Corruption is a complex issue that is embedded in bureaucratic rigidity economic and political power. In some or other way the government is the major promoter of corruption though it concern individual morality. The existing rules and system and institutional mechanism are only aim to punish the corrupt activities but not to eradicate or to reduce the pervasive corruption. The decision making in all level need transparency and not secrecy. These will certainly cater the need in eradicating corruption and promoting human rights.

Money power, muscle power and mafia power have weaken the election process and are hinderant for development and as well as against human rights. Corruption, criminalize-tion, casteism and communalism have further fuelled and damaged the legitimacy of political process. People have fed up with all these kind of pervasive corruption and hence to eradicate all this evil from the Indian political and civil administration and from the clutches of the black money and to make vibrant and transparent, peoples service oriented, it is the right time to have a strong institution to prosecute and reduce corruption in public servant both corrupt politician and bureaucracy it is suggested that to have a strong and independent Lok pal with elected representative of people and civil society will certainly make democracy truly realize and flourishing of human rights.

REFERENCES

[1] Viswanathan, V.N., (Ed), *Human Rights Challenges of 21ˢᵗ Century*, New Delhi: Kalpaz Publications, 2008.

[2] Bagchi, K.K., *Good Governance and Development: An Indian Perspective*, New Delhi: Abhijeet Publications, 2009.

[3] Joseph, T.M., *Governance, Reforms and Challenges Ahead*, New Delhi: Kanishka Publications, 2009.

[4] Venkateshan, V.C., *Public Administration, Principles Practices, Perspectives*, Rajapalayam: V.C. Publications, 2009.

[5] The Hindu.

Corruption and Politics

R. Thilagaraj[1] and S. Latha[2]

[1]Department of Criminology, University of Madras, Chennai-600 005
[2]School of Criminology and Criminal Justice, Tamil Nadu Open University, Chennai-600 005

Political Corruption throughout the world has become a major issue which is to be addressed very seriously.

> *"I would go to the length of giving the whole congress a decent burial, rather than put up with the corruption that is rampant."*

> —*Mahatma Gandhi, May 1939*

This was the outburst of Mahatma Gandhi against rampant corruption in Congress ministries formed under 1935 Act in six States in the year 1937. Politicians are synonymously identified by the public that they are corrupt. A poll conducted by Times *of India* exposed that 1,554 adults in six metropolitan cities reported that 98 per cent of the public is convinced with the fact politicians and ministers are corrupt, with 85 per cent observing that corruption is on the increase. Rarely Mr. and Mrs. Cleans are found in Politics and if they are found they are abandoned minorities. This present paper deals with the nexus between the politics and corruption in detail.

CORRUPTION IN INDIA

The year 2011 has proved to be a watershed in the public tolerance of political corruption in India with widespread public protests and movements led by social activists against corruption and for the return of illegal wealth stashed by politicians and businessmen in foreign banks over the six decades since independence. In 2010, India was ranked 87th out of 178 countries in Transparency International's Corruption Perception Index.

India tops the list for black money in the entire world with almost US$1456 billion in Swiss banks (approximately USD 1.4 trillion) in the form of black money.[1] According to the data provided by the Swiss Banking Association Report (2006), India has more black money than the rest of the world combined[2,3] http://en.wikipedia.org/

wiki/Corruption_in_india-cite_note-10. To put things in perspective, Indian-owned Swiss bank account assets are worth 13 times the country's national debt.[4]

Independent reports published through 1991 to 2011 calculated the financial net worth of India's most powerful and traditionally ruling family (the Nehru-Gandhi political dynasty) to be anywhere between $9.41 billion (Rs. 42,345 crore) to $18.66 billion (Rs. 83,900 crore), most of it in the form of illegal money.[5]

In the present context corruption is so much linked with power that politicians have adopted a cynical attitude toward political morality. Maneuvering the anti-defection law for electoral politics with the help of both money and muscle power and other unfair means for the sake of power have affected the political morality of all the political parties and as such none of them can claim themselves to be faithful to nation in true sense.

India's public campaign-finance laws are not enforced and candidates are regularly backed by donors and corporations that expect favors in return. It's a self-perpetuating cycle of corruption that has carried over since the days of the British Raj, when politicians and bureaucrats expected under-the-table payments. Today, Indians complain that the culture of corruption exists at all levels of government. It's certainly the case in high office.

POLITICAL CORRUPTION

Political corruption is the use of legislated powers by government officials for illegitimate private gain. Misuse of government power for other purposes, such as repression of political opponents and general police brutality, is not considered political corruption. Neither are illegal acts by private persons or corporations not directly involved with the government. An illegal act by an officeholder constitutes political corruption only if the act is directly related to their official duties.

Forms of corruption vary, but   include bribery, extortion, cronyism, nepotism, patronage, graft, and embezzlement. While corruption may facilitate criminal enterprise such as drug, money laundering, and human trafficking, it is not restricted to these activities.

The activities that constitute illegal corruption differ depending on the country or jurisdiction. For instance, certain political funding practices that are legal in one place may be illegal in another. In some cases, government officials have broad or poorly defined powers, which make it difficult to distinguish between legal and illegal actions.

BACKGROUND

The history of corruption in post-Independence India starts with the Jeep scandal in 1948, when a transaction concerning purchase of jeeps for the army needed for Kashmir operation was entered into by V.K. Krishna Menon, the then High Commissioner for India in London with a foreign firm without observing normal procedure. Contrary to the demand of the opposition for judicial inquiry as suggested by the Inquiry Committee led by Ananthsayanam Ayyangar, the then Government announced on September 30, 1955 that the Jeep scandal case was closed [6].

Corruption charges in cases like Mudgal case (1951), Mundra deals (1957–58), Malaviya-Sirajuddin scandal (1963), and Pratap Singh Kairon case (1963) were leveled against the Congress ministers and Chief Ministers but no Prime Minister resigned. As of December 2008, 120 of India's 522 parliament members were facing criminal charges. Many of the biggest scandals since 2010 have involved very high levels of government, including cabinet ministers and Chief Ministers, such as the 2G spectrum scam and the Adarsh Housing Society Scam.[6]

Corruption—the fact itself, but even more important, the talk of it occupies a great place in Indian politics. The sequence of events which culminated in 2011 began before the national general elections in April and May 1996. The only difference between the past and present is the enormity of corruption.[7]

The economic liberalization seems to have increased the demand and supply of corruption, provided new opportunities for corruption through deregulation and state disinvestment, and marketized politics for the poor.[7]

The major cause of concern is that corruption is weakening the political body and damaging the supreme importance of the law governing the society. Elections in many parts of the country have become associated with a host of criminal activities. Threatening voters to vote for a particular candidate or physically prevent voters from going in to the polling booth—especially weaker sections of the society like tribals, dalits and rural women occurs frequently in several parts of the country. Tax evasion is one of the most popular forms of corruption. It is mostly practiced by Government officials and politicians who lead to the accumulation of black money which in turn spoils the moral of the people.

EFFECTS

Corruption poses a serious development challenge. In the political realm, it undermines democracy and good governance by flouting or even subverting formal processes. Corruption in elections and legislative bodies reduces accountability and distorts representations in policy-making; corruption in the judiciary compromises the rule of law; and corruption in public administration results in the inefficient provision of services. It violates a basic principle of republicanism regarding the centrality of civic virtue. More generally, corruption erodes the institutional capacity of government as procedures are disregarded, resources are siphoned off, and public offices are bought and sold. At the same time, corruption undermines the legitimacy of government and such democratic values as trust and tolerance.

Corruption undermines economic development by generating considerable distortions and inefficiency. In the private sector, corruption increases the cost of business through the price of illicit payments themselves, the management cost of negotiating with officials, and the risk of breached agreements or deductions. Although some claim corruption reduces costs by cutting down bureaucracy, the availability of bribes can also induce officials to contrive new rules and delays. Openly removing costly and lengthy regulations are better than covertly allowing them to be bypassed by using bribes. Where corruption inflates the cost of business, it also distorts the playing field, shielding firms with connections from competition and thereby sustaining inefficient firms.

Corruption also generates economic distortions in the public sector by diverting public investment into capital projects where bribes and kickbacks are more plentiful. Officials may increase the technical complexity of public sector projects to conceal or pave the way for such dealings, thus further distorting investment. Corruption also lowers compliance with construction, environmental or other regulations, reduces the quality of government services and infrastructure, and increases budgetary pressures on government.

COMMITTEES ON CORRUPTION

I. Santhanam Committee

The Santhanam Committee, which was appointed by the Government in 1962 to examine the issue of corruption in its report submitted in 1964 observed: "There is widespread impression that failure of integrity is not uncommon among ministers and that some ministers, who have held office during the last sixteen years have enriched themselves illegitimately, obtained good jobs for their sons and relations through nepotism and have reaped other advantages inconsistent with any notion of purity in public life."

II. Vohra Committee Report

The Vohra (Committee) Report was submitted by the former Indian Union Home Secretary, N.N. Vohra, in October 1993. It studied the problem of the criminalisation of politics and of the nexus among criminals, politicians and bureaucrats in India.

The report contained several observations made by official agencies on the criminal network which was virtually running a parallel government. It also discussed criminal gangs who enjoyed the patronage of politicians, of all parties, and the protection of government functionaries. It revealed that political leaders had become the leaders of gangs. They were connected to the military. Over the years criminals had been elected to local bodies, State Assemblies and Parliament. The unpublished annexures to the Vohra Report were believed to contain highly explosive material.

In 1997 the Supreme Court recommended the appointment of a high level committee to ensure in-depth investigation into the findings of the N.N. Vohra Committee and to secure prosecution of those involved.

Government had established the Committee after seeing the reports of our Intelligence and Investigation agencies on the activities/linkages of the Dawood Ibrahim gang, consequent to the bomb blasts in Bombay in March 1993." (2.1 cf. 1993 Bombay bombings, Dawood Ibrahim)

"In the bigger cities, the main source of income relates to real estate—forcibly occupying lands/buildings, procuring such properties at cheap rates by forcing out the existing occupants/tenants etc. Over time, the money power thus acquired is used for building up contacts with bureaucrats and politicians and expansion of activities with impunity. The money power is used to develop a network of muscle-power which is also used by the politicians during elections."

"The nexus between the criminal gangs, police, bureaucracy and politicians has come out clearly in various parts of the country. The existing criminal justice system, which was essentially designed to deal with the individual offences/crimes, is unable to deal with the activities of the Mafia; the provisions of law in regard economic offences are weak (...)"

"Director CBI has observed that there are many such cases, as that of [mafia boss Iqbal] MIRCHI where the initial failure has led to the emergence of Mafia giants who have become too big to be tackled."

"Like the Director CBI, the DIB has also stated that there has been a rapid spread and growth of criminal gangs, armed senas, drug Mafias, smuggling gangs, drug peddlers and economic lobbies in the country which have, over the years, developed an extensive network of contacts with the bureaucrats/Government functionaries at the local levels, politicians, media persons and strategically located individuals in the non-State sector. Some of these Syndicates also have international linkages, including the foreign intelligence agencies."

"The various crime Syndicates/Mafia organizations have developed significant muscle and money power and established linkages with governmental functionaries, political leaders and others to be able to operate with impunity."

"The various agencies presently in the field take care to essentially focus on their respective charter of duties, dealing with the infringement of laws relating to their organizations and consciously putting aside any information on linkages which they may come across."

"In the background of the discussions so far, there does not appear to be need for any further debate on the vital importance of setting up a nodal point to which all existing intelligence and Enforcement agencies (irrespective of the Department under which they are located) shall promptly pass on any information which they may come across, which relates to the activities of crime Syndicates." [8]

CONCLUSION

Every study or survey, academic or governmental, brings out two glaring facts. First, that India's economic growth in GDP terms over the past decade has been as impressive as it has been lopsided It has produces billionaires but it has also increased the numbers of the hungry, the sick and the illiterate and two, that as the total value of the SENSEX goes up does the index of corruption. Higher the GDP, higher the scale and span of corruption.

The political class stands seriously exposed as the fountain head of corruption in India. That of course is not to say that the bureaucracy, judiciary, the legislature or for that matter the defense forces which, till not long ago, were seen to be an island in the middle of the systemic quagmire of corruption that surrounded it, have not tried to keep pace with their political counterparts.

That one thing that needs to be ensured is proper, impartial and unbiased use of various anti-social regulations to take strong, deterrent and timely legal action against the offenders, irrespective of their political influences or money power.

REFERENCES

[1] www.thehindubusinessline.in/2010/08/13/stories/2010081350370900.htm

[2] ibnlive.in.com/news/govt-to-reveal-stand-on-black-money-on-jan-25/141423-3.html

[3] www.currentnewsindia.com/nation-news/govt-to-reveal-stand-on-black-money-on-jan-25.html

[4] www.emirates247.com/news/world/tehelka-says-manorma-group-has-account-2011-02-12-1.355118

[5] Zero tolerance, secret billions.

[6] http://www.southasiaanalysis.org/%5Cpapers3%5Cpaper219.htm

[7] Singh Gurharpal, Political Studies (1997), XIV, 626-638.

[8] http://en.wikipedia.org/wiki/Vohra_Report

A Study about the Realistic Nature of Corruption among the People

M.D. Allen Selvakumar

Department of Criminology and Police Administration, J.H.A. Agarsan College, Chennai-60
Department of Sociology, Manonmaniam Sundaranar University, Tirunelveli-627 012

INTRODUCTION

Corruption is a hidden work present in all type of jobs in all over the world. India also has a big statistics of corruption cases. Our people also get and give for many reasons in all working area. Especially in the government employment field it is high in number. The corruption not only makes the people suffer but also destroy the nation development.

Anti-Corruption in Present Situation

WikiLeaks founder Julian Assange has said the "tremendous" anti-corruption movement "building up" in India is a result of the publication of "cablegate" revelations by The Hindu in recent weeks. Citing the campaign, led by Anna Hazare, as an example of the impact of WikiLeaks cables. Mr. Assange singled out The Hindu's coverage of the leaked U.S. diplomatic cables while speaking in a debate organised by the Frontline Club and New Statesman. Stating that he could "speak for hours" about the reverberations sparked by the cables around the world, the Editor of The Hindu, the most respected paper in India, brought over 21 front pages from the past six weeks that were based on cablegate material. Indian Parliament walked out four times and there's now a tremendous anti-corruption movement that has been building up in that country—something that has not happened since the time of Gandhi."

SOME NEWS AND OPINIONS ABOUT CORRUPTION

- July 19, 2011 FE Editorial: On the wrong track, again: "Just how uphill the government's task will be when it comes to a public procurement policy—one of the things it promised to do when hit by a plethora of scams".

- July 19, 2011 a new anti-corruption device: "From 1 July two webcams—one in Chandy's cabin and the other in his office—have been streaming live pictures, but not audio, that are freely accessible on the official Kerala chief minister website."
- July 19, 2011 Graft Undermines GDP Growth: Narayan Murthy.
- July 19, 2011 Govt. lokpal bill lacks teeth: Kejriwal.
- July 19, 2011 only peoples power can end graft: gurumurthy.
- July 19, 2011 A messy basement and a clean penthouse: "These brazen babus give jobs to the poorest of the poor on paper and pocket their fictional earnings. Clearly, grassroots-level corruption is a growth industry in India."
- July 19, 2011 Kashmir's David *vs.* Goliath battle against corruption: ""The government of India is not sincere about curbing corruption here".
- July 19, 2011 Regulatory body can check corruption in media.
- July 19, 2011 New York Times: Transparent Government, *via.* Webcams in India: "In an India beset by kickback scandals at the highest reaches of government, and where petty bribes at police stations and motor vehicle departments are often considered a matter of course"
- July 17, 2011 Corruption cost India Rs. 1,555 thousand crore: study: "majority of it has been laundered out of India using illicit gateways".
- July 17, 2011 Civil society for referendum on Lokpal.
- July 17, 2011 Corrupt India is a national shame: "According to some estimates, India's parallel economy has risen from a mere 3 per cent of the GDP in the mid 50s to around 50 per cent today."
- July 16, 2011 Wall Street Journal: The Holes in India's Antiterror Armor: "Local police forces suffer from corruption, inadequate training and an unprofessional work ethic. This is aggravated by the fact that India's intelligence model is 60 years old: The data gathering processes at the district and state level are archaic".
- July 16, 2011 India's ugly truth- Corruption followed by doping scandal.
- July 16, 2011 Govt's intentions over Lokpal Bill not good: Anna Hazare.
- July 16, 2011 MP Swamy Offers Prescription to Combat Corruption.
- July 16, 2011 State left parties join hands against corruption.
- July 16, 2011 Indore hospital uses children as guinea pigs: "Gets money from Korean firm, MNCs to conduct clinical drug trials on close to 2,000 children." July 12, 2011 Corruption is a curse on our nation: Neetu Chandra: "I would be lying if I say that I have never bribed a person to get my work done. Every Indian, at some point or the other, has been faced with a dilemma where s/he is expected to shell out money to ensure that the work gets done faster."
- July 12, 2011 India fights corruption the 'Gandhian Way'.
- July 12, 2011 Well-dressed & begging: 43 women from Rajasthan detained: "The women, who have made a city lodge their temporary home, told people they

were begging because they were in trouble and were going hungry in their home state."

METHODOLOGY

With the help of accidental sampling the researchers had conducted the study in Chennai among the public from different position. The main objective of this study is to know the causes, consequences and nature of corruption among the people. The researchers had interviewed 40 respondents from different positions to collect the data related to this study. Case Study method was used by the researchers to collect the required data from the respondents. This is a sensitive study which was related to corruption incidents. So the case study would be the best tool for collecting for these sorts of studies.

IMPORTANT CASES

This study has 40 case studies but there are some interesting and different cases which will reflect the rest of the cases. The important cases are as follows.

Case 1

A principal of a school in Chennai has interviewed for this study and he replied that:

I am working as principal for more than 2 decades in this school. I am facing several problems to run this school in a regular manner since my appointment. I am the mediator between the management and the government officials, the teachers and the management, the parents and the teachers, and so on. I am surprise to hear about asking money for the certificate of clearance of infra structure facilities in the school by the health inspector and educational officer of this region. Then I informed to my management, they asked me to bargain and reduce the money. I was shamed to do such incidents. For my survival I had to be adjusted and do for the sake of running the school in a successful manner. I asked the officers to come and check the school then if there any problem I will clear all the problems. But the officers refused to come to the institution and replied that though your institution is perfect, to get clearance certificate you have to pay such amount. This is happening in all the schools in our region.

Case 2

I am doing M.A. in a college in Chennai. I also met with corruption incident in getting the OBC certificate in the government office. First I went to the office with the required documents. They asked me come after 2 days. Then after 2 days again I went to the same office they replied come after 2 days. I am explaining about the purpose and the deadline date of the OBC certificate. Then one person from that office had asked me to give Rs. 500 for giving the certificate. I told that I can't pay this amount and why should I pay. He suddenly replied if you want you pay otherwise you will be come to this week by weeks to get the certificate. Then I was cornered to pay the amount to get the certificate. I was ashamed of this incident because being a graduate to do this incident.

Case 3

I am working as a lecturer in a private college in Chennai. I had good academic works and qualified the necessary requirements for the lecturer post. One year before, I had an interview in a government aided college in Chennai. I went to the interview and I had replied before the interview board. Then I got a letter from that institution for the appointment of lecturer in that institution. I am happy to see and went to that college. But all of sudden I was shocked to hear that I have to pay some lakhs of rupees for my appointment. Then I refused it to give such amount. Now I am working in a private college with minimum salary as a temporary lecturer. I am very much feeling about the corrupted educational field of our country. If anybody had money he can get certificates, posts in colleges then what is the quality of education.

Case 4

I am an auto-driver. I am driving since 8 years. This is my own auto-rickshaw. I am facing many difficulties for my survival. The traffic problem, increasing petrol rate, passenger's conflict and so on are few difficulties in driving the auto. But the real problem is to give money to the traffic police without any default and without any reason. Though I had no money, I have to give the policemen by getting from others. In this situation my earning money was going to some corrupted policemen without any reason. If I refuse to give they file a wrong petition and disturb me to do my job. I can't complain to high officials because they also warning a time then they would take it this serious matter. So still now it is prevailing in this region.

Case 5

I am completed B.Ed in an educational institution. I was restless during my B.Ed course due to the assignments and works in my study. In the practical time, I haven't slept for more than a month to finish the records and preparing charts. Though I had done it sincerely I got scold from my teachers. I am very regular to my class. In the practical examination, I had seen a person who never came to my institution and attended the classes, he is with the uniform and having some record books which is circulated by the finished candidate. That person finished the practical exam and appeared the written exam also. On that day my brother came to my college to pick up me to home. He saw that person and asked him what you are doing here. That person replied I am doing B.Ed. by giving 2 lakhs to the management to free from attending classes and practical works. I was shocked if he became a teacher what will be position of the students.

CONCLUSION

The position of the job, urgency of work, money motive and lack of strict law were the main causes for corruption. The people suffer economically, psychologically and physically to finish their simple work. The white-collar crime was highly found among the government officials. The corruption is a shameful work. But the offenders do it in a normal way. They never felt it as a crime. Because many of the offenders are working with them, this might leads to do the corruption without fear. In daily newspapers, at least one corrupted cases was found from any region of our country. But the result of the corrupted cases was not known to us. The politician, government officials and law authorities are highly involved in corruption in our country. Crores and crores of money was valued for the corruption in the 2G spectrum and it was going like a snake. The strict law and the future generation can change this scenario.

REFERENCES

[1] http://ibnlive.in.com/videos/167607/indore-hospital-uses-children-as-guinea-pigs.html

[2] http://www.dnaindia.com/analysis/report_corruption-is-a-curse-on-our-nation-neetu-chandra_1564836

[3] http://news.outlookindia.com/item.aspx?728259

[4] http://www.csmonitor.com/World/Asia-South-Central/2011/0718

[5] http://www.nytimes.com/2011/07/18/business/global/in-india-an-official-puts-a-webcam-in-office.html?_r=1

[6] http://zeenews.india.com/news/nation/civil-society-for-referendum-on-lokpal_720306.html

[7] http://kanglaonline.com/2011/07

The Linkage of Corruption with Economic Backwardness and Poverty in India

Jomon Mathew

Department of Economics, E.K.N.M. Govt. College Elerithattu, Elerithattu PO, Kasaragod District, Kerala–671 314

E-mail: jomonmathew.k@rediffmail.com

The word corruption stands for an evil or immoral or the willingness to act dishonesty in return for money or any gift. The word *corrupt* when used as an adjective literally means *utterly broken* There exist different types of corruption such as political corruption, police corruption, corporate corruption etc. Though the term is used in different contexts, in general, we do mean it the political corruption. Public sector corruption is commonly defined as *the misuse of public office for private gain.* The USAID Handbook for Fighting Corruption (1999)[1] describes the various forms that corruption can assume. It includes unilateral abuses by government officials such as embezzlement and nepotism, as well as abuse slinking public and private actors such as bribery, extortion, influence peddling and fraud. Corruption arises in both political and bureaucratic offices and can be petty or grand, organized or disorganized. Corruption is inherently a secretive transaction and, thus, difficult to observe and measure.

Several organizations including the World Bank, have attempted to develop corruption indicators; all of them depend on aggregate surveys of citizens, businesses or experts and therefore base their results on perceptions of the problem as opposed to more objective data. While these measurement approaches have acknowledged reliability and validity problems, they are the best that we have for the time being (Johnston and Kpundeh, 2002).[2] The task of measuring corruption is statistically difficult and a Himalayan task mainly due to the illicit nature of the transaction and imprecise definition of corruption.[3] The present study, however, aims to focus attention on reviewing the earlier studies linking corruption with poverty and analyzing the linkage of corruption with the economic backwardness and poverty in the context of Indian economy.

REVIEW OF STUDIES LINKING CORRUPTION WITH POVERTY

It is the requisite of the time to check the linkages between corruption and poverty of the country. A large number of recent studies have examined the relationship between poverty and corruption to clarify the ways in which these corruption and poverty interact. A World Bank study (2000c)[4] of poverty following the transition to a market economy in Eastern Europe and Central Asia (ECA) produced important findings concerning income distribution and corruption. The study analyzes data on firms' perceptions of corruption and notes that more firms in ECA report that corruption is a problem than in most other geographic regions. There is evidence that the absence of economic growth increases poverty. Quibria's study (2002)[5] suggests that the burden of rapid economic retrenchment, such as seen recently in Thailand and Indonesia, hurts the poor most heavily.

Another World Bank study (2000a)[6] suggests that higher levels of corruption reduce growth through decreased investment and output. This comprehensive study looked at 22 transition countries and examined various forms of corruption and their impact on selected economic and social indicators. Another study conducted by Mauro (2002)[7] used a composite of two corruption indices and multiple regression analyses with a sample of 106 countries to show that high levels of corruption are associated with lower levels of investment as a share of Gross Domestic Product (GDP) and with lower GDP growth per capita.

A very significant research on the relationship among corruption, governance and poverty has been conducted at the World Bank by the team of Kaufmann, Kraay and Zoido-Lobaton[8]. They put forward the suggestion on the basis of their study that an association between good governance i.e., governance without control of corruption will lead to poverty alleviation. They further studied the effect of governance on per capita income in 173 countries, treating control of corruption as one of the components of good governance.

MAGNITUDE OF BLACK MONEY IN INDIA

According to the data provided by the Swiss bank (2006)[9], India has more black money than the rest of the world combined. India topping the list with almost $1891 Billion black money in Swiss banks. Swiss Banking Association report, 2008 provides the details of bank deposits in the territory of Switzerland by nationals of following countries.

It has been shocking news that the world's largest democratic country has got such huge collection of black money earned through illegal activities and kept away from the country's rules and legal set up. It is again a surprising fact that this huge amount of black money i.e., $ 1891 billion is thirteen times larger than the foreign debt of the nation. No wonder, the amount of black money accounts for around 40 per cent of India's Gross Domestic Product. It has simply been a known fact that the money which belongs to the nation and its citizens is taken away by the corrupt politicians (or officials) and kept in illegal personal accounts. In the circumstance the money comes back to India, it could result in growth achievement for the economy and thereby radical change in the life of India's common man.

Table 1: Amount of Black Money in Swiss Bank by Leading Countries

Sl. No	Country	Amount of Black Money	Country Wise Share of Black Money (in %)
1.	India	$ 1891 billion	56.2
2.	Russia	$ 610 billion	18.14
3.	China	$ 213 billion	6.34
4.	United kingdom	$ 210 billion	6.24
5.	Ukraine	$ 140 billion	4.16
6.	The rest of the world	$ 300 billion	8.92
	Total	$ 3364 billion	100

Source: Swiss Banking Association Report, 2008.

The World Bank and the Transparency International which is a civil organization have made attempt to publish the *Corruption Perceptions Index (CPI)* thereby giving each country's position in the corruption ranking. The CPI orders the countries of the world according to the degree to which corruption is perceived to exist among public officials and politicians. Accordingly, India stands 87th among 180 countries in CPI in 2011. It can be noticed in the CPI ranking that the most of the least corrupted countries are European Union countries, USA, Canada, Australia etc. while the most corrupted countries are from Africa and Asia. This shows that the least corrupted countries are economically rich and the least corrupted countries are economically backward and poor. Thus, there exists very strong positive correlation between corruption and economic backwardness and poverty. The key message form the 2011 survey was that corruption is a major cause of economic backwardness of India and therefore, steps are to taken to overcome this evil.

CORRUPTION AND POVERTY: A PEEP INTO INDIAN ECONOMY

Large number of studies conducted in the international arena brings out the fact that the relation between corruption and poverty is importantly an indirect one. Though corruption does not produce poverty directly, it has got direct consequences on the economic as well as governance factors that in turn produce poverty in the society. The fact, therefore, is that whether the corruption directly or indirectly produces a state of poverty in the country, the ultimate targeted and worst affected group of this evil is the marginalized poor in any country.

India being the largest economy known for its democratic values will be completing 64 years of freedom on 15 August, 2011. In spite of the attempts made by governments of free India, one fourth of her population live below poverty line and around half of the total 121 crore populations live a poverty affected life. We have already seen the magnitude of corruption in India in the form of black money kept in Swiss bank (Table 1). It has to be kept in mind that the corrupted money never comes in the light and hence, the known figures may count only a minute percentage. Though there were attempts made by a few governments to plough back black money like VIDS, the freedom from corruption still remains a long lasting hope. Corruption in India is acknowledged as a complex problem. The reason for this is that the political, legal and judiciary system cannot be fully relied upon. The recent stake by Anna Hazare to enact the *Jan Lokpal Bill,* that prevents Corruption of politicians and the array of protests that followed are kinds of freedom struggle against corruption in India. The growing concern is that the incidence of corrupt economic practices has been increasing over the years at high rates.

As already mentioned the practice of corruption and the outflow of money from the domestic economy affect the economic growth in a variety of ways. It may be noted that corruption hinders economic progress in the following manner:

- It reduces domestic and foreign investment
- It reduces the volume of tax revenue of the government
- It reduces the quality of public infrastructure
- It takes away huge amount of income from the domestic economy
- It shrinks the volume of non tax revenue of the government
- It discourages the young entrepreneurs from undertaking new business.

Thus it can be learnt from the above stated facts that the practice of corruption leads to economic backwardness and possess vast negative impacts on the economic upliftment of the people, the Indian economy suffers a lot from this evil. The backwash effect of this economic backwardness will be beyond explanation. The solution of corruption can be made possible through the passing of the proposed *Jan Lokpal Bill* in the parliament. It can help improving India's CPI ranking. Using the public money for public utility purposes in turn improve the living conditions of the crores of poor in India.

CONCLUDING REMARKS

The overall literature reviewed in this paper demonstrates that corruption does exacerbate and promote poverty, but this pattern is complex and therefore, generates several economic distortions. It hinders the normal running of the economic system by way of withdrawal of a part of money from the economy, which otherwise could have utilized for the general upliftment of the poor people. Though corruption and its other form of black money do not directly lead to poverty, the phenomenon indirectly results in loss of income, low per capita income and reduced GDP. Thus corruption produces a kind of vicious circle of poverty. All these, therefore, link the evil of corruption with poverty in India, as in the case of other countries of the world. The CPI ranking of India and the living standards of crores of Indians can effectively be improved through strict actions in the formulation of anti corruption laws like *Jan Lokpal Bill.* The immediate requirement should be bringing back the black money to the domestic economy and make it white. It necessitates sincere efforts from the ruling politicians backed by courage.

REFERENCES

[1] USAID, 1999. "A Handbook on Fighting Corruption." Technical Publication Series, Center for Democracy and Governance.

[2] Johnston, Michael and Sahr Kpundeh, 2002. "The Measurement Problem: A Focus on Governance." Unpublished, January.

[3] A Users' Guide to Measuring Corruption". Global Integrity. September 5, 2008. Retrieved 2010–12–11.

[4] World Bank, 2000c. Making Transition Work for Everyone: Poverty and Inequality in Europe and Central Asia. Washington D.C.

[5] Quibria, M.G., 2002. "Growth and Poverty: Lessons from the East Asian Miracle Revisited." Asia Development Bank Research Paper 33.

[6] World Bank, 2000a. "Anti-Corruption in Transition: A Contribution to the Policy Debate." Washington D.C.

[7] Mauro, Paulo, 2002. "The Effects of Corruption on Growth and Public Expenditure." Chapter 20 in Heidenheimer and Johnston, 2002.

[8] Kaufmann, Daniel, Aart Kraay and Pablo Zoido-Lobaton, 2002. "Governance Matters II, Updated Indicators for 2000/01." World Bank Policy Research Working Paper 2772.

[9] Swiss Banking Association Report, 2008.

A Study on the Economic Rights of the People and Corruption in India

P. Arunachalam

Department of Applied Economics, Cochin University of Science and Technology, Kochi-22
E-mail: arunachalam14@yahoo.co.uk

Prof. Irma Glicman Adelman, an Irish Economist working in California University at Berkely, in her research work on 'Development Over Two Centuries', which is published in the Journal of Evolutionary Economics, 1995, has identified and concluded that India, along with China, would be one of the largest economies in this 21st Century. She has stated that the period 1700–1820 is the period of Netherlands (Holland), the period 1820–1890 is the period of England, the period 1890–2000 is the period of America and this 21st Century is the century of China and India. World Bank has also identified that India would be a one the leading players of this century after China and USA (third largest economy). India (\$ 1.5 trillion) will challenge the Global Economic Order in the next 15 years. India will overtake Italian economy (\$ 2.18 trillion) in 2015, England economy (\$ 2.29 trillion) in 2020, Japan economy (\$ 5.45 trillion) in 2025 and USA economy (\$ 14.77 trillion) in 2050 (China with \$ 5.88 trillion already overtook Japan economy in 2010 and will overtake USA economy in 2027). India has the following advantages compared with other economies. India is 4th largest GDP in the world in terms of Purchasing Power. India is third fastest growing economy in the world after China and Vietnam. Service sector contributes around 57 per cent of GDP. The share of agriculture is around 17 per cent and Manufacture is 16 per cent in 2005–06. This is a character of a developed country. Expected GDP growth rate is 10 per cent shortly (It has come down from 9.2 per cent in 2006–07 to 6.2 per cent during 2008–09 due to recession). India has \$ 209 billion as Foreign Exchange Reserve as on today. India had just \$ 1 billion as Foreign Exchange Reserve when it opened its economy in the year 1991.

India ranks 13th among the richest countries in the world, she has the highest number of representatives among the countries in the top 20 list of world's richest persons, India among global top 10 in industrial production according to United National Industrial Development Organization Year book on Industrial statistics 2010 (China is now the World's second largest producer of manufactured goods). India's high growth rates have been a matter of boastful self-congratulatory publicity for the Indian Government. The latest Human Development Report released by the UNDP in India recently serves to confront and challenge the tall claims with the rude realities of India's sorry human development performance in the very midst of its much-touted economic success story. Undeniably, in the very phase when the Manmohan Singh Government is boasting of high growth rates, India's performance in terms of providing the basics required for a life of dignity continued to slide steeply. Another major issue striking the economy is corruption charges and the amount of money involved with it. India has been placed at 87th position in Transparency International's Corruption Perceptions Index 2010, in the company of Albania, Jamaica and Liberia. Countries like China (78), El Salvador (73), Rwanda (66) and Bhutan (36) fare better than us; only countries like Burkina Faso (98), Kazakhstan (105) and Pakistan (143) are worse than us.

According to Baker from 2004 to 2008, "approximately $89 billion was moved out of India through mispriced trade alone. Not only this corruption but also nearly 200 million Indians are living with hunger. About 49 per cent of our children are suffering from underweight, about 42 per cent suffering from malnutrition, 23 million children in India simply wasted or stunted, and millions of tons of food grains are simply wasted or destroyed due to lack of storage facilities. These are the reasons why great economists have stated that in India rates are healthier than people. Great challenges remain as the Economist journal has reported that half of 10-year-old rural children can't read at the basic level, over 60 per cent is unable to do simple division and half drop out by the age 14. Fewer than 40 percent of adolescents in India attend secondary schools. Around 1 in 10 young person's has access to tertiary education. Mercer consulting estimates that only a quarter of graduates are "employable". India's commitment to 'provide for and ensure Universal Elementary Education for all children' up to the age of 14 has been reiterated time and again. The Kothari Commission (1964–1966), the Acharya Ramamurthy Committee (1990), the Prof Yash Pal Committee (1993), the Saikia Committee (1997) have all reiterated the need for free and compulsory universal elementary education (UEE) and quality education. In 1993, the Supreme Court clearly declared education a fundamental right. To make any real impact on children's lives, the country needs to spend at least 10 per cent of GDP on school education and health. Currently, the spending on schooling is 1.28 per cent (the total government outlay is 3.3 per cent) of GDP.

Nothing is easier than to recognise a poor person when you see him or her. Yet the task of identifying and counting the poor seems to elude the country's best experts. Take for instance the "headcount" of rural poverty—the proportion of the rural population below the poverty line. At least four alternative figures are available: 28 per cent from the Planning Commission, 50 per cent from the N.C. Saxena Committee report, 42 per cent from the Tendulkar Committee report, and 80 per cent or so from the National Commission for Enterprises in the Unorganised Sector (NCEUS) (Jean Drèze, 2010). The 2005 ICP updates PPP rates last calculated in 1993 to produce an international poverty line of $ 1.25 a day. According to this, the proportion of the world's population living in poverty has fallen by approximately one percent a year since 1990. At this rate, it is unlikely that the developing world outside China will reach the MDG poverty goal. In this context, the article estimates India's poverty according to both the $ 1.25 a day international poverty line and India's national poverty line of $ 1.00 a day (at 2005 PPP) to find that: 42 percent of the population were living below $ 1.25 in 2005 (24 percent below $ 1.00) as compared to 60 percent twenty-five years ago (42 percent below $ 1.00) the number of people living below $ 1.25 rose from 421 to 456 million during 1981–2005 the number of people living in the 25 cent interval between $ 1.00 and $ 1.25 rose from 124 million to 189 million during 1981–2005 India's overall rate of poverty reduction during 1981–2005 according to both poverty lines was lower than the average for the developing world.

When we look at the amount of money earmarked for infrastructural development (only 7.8 per cent of GDP, expected to be 14 per cent), health sector development (only 1 per cent of GDP, expected to be 3 per cent, America spends nearly 16 per cent of GDP), agriculture-research and development (0.67 per cent of GDP, expected to be 3 per cent), due to lack of world class higher educational institutions nearly 5 lakh Indian students going abroad for higher education taking nearly $ 12 billion as fees, travel cost and other expenditures. If we have enough money India could provide all these facilities for the common people. But we don't have enough money for the same. So budget allocation is very less for these sectors. When these essential sectors are suffering for want of money one side the amount of money involved in corruption is increasing year after year. If we brought the black money kept outside India by corrupt means and other corrupt amount within India we could provide world class facilities within India itself.

All levels of education in India, from primary to higher education, are overseen by the Ministry of Human Resource Development, Department of Higher Education, India and Department of School Education and Literacy, and heavily subsidized by the Indian government.

HUMAN RIGHTS ON FOOD

The World Food Summit held in 1999 has accepted in principle the right to food. The UN committee on Economic, Social and Cultural Rights of its General Comment 12 talks about the right to adequate food. But in India nearly 200 million populations are living with hunger.

HUMAN RIGHTS ON EDUCATION

Recently Government of India brought an Act on Free and Compulsory Education. If India intended to provide education to all 220 million school going children it had to spend nearly 10 per cent of its GDP on education. But actually 3.5 per cent earmarked for the same. But only 12.5 percent of our children were getting the opportunity to enter into college level. The right to education is denied to nearly 87.5 per cent of our children.

We are not able to provide justice to people by denying food, education and infrastructural development needed for our people due to lack of budget. At the same time we come across very huge amount of money involved in each corruption case. If the total amount of money involved in corruption is properly utilized we could provide sufficient quantity of food to our people and better educational facilities to our children.

In this research paper an attempt has been made to analyze the economic impact of ever increasing corruption on Indian economy.

WHAT IS CORRUPTION?

The word corruption means the destruction, ruining or the spoiling of a society or a nation. A corrupt society stops valuing integrity, virtue or moral principles. It changes for the worse. Such a society begins to decay and sets itself on the road to self destruction. Corruption is an age old phenomena. Selfishness and greed are the two main causes of corruption. Political corruption is the abuse of their powers by state officials for their unlawful private gain. Lack of integrity or honesty—especially susceptibility to bribery

When countries tackle corruption they increase their national incomes by as much as four times in the long term. Business can grow as much as 3% faster, and child mortality can fall as much as 75%.

Major reasons for corruption are:
1. *Opportunity:* People get involved in corruption when systems don't work well and they need a way to get things done regardless of the procedure and laws.
2. *Little chance of getting caught:* A lack of accountability comes when there is little transparency (for example, public officials who don't explain what they are doing, how and why), and weak enforcement (law agencies who don't impose sanctions on power holders who violate their public duties).

3. *Bad incentives:* For example, a clerk not earning enough to live on, or not sure that he will have a job tomorrow, might supplement his income with bribes.
4. Certain attitudes or circumstances make average people disregard the law. They may try to get around laws of a government they consider illegitimate. Poverty or scarcity of key goods such as medicine may also push people to live outside the law. Instead of thinking about bribing officials to obtain something that may be valuable to them personally (like having a phone line installed), people should realize that giving a bribe contributes to corruption in their country. Instead they should work to change the circumstances and curb corruption. Fighting corruption is closely related to improving governance in a country. It's about improving how the government is set up and managed.

Corruption has prevailed in all forms of government. Various forms of corruption include extortion, graft, bribery, cronyism, nepotism, embezzlement and patronage. Corruption allows criminal activities such as money laundering, extortion and drug trafficking to thrive. Corruption in several forms prevails all over the world with bribery alone crossing one trillion US dollars annually. A state of unchecked political corruption is known as kleptocacy, which literally means "rule by thieves". At times, bribes are given to avoid punishment. For some people, being corrupt is a way to get what they desire. In societies which ignore corruption, it becomes a way of life. People getting very low wages feel they have to demand bribes in order to lead decent lives. But they do not realize that corruption causes suffering to others.

India has been listed as one among 88 countries where people live with hungry. In the Global Hunger Index 2008, India occupied 66th position out of 88 countries listed by International Food Policy Research Institute, Washington, USA. It has stated that more than 200 million people in India facing hunger. According to the latest Human Development Index that was released globally on 5th October 2009 India ranks 134th out of 182 countries in the world, with the Human Development Index (HDI) estimated at .612 based on 2007 data in terms of a long and healthy life, access to knowledge and a decent standard of living to its citizens. The Human Poverty Index (HPI-), focusing on the proportion of people below certain threshold levels in each of the dimensions of the HDI, is estimated at 28 per cent of Indians are living below the poverty line and placing the country in the 88th slot among 135 countries for which the index has been calculated.

India's commitment to 'provide for and ensure Universal Elementary Education for all children' up to the age of 14 has been reiterated time and again. The Kothari Commission (1964–1966), the Acharya Ramamurthy Committee (1990), the Prof Yash Pal Committee (1993), the Saikia Committee (1997) have all reiterated the need for free and compulsory universal elementary education (UEE) and quality education. In 1993, the Supreme Court clearly declared education a fundamental right.

In the field of education we have achieved: Increase in literacy rates from 18.33 per cent in 1951, to 65 per cent in 2001, Decrease in dropout rates from 62.7 per cent in 1977–78, to 39.37 per cent in 1995–96, Increase in enrolment at primary school from 19.2 million in 1950–51, to 109.8 million in 1995–96, Increase in primary schools from 209,671 in 1950–51, to 590,421 in 1995–96. And yet Only 65 per cent of children reach Grade 5, It is estimated that between 40–60 per cent of children in the 6–14 age group are out of school, About 40 per cent of children drop out of school before they reach Class V, Fifty-four per cent of children drop out of school before they complete their elementary education. Of them, 51 per cent are boys and 59 per cent girls, Enrolment rate at the primary level is 88 per cent: 98 per cent for boys and 81 per cent for girls. The enrolment rate at the middle level drops to 59 per cent–67 per cent for girls and 50 per cent for boys, As far back as 1962, the Kothari Commission had recommended a minimum of 6 per cent of the GNP as allocation for education. Four decades later, our allocation for education is a mere 3.5 per cent, Twelve per cent of primary schools have only one teacher, 58 per cent had only two rooms, 60 per cent had leaking roofs, and only 25 per cent of teachers were found teaching (Enakshi Ganguly Thukral, Bharti Ali, Saloni Mathur).

It is a lesson in misplaced enthusiasm. While the Centre has been busy tom-tomming its efforts to send more children to school, enrolment in primary classes across the country has, in actuality, dropped since 2007. Between 2008–09 and 2009–10, enrolment in classes I to IV in Indian schools dropped by over 2.6 million. The biggest setback was witnessed in Uttar Pradesh, where admissions plummeted by over a million in the last two years, according to the latest data released by the ministry of human resource development.

Comparative Literacy Data

Country	*Adult Literacy Rate*	*Youth Literacy Rate*
China	93.3% (2007)[11]	98.9% (2004)[12]
Sri Lanka	90.8 (2007)	98.0
Burma	89.9% (2007)[13]	94.4% (2004)[14]
Iran	82.4% (2007)[15]	95% (2002)[16]
World Average	84% (1998)[4]	88% (2001)[17]
India	**74.04% (2011)**[18]	**82% (2001)**[3]
Nepal	56.5 (2007)	62.7
Pakistan	62.2 (2007)[19]	73.9
Bangladesh	53.5 (2007)	74

Source: wikipedia.org

Data from a Demographic and Health Survey (DHS) show in 2000, 76 per cent of all children of primary school age (6–10 years) were in school. By 2006, this value had increased to 83 per cent (see Table 1). However, close to 17 per cent of all children of primary school age continue to be out of school.

Table 1: Children of Primary School Age in School (per cent), India 2000 and 2006

	2000	*2006*	*Change 2000 to 2006*
Male	79.2	85.2	5.9
Female	72.3	81.4	9.1
Urban	82.5	88.5	5.9
Rural	73.8	81.5	7.7
Poorest 20%	66.1	69.4	3.2
Second 20%	69.2	81.2	12.1
Middle 20%	78.8	87.5	8.7
Fourth 20%	82.1	92.2	10.1
Richest 20%	89.1	95.7	6.6
Total	75.9	83.3	7.5

Data Sources: India Multiple Indicator Cluster Survey (MICS) 2000, India DHS 2005–06.

As a result of the increase in primary school attendance, the number of children out of school fell by almost one third from 30 million in 2000 to 21 million in 2006 (Friedrich Huebler, 2007) (see Table 2).

Table 2: Children of Primary School Age out of School (million), India 2000 and 2006

	2000	*2006*	*Change 2000 to 2006*
Male	13.0	9.5	–3.5
Female	16.4	11.2	–5.2
Urban	5.0	3.7	–1.3
Rural	24.5	17.0	–7.5
Poorest 20%	9.4	9.8	0.5
Second 20%	8.5	5.3	–3.2
Middle 20%	5.2	3.1	–2.1
Fourth 20%	4.3	1.7	–2.6
Richest 20%	2.0	0.8	–1.3
Total	29.5	20.7	–8.7

Data Sources: India MICS 2000, India DHS 2005–06.

The 86th Constitutional Amendment Act was passed by the parliament to make the Right to Elementary Education a fundamental right and a fundamental duty. Education is the primary vehicle for children to drive towards economic and social upliftment.

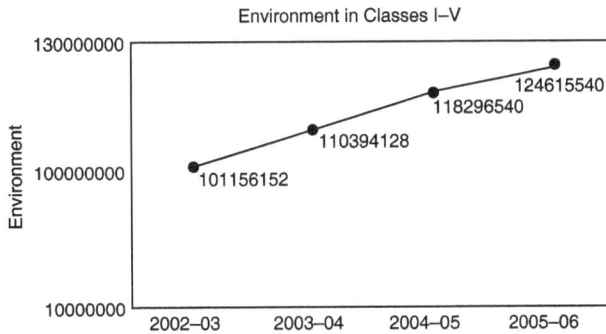

Source: schoolreportcards.in/Media/m52.html

There is no doubt that the average drop-out rate in primary classes suggests a consistent decline; but the same is still too high to attain the status of universal retention at the primary level of education. Universalisation comprises four components: 1. universal access, 2. universal enrolment, 3. universal retention and 4. universal quality of education. The flagship Sarva Shiksha Abhiyan (SSA) programme of the Government of India launched in 2001 in this direction has also this objective of universal retention by 2010. The drop-out rate indicates an average rate of 9.96 percent in primary grades. In many states, drop-out rate in Grade I is noticed to be alarmingly high. The very few exceptions, however, are visible in states like Tamil Nadu, where retention rate is 100%; it is more than 95 per cent in Kerala as well. Around 69,353 schools in the country have enrolment less than 25, out of which 94% are located in rural areas. One in three primary schools has enrolment less than 50. The enrolment of students in classes I to VIII in 2005–06 was 168.29 million, an increase of 12.28 million from the previous year (School report cards.in).

The number of out-of-school (OOS) children in the 6–14 age group has come down dramatically from 1.34 crore in 2005 to 80.4 lakh in 2009. In percentage terms, 4.22% of the total children in this age group are not going to school as per the latest figures. The first survey of 2005 had showed that 6.94% children in this age group were OOS. Survey by Social Research Institute of Indian Market Research Bureau of OOS children in the country. The survey, done for HRD ministry, corroborates the prestigious private survey by Pratham. In early 2009, Pratham had put OOS children at 4.3%. The big news is Bihar's success story and Rajasthan and UP's poor performance. The north-south divide is also clear. Kerala, Karnataka, Andhra Pradesh and Tamil Nadu have OOS children ranging between just 0.38% in Kerala to 1.4% in AP (Akshaya Mukul, 2009).

According to Ashok K. Chauhan (2010) "Primary education seems to be the focal point of Budget 2010–2011. The planned allocation for school education has been increased by 16% from Rs. 26, 800 crore in 2009–10 to Rs. 31, 036 crore in 2010–11 and states will have access to Rs. 3, 675 crore for elementary education under the 13th Finance Commission grants,.

India needs to increase its spending on education to 6% of its GDP which has been reiterated year after year by every government since independence. The Economic Survey 2007–08 also refers to this elusive goal of allocating six per cent of the GDP to education.

DEFINITION OF POVERTY

In India, the first official definition of poverty was given in 1962. This pegged the rural poverty line at a monthly family income of Rs. 100 and the urban one at Rs. 125. In 1971, V.M. Dandekar and Nilkanth Rath used a different measure to estimate poverty. They used an average calorie norm of 2250 calories per capita per day for both rural and urban areas as a criterion to define the poverty line. The current poverty line was fixed in 1979, when a Planning Commission talk force defined the poverty line as the per capita expenditure level at which the average per capita calorie intake was 2400 and 2100 calories for rural and urban areas respectively. Different levels of calorie intake were fixed for rural and urban areas taking into consideration the fact that the calorie requirement in rural areas, where more people were engaged in manual labour, was more than in urban areas.

Poverty has also been falling far more slowly in India than in other high-growth developing countries, such as Vietnam and Brazil. Watkins believes that part of the problem is that the benefits of growth have been "highly skewed". "While wealth has been flooding into urban areas and middle-class suburbs, it has been trickling down in small doses to rural areas, poor states in the north of the country, rural labourers and low-caste groups, Watkins has stated that India's children did not receive the basic medication they so badly need such as immunisation, drugs for treating childhood diarrhoea and nutritional supplements. "Fewer than half of India's children are fully immunised and the share has barely changed in a decade," Gender inequalities are also still rife in India, with boys getting access to food and medicine before girls, according to Watkins. "Being born a girl carries high risks: it raises the chance of premature death between the ages of one and four by about one-third" (Kathryn Hopkins, 2008).

Political and bureaucratic corruptions in India are major concerns. A 2005 study conducted by Transparency International in India found that more than 45% of Indians had first-hand experience of paying bribes or influence peddling to get jobs done in public offices successfully. Transparency International estimates that truckers pay US$5 billion in bribes annually. In 2010 India was ranked 87th out of 178 countries in Transparency International's corruption (Wikipedia).

The year 2011 has proved to be a watershed in the public tolerance of political corruption in India, with widespread Public protests and movements led by social activist against corruption and for the return of illegal wealth stashed by politicians and businessmen in foreign banks over the six decades since independence.

India tops the list for black money in the entire world with almost US$1456 billion in Swiss banks (approximately USD 1.4 trillion) in the form of black money. According to the data provided by the Swiss Banking Association Report (2006), India has more black money than the rest of the world combined. To put things in perspective, Indian-owned Swiss bank account assets are worth 13 times the country's national debt.

"The recent scams involving unimaginably big amounts of money, such as the 2G spectrum scam, are well known. It is estimated that more than trillion dollars are stashed away in foreign havens, while 80% of Indians earn less than 2$ per day and every second child is malnourished. It seems as if only the honest people are poor in India and want to get rid of their poverty by education, emigration to cities, and immigration. It seems as if India is a rich country filled with poor people. "As on March 31, 2010, unutilised committed external assistance was of the order of Rs. 1,05,339 crore." (Wikipedia)

According to Amartya Sen, "India needs to spend more on basic health care and education if economic growth is to benefit all members of society. Higher public spending must also be part of Prime Minister Manmohan Singh's efforts to restore public confidence following a corruption scandal involving the sale of mobile-phone licenses. "The reform process has not stopped, it has halted and it will start again if the government survives. "It will also have to make the growth much more inclusive. Education and health-care expansion are the biggest part of that because an illiterate laborer with very indifferent health is not in a great position to seize the opportunities that globalized economic relations provide today." India's democratic agenda is increasingly concerned with narrower issues such as corruption and inflation. "There isn't enough voice in India about the totally urgent need for expansion of basic education and basic healthcare, particularly basic health care, much further than has happened. The increasing exposure of corruption in the economy, which had been present for a long time, would have caught whichever government had been in power. "So the first priority is to ride out the present crisis, to generate confidence in his government. "Economies of countries such as India, China and Brazil won't be much affected by the sovereign debt crisis because of their focus on economic growth (Peter Woodfiled, 2011).

The consequences of corruption for social and economic development are bad. Corruption hinders economic growth and deters investment. The impact of development assistance is reduced and natural resources are overexploited causing further harm to a country's environmental assets. Resources are diverted from sectors such as education and health to less important sectors or personal enrichment. The rule of law is eroded and the people no longer respect or trust the state. A few people manage to get rich at the expense of society as a whole, while the poor suffer terribly. In the long run unchecked corruption pushes more and more people into poverty which often destabilizes a society.

The effects of corruption in India include poor social sector performance and failing infrastructure. Corruption discourages the investments needed for economic progress. According to KPMG in India high-level corruption and scams are now threatening to derail the country's credibility and its economic boom.

It has bad effects on foreign investors. Social effects, initiative and ambition shrivel evaporation of respect for authority Anger and resentment build Grievance leading to movements. In India found that more than 15% of Indians had first-hand experience of paying bribes or influence peddling to successfully complete jobs in public office, taxes and bribes are a fact of daily life and common between state borders, transparency International estimates that truckers pay US$ 5 billion in bribes annually.

Corruption Perceptions Index (CPI): This index orders the ordering the countries of the world according to "the degree to which corruption is perceived to exist among public officials and politicians". A higher score means less (perceived) corruption. The results show seven out of every ten countries (and nine out of every ten developing countries) with an index of less than 5 points out of 10. India stands 87th among 180 countries in CPI. Average rating for India since last three year is between 3.3 to 3.4 which is far behind than the top ranking countries at CPI of 9.3

The judiciary, the law enforcement agencies and the education sector have an important role to play to fight corruption by changing the prevailing laws, punishments and the education system. Societies can fight corruption by letting the state know that they have had enough of it. The authorities move very quickly when the press or the television highlights instances of corruption. Education spreads political and social awareness and these are some factors that help curb the menace of corruption.

India has to take two simple steps and we will transform our nation. The first is to introduce complete transparency in government and in all its actions other than national security. Nothing but public exposure ensures accountability. Corruption breeds in dark corners. The second is to have enforcement of the law without fear or favour. Prosecute and punish the guilty regardless of their standing. This means law enforcement agencies have to stop being the handmaidens of those in power. Power not only corrupts. It also protects the corrupt.

How Proposed "Jan Lokpal Bill" can help improving CPI ranking: Controlling the corruption will lead to gaining the numeric points in CPI. Following steps will come into existence when this bill is passed:

1. Anti-corruption institution called "Lokpal" by central government will be established and will be supported by state institutions called "Lokayukta.

2. Janlokpal bill will ensure free, fair and time bound investigation against corrupt person/organization. Investigations in each case will have to be completed in one year. Trials will be completed in the following year, meaning the total process will take place within two years.
3. It will be completely independent entity like CEC.

REFERENCES

[1] Enakshi Ganguly Thukral, Bharti Ali, Saloni Mathur Children : Background and Perspective infochangeindia.org/.../Children/.../Children-Background-Perspective.html

[2] Friedrich Huebler (2007). International Education Statistics: India has 21 million children, Tuesday, November 13 ...India has 21 million children out of school huebler.blogspot.com/.../india-has-21-million-children-out-of.html

[3] India Progressing Towards Universal Elementary Education: Where goes missing 40% efficiency? May-2007, schoolreportcards.in/Media/m52.html

[4] Akshaya Mukul (2009). Sharp decline in out-of-school children, TNN, Sep 13, 2009, 01.47am IST, timesofindia.indiatimes.com › India

[5] Siba Sankar Mohanty (2009). Union Budget 2009–10 Does Not Have A Pro Poor Orientation, 16 July, Countercurrents.org

[6] V. Mohan Rao India and its Literacy Mission, Monday, September 7th, 2009 nvonews.com/2009/09/07/india-literacy-mission

[7] Sushma (2009), Education Budget 2008–09, Viewpoint, Berlia President, Apeejay Stya Group and Vice President, Apeejay Education Society, New Delhi, Delhi, March 6, 2008, India PRwire—Summary www.indiaprwire.com/.../education/200803067868.htm

[8] www.indiaedunews.com

[9] Read more: http://www.ganpatinews.com/2010/02/27/budget-2010-allocation-of-25-more-funds-for-education-72930#ixzz0goI84NpF

[10] Puja Marwaha (2009). "Right to Education Bill, 2009: Will it help all Indians make the grade? http://www.thehindubusinessline.com/2009/07/24/stories/2009072450160800.htm

[11] Jean Drèze (2010). Poverty Estimates *vs.* Food Entitlements, Tuesday, March 2, newage.communistparty.in/.../poverty-estimates-vs-food-entitlements.html - 19 hours ago

[12] Karin Hulshof (2009). "Child Undernutrition in India is a Human Rights Issue" www.hindu.com/2009/12/10/stories/2009121051270900.htm

[13] Food Security Bill (2009). India eIndia2007, Wednesday, July 22, 2009 http://eindia2007.blogspot.com/2009/07/food-security-bill-india.html

[14] Jayati Ghosh (2006). "Introduction: Increasing Food Insecurity in South Asia", InfoChange News and Features, October, inforchangeindia.org/2006-10225659/Agenda/ Hunger-Has-fallen-Off-The-Map/Introduction-increasing-food-insecurity-in-South-Asia.html.

[15] india.gov.in/citizen/health/national_rural.php

[16] 28,000 Health Centres Short In India Indian Economic Survey, Last Updated: 2009-07-02T16:20:47+05:30www.india-server.com/.../national-rural-health-mission-allocated-8575.html

[17] Karin Hulshof (2009). "Child undernutrition in India is a human rights issue" www.hindu.com/2009/12/10/stories/2009121051270900.htm

[18] www.unicef.org/india/media_3766.htm

[19] UN (2007). Says India Must Reduce Child Mortality Rates, New Delhi 10 December 2007, www1.voanews.com/.../a-13-2007-12-10-voa58-66534097.html

[20] Thaindian.com India worst in cutting child mortality rates despite fast economic growth http://www.thaindian.com/newsportal/south-asia/india-worst-in-cutting-child-mortality-rates-despite-fast-economic-growth_10018985.html#ixzz0h89ySKwD

[21] Kathryn Hopkins (2008). The Guardian, Monday 28 July 2008 Human development: Child mortality stays high despite India's boom, www.guardian.co.uk/.../india.inter nationalaidanddevelopment

[22] blog.taragana.com (2009). India's neighbours debunk myths on reducing child mortality, October 5th, blog.taragana.com/.../2009/.../indias-neighbours-debunk-myths-on-reducing-child-mortality-12977

[23] www.unicef.org/india/overview_3705.htm

[24] BBC NEWS | Health | Child mortality drop 'too slow' Child mortality drop 'too slow' news.bbc.co.uk/2/hi/health/8249786.stm

[25] India needs political will to reduce maternal mortality: WHO http://www.thaindian. com/newsportal/health/india-needs-political-will-to-reduce-maternal-mortality-who_10033862.html#ixzz0hCEcN8GO

[26] India grapples with high maternal death rate Mon Jan 26, 2009 6:in.reuters.com › Home › News › Top News.

[27] Ananta Basudev Sahu and Sandhya Rani Das (2007). "On Gender Issues and Empowerment of Women", Platinum Jubilee of Indian Statistical Institute, 1–2 February.

[28] June Lennie (2002). Rural women's empowerment in a communication technology project: some contradictory effects, Paper published in Rural Society, Vol. 12, No. 3, 2002, pp. 224–245.

[29] Vinita Pandey (2005). Empowering Women in India: Changing Horizons—The Kalanjiam Experience, *Journal of South Asian Women Studies*,Vol. 10, No. 1 March, http://asiatica.org/jsaws/vol10_no1/empowering-women-india-changing-horizons-kalanjiam-experience

[30] www.awid.org, India: Women's Political Empowerment, Yes; Better Lives, No ... IPS News 26/11/2009, www.awid.org/.../INDIA-Women-s-Political-Empowerment-Yes-Better-Lives-No.

[31] India Directory - Maps of India) india.mapsofindia.com › India Forum

[32] www.wikigender.org/index.php/India

[33] Nageshwar (2010). indiacurrentaffairs.org/political-empowerment-of-women-special-article-prof-k-nageshwar-2.

[34] Lalit kishore where do we stand in empowering women in India? Dr., www.merinews.com › Lifestyle - Cached.

[35] Raichel Matthai (2006). Political Status of Indian Women: Progress since independence Vol. XLV, No. 01, Tuesday 24 April 2007, by www.mainstreamweekly.net › 2006 › December 23, 2006.

[36] Rasheeda Bhagat (2009). Editorial, Women and Indian Politics, Business Line, Vol. 16, No. 229 Aug. 18.

[37] Hemali Chhapia (2011). Enrolment in Primary Schools Plunges 2.6 million in 2 years TNN Mar 21, 2011, 12.24 am IST, http://articles.timesofindia.indiatimes.com/2011-03-21/india/29171057_1_enrolment-indian-schools-education-act

[38] "University Education Commission", 1948–49. http://www.education.nic.in/higedu.asp, Higher Education in India: Issues Related to Expansion, Inclusiveness, Quality and Finance-UGC http://blogs.sungard.com/he_india/2011/06/06/indian-higher-education-%

[39] John A. Gardiner (1993). "Defining Corruption." In: Corruption and Reform, http://elaine.ie/2009/07/31/definitions-and-types-of-corruption

[40] What is corruption? http://www.thegeminigeek.com/what-is-corruption

[41] http://youthink.worldbank.org/issues/corruption

[42] http://www.indiastudychannel.com/resources/138785-The-different-types-Corruption.aspx

[43] www.karmayog.org/anticorruption/anticorruption_868.htm

[44] Introduction to Corruption info.worldbank.org/etools/docs/library/35970/mod03.pdf

[45] Aroon Purie, Editorial (2010). India today, http://indiatoday.intoday.in/site/story/from-the-editor-in-chief-aroon-purie/1/125133.html

[46] http://www.facebook.com/pages/Support-The-Anti-Corruption-Revolution-of-India-2011/185777968122444?sk=info

[47] Corruption Perceptions Index (CPI) and Jan Lokpal Bill-The relevance in Indian Prospective April 9, 2011 http://asseer.wordpress.com/2011/04/09/corruption-perceptions-index-and-jan-lokpal-bill-the-relevance-in-indian-prospective.

[48] Ankit Agarwal (2010). Corruption in India: A Billion Dollar Industry, on January 16, 2010.

[49] http://trak.in/tags/business/2010/01/16/corruption-in-india-a-billion-dollar-industry

[50] Graft Undermines GDP Growth: Narayan Murthy http://news.outlookindia.com/item.aspx?728259

[51] Peter Woodfiled (2011). India Needs More Health, Education Spending for Inclusive Growth, Sen Says http://www.bloomberg.com/news/2011-07-19/india-needs-more-health-education-spending-for-inclusive-growth-sen-says.html

Combating Economic Fraud in Global Sphere with Reference to Role of UNCAC

D.S. Makkalanban

Department of Political Science, Presidency College (Autonomous), Chennai–600 005

PROLOGUE

In the past few decades, as the number of International Organizations (IOs) steadily increased, interaction among them has become a common place. They are initially created by states to deal with specific collective action oriented problems. They often also tend to take on additional tasks and may find themselves caught up in issues that other organizations are also dealing with. The realm of corruption is chosen because none of the organizations that deal with it were specifically designed for this grievous task. Therefore, a number of international organizations (both intergovernmental and non-governmental) have recently developed strategies for dealing with corruption in states. The IOs especially like the United Nations (UN), World Bank, International Monetary Fund (IMF), European Union (EU), Council of Europe, as well as very active NGOs such as Transparency International or the Open Society Institute have been devising and funding anti-corruption programs. The present paper tries to highlight one of legal instruments of IO that tries to combat corruption in global sphere. The United Nations Convention against Corruption (UNCAC) is the only legally binding universal anti-corruption instrument. The Convention's far-reaching approach and the mandatory character of many of its provisions make it a unique tool for developing a comprehensive response to a global problem. The UNCAC covers five main areas: prevention, criminalization and law enforcement measures, international cooperation, asset recovery, and technical assistance and information exchange. The UNCAC covers many different forms of corruption, such as trading in influence, abuse of power, and various acts of corruption in the private sector. The rapidly growing number of States that have become parties to the Convention is further proof of its universal nature and reach. As such the paper will highlight the importance of UNCAC in combating corruption and secondly, it will explore the problem from an economic perspective dealing with international economic fraud and abuse.

THE THEORETICAL ISSUES

Even though there are a number of international instruments the UNCAC is the only legal binding agreement under the United Nations Office on Drugs and Crime (UNODC). In international relations theory According to Cox and Jacobson, three types of decisions fall in circle of autonomous policy making by international organizations. They are based on the importance given to authority and autonomy of an organization. They are; rule-creating, rule-supervisory and rule enforcement decisions.

Rule-creating deal with the way the UNODC frames policies and programs with rules and regulations over its constituent's states. It defines rules and norms laid down in agreements, conventions or resolutions adopted by its member states.

Rule-supervisory decisions apply approved rules in a variety of ways through acting as a broker in providing technical assistance to the needy states from those who can provide international cooperation and information exchange to deal with anti corruption methods and strategies.

Rule-enforcement is the most important function of the IO that denotes the strength of the UNODC, weather it's enabled rule creating an rule supervisory functions are worth or not. It depends upon a significant number of variables that decide the autonomy of the influence exerted by the UNODC. The key variables are:

1. *dominant actors* that involves representatives of powerful states
2. *dominant type of decisions* involves rule-creating, rule supervisory and rule enforcement
3. *dominant type of subsystems* denotes representative subsystems (oligarchic) or direct participation
4. *environment* involves both specific/general like regional integration, breakdown of USSR, rise of American hegemony etc
5. *actors' sources of influence* highlights the actor's position in international relations, nationality, control over vital resources etc.

These five variables often influence and decide the course and action that a particular IO or an agency of IO is involved at a specific time period. This influence may be complete or marginal or sometimes zero depending upon the variables roles played at a particular time. The significance and area covered by the UNCAC directly relates to the organizational autonomy on UNODC with roles of variables taken into account. International agencies that make and apply rules have the greatest implications for the behavior of the major states. With this theoretical background, the further research study is carried out with exploring the dynamics of exerting influence on its member nations worldwide to combat economic fraud/corruption.

ECONOMIC FRAUD/CORRUPTION ANALYSIS IN GLOBAL SPHERE

Economic crime is a truly global phenomenon. Despite the attention of nations and companies investment in controls, fraud remains one of the most problematic issues for nations around the world. The actual level of economic crime and associated financial and non-financial losses has not decreased. Many of economic crime are intractable because of the many kinds of fraud and the broad range of employees, including senior executives, who commit them. Many factors play a vital role in causing economic fraud as per Global Economic Crime Survey 2009; they are represented as below in Table 1.

Table 1: Global Causes for Economic Fraud

Sl. No.	Reasons for Economic Fraud	% of Global Economic Fraud Committed
1.	Financial targets more difficult to achieve	47
2.	Fear of losing jobs	37
3.	Desire to earn personal performance bonuses	27
4.	For senior executives to achieve desired financial results	25
5.	Bonuses not paid this year	23
6.	Maintain financial performance to ensure lenders do not cancel debt facilities	18
7.	There is a belief that competitors are paying bribes to win contracts	13
8.	Others	14

On the other hand economic crime takes many different forms, some more common than others. The following table represents the economic crime suffered commonly. The following table depicts the Types of Economic Fraud suffered as per Global Economic Crime Survey 2009.

Table 2: Types of Economic Fraud

Sl. No.	Types of Economic Crimes	% of Types Committed
1.	Asset misappropriation	67
2.	Accounting fraud	38
3.	Bribery and corruption	27
4.	IP infringement	15
5.	Money laundering	12
6.	Tax fraud	5
7.	Illegal insider trading	4
8.	Market fraud involving cartels colluding to fix prices	3
9.	Espionage	3
10.	Others	5

The Table 2 shows about 27 percentages of them suffer due to bribery and corruption in economic transactions. A separate analysis regarding corruption trends shows that it has increased in past few years in global sphere. The following table illustrates the percentage of people suffered due to corruption in global transactions as per Global Economic Crime Survey 2009.

Table 3: Percentage of People Suffered Due to Corruption

Sl. No.	Bribery and Corruption	% Affected
1.	2003	14
2.	2005	24
3.	2007	30
4.	2009	27

The risk of bribery and corruption is most in the governmental transactions involving public sector companies and between governmental officials across nations in which organisations operate. However in recent years there has been a sea change in attitude dealing with corruption. Increased regulations in most part of the world have brought immense pressure due to efforts of IOs like OECD, UN, UNODC, World Bank and other prosecutors in international commerce. An action taken by external relevant regulatory authorities is only 24% for internal fraudsters within organization and for external fraudsters outside the organization is 46%.[1] However, large number of economic frauds rests with large organizations in countries such as Russia, South Africa, Kenya, Australia and others that have 40% or above economic frauds committed in their territory and India has low level of fraud committed in its territory i.e. 18%.[2] The following Table 4 shows the frauds by various types of organizations as per Global Economic Crime Survey 2009.

Table 4: Types of Organizations Involved in Economic Fraud

Sl. No.	Frauds by Various Types of Organizations	% Committed
1.	Private Sector	28
2.	Government/Sate Owned Enterprises	37
3.	Listed in Stock Exchange	31
4.	Others	21

Communication, financial services, insurance and, hospitality and leisure (Private Sector and Listed in Stock Exchange) tops the list of economic frauds committed more than

---

[1] Global Economic Crime Survey, November 2000, p. 14.
[2] Ibid, p. 10.

40% to its credit were external frauds play vital role. Government and state owned enterprises economic fraud share is 37% and it is almost in bribes form where the internal frauds play the role.[3] The economic frauds are often disclosed by internal audit, tip off (both internal and external), whistle-blowing system, suspicious transaction reporting, rotation of personal, accident and law enforcement. To the hard reality, the law enforcement detection of economic fraud is only 3%. This shows the lacuna in the functioning of the system in global sphere. However, The UNODC through its Thematic Programme on Action against Corruption and Economic Crime acts a catalyst and a resource to help States effectively implement the provisions of the Convention. It assists States with vulnerable developing or transitional economies by promoting anti-corruption measures in the public and private sector. The primary goal of the anti-corruption work done by UNODC is to provide States with practical assistance and build the technical capacity needed to implement the Convention. Efforts concentrate on supporting Member States in the development of anti-corruption policies and institutions, including preventive anti-corruption frameworks. As the Guardian of the United Nations Convention against Corruption, UNODC has resident in-depth knowledge on the Convention emanating from having negotiated the treaty.

THE ROLE OF UNCAC

Under UNCAC States Parties are gratified to adopt coordinated policies that prevent corruption and assign a 'body or bodies' to coordinate and supervise their performance. The preventive policies covered by the Convention include measures for both the public and private sectors. These include, among others, transparent procurement and sound financial management, a merit-based civil service, effective access to public information, auditing and other standards for private companies, an independent judiciary, active involvement of civil society in efforts to prevent and combat corruption, and measures to prevent money-laundering. States are to criminalise bribery (both the giving of an undue advantage to a national, international or foreign public official and the acceptance of an undue advantage by a national public official), as well as misappropriation of public funds. Sanctions extend to those who participate in or attempt to commit corruption offences.

As for as India is concerned the 'fundamental principle' of the Convention, and one of its main innovations, is the right to recovery of stolen public assets. India initially had reservation to sign the agreement later ratified it on 12th may 2011. UNCAC provisions also lay a framework for countries to adapt both their civil and criminal law in order to facilitate tracing, freezing, forfeiting, and returning funds obtained through corrupt activities. The requesting state will in most cases receive the recovered funds as long as

---

[3] Ibid, p. 15.

it can prove ownership. In some cases the funds may be returned directly to individual victims.

UNODC is also mandated to take other necessary actions to combat corruption through following measures often. They are: strengthening the integrity of the judiciary, international anti-corruption academy, technical assistance tools, manuals and publications, tools and resources for anti-corruption knowledge (TRACK) and UNCAC legal library, stolen asset recovery assistance, awareness-raising and outreach, and importantly working with the private sector. The responsibility of the private sector in the fight against corruption is regarded as decisive, underscoring the role that the private sector has to play in preventing and fighting corruption.[4] UNODC contributes actively to the implementation of the 10th principle of the United Nations Global Compact, which states that "Business should work against corruption in any form, including bribery and extortion."

CONCLUSION

Despite the Convention's comprehensiveness, there are several weak areas. For example, the Convention fails to vigorously tackle political corruption, one of the major concerns of citizens around the world. The Convention also refrains from referring to any specific political system and omits the important role parliaments can play in holding governments to account. The UNCAC is not a blueprint for anti-corruption reform, it is a mere compilation of important measures that lacks any prioritisation or sequencing. Ratification of the UNCAC does not constitute political will in itself. Some states may ratify just to deflect criticism from political opponents. Thus it performs the rule creating and rule supervisory functions but fails to perform rule enforcement function which is the hall mark of independence and autonomy of international organization. Even otherwise the functioning of UNODC is determined by the key variables such as dominant actors, dominant types of decisions, environment, and nature of subsystem and actors source of influence at a specific time period. Even ECOSOC also encourages member states to make full use of modern technologies to prevent and combat economic fraud and identity-related crime.[5] But it does not have mechanism to punish the offenders strongly as UNCAC. Hence forth following measures can be taken to Combat Corruption in Global Sphere:

1. High-level policy dialogue between partner governments, donors and civil society.
2. Identifying technical assistance needs.

---

[4]The Conference of the States Parties to the United Nations Convention against Corruption adopted resolution 3/2 at Third Session.

[5]Resolution 2007/20, International cooperation in the prevention, investigation, prosecution and punishment of economic fraud and identity related crime.

3. Inviting civil society to participate.
4. Inviting reviewers to a country.
5. Publishing the full country reports.
6. Think-thank Advisors and mentors assistance.

As a final remark, UNCAC provides not only a global legal basis for cooperation, but also a political tool for discourse between countries and between governments and their citizens with unanimously agreed concepts of corruption and ways to deal with it within one framework nurturing international exchange of expertise, good practices be instrumental in coordinating international backing.

The Role of Civil Society in Combating Corruption

S.M. Arasu

Secretary, Anti-Corruption Movement, Chennai

INTRODUCTION

It is ironical that, in to days advanced world, the most dreaded social disease is 'Corruption' and following that, to a slightly lesser extent, the violation of 'Human Rights'. It is all the more serious that these two elements happen to be the most vital components of a civil society in a country, whatever be the form of governance, the latter signifying the embodiment of reverential existence of the human race and the former providing or denying the economics for the same by its absence or presence.

It is therefore no wonder that the whole international community is of late fully seized of the matter, the United Nations itself declaring an Anti corruption convention.

A number of countries have signed the declaration, raising the hope for effective global actions against corruption.

CORRUPTION DEFINED

Dictionaries define corruption as 'moral depravity', which obviously means that any thing that cannot be passed of as an acceptable right conduct, is a corrupt practice. And that encompasses all vices. Bribe is one such component. Bribe itself is explained as 'the compensation paid for doing a wrong thing—repeat, for doing a wrong thing—to the person who does it, by the one who benefits by it'. So actually, bribe is that which is given and not one demanded. In any case, it is the greed for money which impels one to make it in plenty by hook or crook. The United Nations has rightly given it an apt one line definition—'Misuse of public office for personal gain'.

CAUSES FOR CORRUPTION

One need not delve deep into this for exploring the cause for one to indulge in corruption. It is simply the craving for money, more money and much more money. It is only man's innate craving for abundant affluence that drives him to adopt dubious means to amass wealth, which is rightfully not his. It is illogical to expect such men to mend by themselves. Therefore corruption and bribery need to be combated with forceful legal weapons by the State and through volatile public upheaval. Going by the survey conducted by the Transparency international, India finds itself in the comity of Nations with high levels of corruption. Thus it becomes imperative that the task of containing corruption has to be taken up in all seriousness as a National assignment.

AVENUES OF CORRUPTION

Corruption finds its roots where there are rules and restrictions as in government functioning, where there is plenty of room for authority sans accountability. Most of the Government departments have service delivery to the public for one thing or the other and the general public have to frequent the government offices for a number of such services, like getting ration cards, driving licenses, community certificates, electrical service connections, passports, to mention a few. Besides there are certain discretionary powers given to certain officials which they misuse for pecuniary advantage. When the money at stake is small, it can be classified as bribe and when large amounts are involved, like in the scams, then, it may be christened as corruption.

HUMAN RIGHTS DEFINED

Human rights are "basic *rights* and *freedoms* that all people are entitled to, regardless of nationality, sex, national or ethnic origin, race, religion, language, or other status." Human rights are conceived as *universal* and *egalitarian*, with all people having equal rights by virtue of being human. These rights may exist as *natural rights* or as *legal rights*, in both national and *international law*.

CORRUPTION AND HUMAN RIGHTS VIOLATION

The human rights can easily be defused by corruption. The equality of rights by virtue of being human can be off set by employment of money in favour of one, less deserving than another. Interference of corruption in human rights is more apparent than vice versa. In other words it can be said that corruption always involves violation of human rights in one way or the other. Besides corruption, violation of human rights emanates from one's personal biases, likes and dislikes and disregard for civility.

EFFECTS OF CORRUPTION

Corruption *per se* is morally degrading and presents one in poor light. At the national level, corruption impacts economy. The prices of commodities are determined by market demand and consumers response. A section of people with unlimited black money accrued through dubious means, on a spending spree, tend to raise the price line which contributes to inflation. They also don't hesitate to shell out some extra money for getting some thing done in government departments to their convenience. The common man, who needs to stand almost daily at the door step of Government offices for a number of services is the most affected, when he is compelled to grease the palms of officials for getting such services done.

WHO WANTS TO DO AWAY WITH 'CORRUPTION'?

This is the million dollar question. Apparently it is not the rulers in the government who die to get rid of corruption. Experience has made it known that those who are in authority in the Government would really like to take advantage of the facilities that a corruptive system offers. Probably it is actually a hidden agenda for such power centres. We can say with certainty almost, that corruption in any country has flourished with the tacit blessings of the ruling community. Otherwise corruption would not have proliferated to the extent to which we find it today. Their attempts at creating Anti-corruption awareness among the public don't seem to be whole hearted at all. Some time ago, when an NGO approached the State run transport corporation for pasting stickers containing the slogan 'Shun corruption-feel proud' on the buses, they were told pay a monthly royalty. When the matter was taken to the Government, it was responded with a reply that the government had taken all the steps needed to curb corruption and that there was no need to use the stickers. Well, so much for the government's commitment to eradicate corruption. And then, think of the efforts the governments are taking for, and the enormous money spent on campaigns for HIV and the like. All this go to expose the low priority that governments are assigning for the task of eradicating corruption. Thus, the fight against corruption has to come from the bottom, from the common people, who are at the receiving end. It is only them, and some patriotic nationalists who want to see the back of the demon 'corruption'. The civil society has a major role to play in this crusade.

STATE'S RESPONSIBILITY IN ERADICATING CORRUPTION

Theoretically, it is the bounden duty of the government to take all out efforts to see that the society and the country are not afflicted with corruption. But in reality not much is seen to be done. Governmental projects are, by design, allowed to be influenced by monetary considerations which tend to erode their level of performance. By facilitating the mushrooming of corrupt officials, governments have tacitly ensured that all the government services carry a price tag. There are government circulars and circulars against corruption and bribery perhaps to satisfy the critic, but none is really implemented. If only the Governments take a strong initiative with genuine desire, corruption would come down enormously.

STATE'S INFRASTRUCTURE IN COMBATING CORRUPTION

India's fight against corruption started in early sixties following the recommendations of Santhanam Committee. Central vigilance commission and State vigilance commissions were put in place. At the states level, directorates of vigilance and anti corruption were set up to tackle corruption. Though these agencies take continuous action to trap and arrest officials taking bribe and indulging in large scale corruption, the net effect is insignificant due to the provision for long drawn legal process and lack of stringent punishment. The loop holes in the system have helped to ensure that the conviction percentage in the trap cases is not more than 10. The vigilance wing itself, with some exceptions, is manned by men of questionable integrity drawn from the regular police force. It is no secret that in a survey the police was found to occupy the first place in the ranking of most corruptive departments. A number of representations from various NGOs suggesting ways of improvement in the functioning of the vigilance directorate have not borne fruit. Adding fuel to the fire, Government of India has recently issued orders exempting CBI from the purview of the RTI Act. The state government for its part has given exemption to the state vigilance directorate. The anti corruption activists all over the country hope that the much talked about 'Lokpal Bill' which is on the anvil will make a vigorous emergence strong enough to counter the Goliath of corruption.

PEOPLE'S APPROACH TOWARDS CORRUPTION

The apparent lack of enthusiasm among the masses in the fight corruption should not be misconstrued as an indicator of acceptance of the evil. On the contrary it is otherwise. The point in simple is that the average Indian lacks the initiative to protest, chooses the easiest way of keeping complacent and prefers to go by the compulsions of the environment until he gets hit himself. More than this many don't seem to recognize corruption as a sin. They tend to adore the sinner. When the man next door, takes to an adventurous foray into the political field and manages to make some fast buck by corruptive means, people begin to adore him as an achiever. But despite all this when confronted openly to speak about corruption all in one voice will agree that 'corruption should go'. Their only concern is that who is there to bell the cat?

NGOS FIGHTING CORRUPTION

In the absence of concerted efforts by the Government to eradicate corruption, it is laudable that a number of organizations have been started to involve people in the fight against corruption. There are organizations that are more than 10 years old. The Vth pillar, Anticorruption Movement, Lanjam kodathor Eyakkam (Non-bribe givers Movement), are some of the more popular associations which have bases in the districts of Tamilnadu and functioning effectively. Transparency International Chennai chapter, and Catalyst Trust are also lending a helping hand in the process. These organizations take action to conduct public awareness meetings against corruption and also address the students in educational institutions. Whenever members of the public who get harassed by the demand of bribe in Government offices approach them they render all assistance to get their job done without paying bribe money. In many cases even the money taken as bribe were made to be returned. The Movements also report cases when required to the vigilance directorate and cause trapping and arrest of the corrupt officials.

The RTI Act 2005 has come handy in a number of cases to get information about pending services in Govt. offices as a result of which the issues are settled in the normal course.

SCOPE FOR FIELD WORK BY THE VOLUNTEERS FIGHTING CORRUPTION

The Anti corruption volunteers should have absolute conviction in their fight against corruption. They should be bold and motivated. Normally the members are provided with identity cards by the respective organizations. When people approach them with complaint of extortion of bribe, they should satisfy themselves with the genuineness of the allegation. They may then directly accost the official concerned or report the matter to the higher authority. The acknowledged irony in most cases is that the higher officer himself is hand in glove with the corrupt official and the job becomes difficult. In cases involving high stakes this chain may extend to the level of political bosses, where it gets stonewalled. This is the situation in which the Anticorruption volunteers work today not to mention other kinds of risk.

DIFFICULTIES FACED BY ANTICORRUPTION VOLUNTEERS

Instances are not lacking where the volunteers questioning bribe takers or exposing major fraud in contract works have been threatened and in a few cases fatally attacked. The case of Young Engineer. Sathyendra Dubey who was shot dead for bringing to light certain irregularities in the Golden quadrilateral road work in Bihar and Mr. Amit Jethwa who was killed for raking questions under the RTI Act, 2005 are cases in point. Back home in Chennai, Anticorruption activists in Chengalpattu and Namakkal were seriously knife attacked for exposing corruption in high places. These cases take a long time in courts to finish at the end of which the culprits go invariably scot free. The NGO's fight against corruption is thus a thankless job which deserves to be complimented. More than compliments, it would be greatly helpful if the volunteers are adequately protected. Of course we could expect this only of a government with deep commitment to eliminate corruption.

TACKLING BRIBERY IN GOVERNMENT OFFICES

Government offices are the most notorious places where corruption is largely prevalent. These are outlet points of the Government to provide public services. A Govt. for the people, collecting taxes for various items is duty bound to provide the much needed services for the people at the right times without any hitch or harassment. The Government employees who are appointed for this purpose are paid salary from the State's tax revenue. They should perform their duties diligently befitting a true public servant as they are christened. Government has prescribed certain fees and time frame for accomplishing each type of service. The employees have to faithfully go by the guide lines. But in practice it is not so. Any job has a price other than the prescribed fee. This is utterly ridiculous. Governments do not seem to take note of this. For services like getting ration cards, different kinds of certificates and licenses in various departments people have to run from pillar to post, not knowing whom to approach and how. It is this ignorance and urgency in some cases that the officials take advantage of for extracting bribe from the gullible public. If this has to stop people have to rise up and start asking questions. They should not succumb to the pressure of greasing palms. Initially they should confront the official face to face. If he is not amenable the matter should be taken to the notice of the higher officer. In spite of all this if one due to exigencies of the situation, has to cough up some money and get his service fulfilled, he should immediately make a written complaint to the Head of department and vigilance narrating the incident and naming the corrupt individual. One should on no account take it lying down. But the better course indicated is to refrain from paying bribe and taking up the matter with the vigilance wing for trapping and arresting the corrupt individual under the prevention of corruption Act. The help of Anticorruption NGOs may also be sought who would be too glad to oblige. For this, of course, the individual should have patience and determination.

This is the biggest menace afflicting the general public which for reasons (not) unknown the Governments have been slack in tackling though it is easy to control by proper monitoring.

RTI ACT-2005 AN EFFECTIVE TOOL TO TACKLE CORRUPTION

The RTI Act 2005 is indeed a boon in the hands of the people to ensure improvement in the level of public service. The Act provides that any information sought for has to be given within 30 days. There are appeal procedures in case of default. The Act provides for penalty of Rs. 250 a day of delay subject to a maximum limit of Rs. 25000. Questions can be asked seeking reasons for not issuing a document or certificate for a long time without valid reason. But the Activists have found that the Act has not been given due importance by the Governments. Nevertheless the Act has proved its usefulness in tackling corruption in a number of cases.

CASE STUDIES

An Inspector of police was demanding a monthly *mamool* of Rs. 5000 from a tea stall owner for issuing a permission to run the stall. By the help of the volunteers of the Anticorruption Movement he was trapped and arrested by the Vigilance police wing. This happened a few years ago and the case is still going on, but the accused in active service perhaps carrying on his habitual chores.

Very recently at the instance of a medical shop owner two officers of the commercial department were caught red handed while receiving the bribe money.

An Anticorruption volunteer who brought out blatant corruption in the execution of rural employment guarantee works by the Panchayat president in his village is under constant threat to his personal safety and has taken to hiding.

The irony of it all is that such actions have failed to deter the corrupt officials from indulging in bribery. The reason is not far to seek. In most cases (up to 90%) the culprits manage to extricate themselves from the case with the help of lawyers. The temporary discomfiture they undergo is nothing compared to the enormous benefit they enjoy from bribes. It is therefore necessary that the laws and punishments are made more stringent. In this context the demand by Anticorruption Activists like Anna Hazare for a strong Lokpal bill is quite relevant for eradicating corruption.

POLITICS AND CORRUPTION

Politics may not be the birth place of corruption, but it has provided the much needed asylum for this social evil. It can be recalled that in the fifties and early sixties of the 20th century things were not so bad though there surfaced sporadic incidents of corruption here and there. The decline began from that point in time. A senior politician lamented that virus had entered politics. Time has proved this prophecy. Virus did enter in the form of a clan of politicians whose only goal was to mint money for self by hook or crook and lo they have done just that. During this phase of governance we had come across politicians who had openly supported corruption in.

The Anti corruption Activists have realized that if corruption should go corrupt politicians should go. The best way to achieve this is to impart training to dedicated youth in all aspects of politics-clean politics- and encourage them to enter the political field. A few Movements have joined together and started 'An Academy of Honest politics' and providing this training free of cost to aspiring youth.

The electoral laws need to be amended to ensure that people with criminal record are kept out of the political stream. The recommendations of the election commission n in this regard have not seen the light of the day. No one can deny the fact that the parliament and State assemblies are replete with criminals, or at least those charged with criminal offences to the extent of 30% and more. People should exercise their franchise in the elections without fail and vote for men of integrity and patriotism. In this context it is also relevant to consider the wise suggestion from various quarters that the Prime Minister of the Country and Chief Ministers of the States should be elected directly. This will help to ensure complete authority for the incumbents and do away with horse trading and such maneuvers.

CONCLUSION

In the present context, it appears that in the absence or in spite of total commitment on the part of the Governments, the Non governmental organizations fighting corruption have a heavy responsibility. The role of the civil society can be reflected only through the actions of the representative associations. Therefore conscientious people who want to see a corruption free India with good governance should associate themselves with any of the organizations and contribute their efforts in different ways in fighting corruption. At a personal level, every citizen should take an oath that he would never indulge in paying a bribe or involve himself in a corruptive activity, come what may. He should readily come forward to report such happenings to authorities and pursue the same to the logical end.

In short people particularly youth of the country should realize the value of Gandhian thoughts and adhere to them. This alone will pave the way for a prosperous and powerful India.

Good Governance and Human Rights

L.S. Jeganathan

T.N. Lanjam Kodathor Iyakkam, Srinivasapuram, Korattur (R.S.), Chennai–600 076
E-mail: ellesjelsj@yahoo.com

One of fundamental rights enshrined in our Constitution is right to life which means not only one to be alive but also one's right to liberty, security and a dignified livelihood with assured food, cloth, shelter, education, health, recreation *et al.* Human Rights are inclusive of these fundamental rights. U.N. Universal Declaration of Human Rights includes civil, Political, economic, social and cultural rights. A corrupt and inefficient Government cannot guarantee these rights as the benefits of its welfare schemes and development programmes will not reach the targeted population in full measure; or sometimes even minimum extent depending upon the level of corruption. Hence to ensure human rights, good and clean governance with transparency and accountability is sin qua non. The means of achieving such good governance have been detailed below:

To our dismay and disappointment, the quality of our politics and for that matter governance has been continuously deteriorating to reach its nadir. It is anyone's obvious expectation that with the increase of the percentage of educated, the standard of ethics of politics and quality of governance would commensurably enhance in any nation. But alas! Here the situation is diagonally opposite. Also the caliber of our educated population is much to be desired. As one philosopher said any people will get a government that deserves to them for which our nation stands a clear testimony.

Our educated population is squarely responsible for fast deterioration of politics and governance of this nation. They miserably failed to cultivate citizenship among themselves and among their fellow citizens and act as responsible citizens. They do not evince enough interest even to enrol themselves and their family members in electoral rolls and discharge their basic democratic duty of exercising their franchise in all elections.

All ills of governance flow from periodical elections to our legislative bodies of states and Central Parliament. The elections are fountain—head of black money. These elections to our august democratic bodies have been rendered mockery due to free practice of all sorts of irregularities and atrocities like fake electoral rolls, selection of candidates on the basis of their religion or caste or their monetary strength not withstanding their criminal background, spending extravagantly with no limit whatsoever, bribing voters with huge sums, scaring voters with high voltage violence, including murder, playing vote-bank politics suited to each party, booth capturing, contravening election rules and code of conduct with impunity, promising improbables including mega free-bies unmindful of the economic consequences in the long run, not to speak of our rotten and spineless administration which is hand in glove with rulers. Can this poor nation afford to bear such exorbitant expenditure frittered away by political parties in elections? The stated objectives, economic policies and development programmes of respective parties are discussed only for 10% of the time of their election meetings while 90% of the time is spent on calling names of political rivals. Political parties capable of scoring even 25% of total votes polled in any election manage to catch the seat of power, because of multi-corner contests.

Not only the people are fast loosing faith in political parties and elections and thereby democratic governance due to continuous declining of their moral ethics and ever increasing electoral irregularities, but also it has paved way for the growth of extremism and terrorism for which state of affairs no political party feels sorry.

There was once a time when constructive debates with clash of innovative ideas were held in healthy and harmonious environment by our elected representatives in our legislative bodies. But for the past few decades, our august legislative bodies have been rendered as pandemonium where noisy scenes and physical clashes are common. It is highly reprehensible that our elected representatives have no qualm whatsoever to demand bribe even to ask questions in the legislative bodies or to allot funds from their Constituency development funds for the felt needs of their clientle population.

Can we make bold that we have achieved all intended targets fixed in our five year plans? If not, why? Our former Prime Minister Rajiv Gandhi himself confessed that out of every rupee spent on a development programme only 15 paise reach the targeted population. Success of any Government can be decided on the basis of the following factors:

1. The extent of successfulness of the efforts taken to boost tax revenue without enhancing the rate of tax/duties/toll affecting common man.
2. Maximise Plan part of expenditure, thereby bringing share of Non-plan part to the minimum extent possible.
3. Avoiding unnecessary and unproductive expenditure.
4. Provision of adequate funds for farsighted schemes for ensuring sustainable, all-round inclusive and balanced growth.

5. Avoidance of budget deficits or at least maintaining it at reasonably minimum level.

In Plan Part of the budget the following items should be accorded preference:
1. Productive and employment-oriented schemes.
2. Schemes meant for infrastructural development.
3. Programmes for fulfilling the basic needs and felt-needs of people of various regions.
4. Reasonable provision for human resource development (education).
5. Poverty alleviation programmes and social welfare/security schemes.
6. Far-sighted schemes.

The question is whether schemes are chosen on the basis of above-said factors or schemes are selected for cheap popularity or for political gains and to satisfy its vote bank. A welfare state will not encourage unproductive schemes or free-bies. But it is disheartening that even the so called educated population praise such schemes because of their instant gains.

Without building healthy and responsive society, good governance is not feasible. To uproot all social evils particularly corruption in public life and ensure such healthy society we should bring major reform in our education system by way of:
(a) introducing value-based education with moral and ethical aspects.
(b) appointing adequately qualified and disciplined teachers with dedication and devotion in their sacred profession.

Apart from above-said suggestions, the following reforms are badly needed for immediate implementation to ensure good governance at Central and State levels:
1. (a) Electoral reforms as already suggested by various commissions and other bodies in a bunch in toto—not in piece-meal manner.
   (b) Those with criminal background should strictly be prohibited from contesting any election.
2. Democratic decentralization of governance should be ensured by downloading maximum administrative and financial powers from Central level upto bottom most unit of village panchayat level, inclusive of empowering of rural and urban local bodies as enshrined in the 73rd and 74th Amendments of the Constitution of India.
3. Anti-defection law should be made more stringent.
4. All elected representatives of people of all states legislatures and national Parliament should be subjected to Lok Ayukta or Lok Pal enquiry in the event of receipt of any complaint of financial irregularity or corruption charges with adequate prima-facie against them.
5. The entire Central and State Government machinery should be computarised and e-governance introduced at all levels to ensure transparency and speed.

6. All loopholes in the Right to Information Act, 2005 should be plugged and implemented strictly and the Act should be included in the job-chart of all officials.
7. All performing officials showing exemplary achievements continuously should be commended and given suitable incentives including out-of-turn promotion.
8. Non-performing and corruptive officials should be punished suitably. All disciplinary proceedings initiated against them should be completed within six months.
9. Cases of corruption caught red-handed by Vigilance Department should be conducted on the lines of Court Martial on day-to-day basis as suggested by Santhanam Commission and finalised within one year.
10. All Government activities should be assigned reasonable time-limits. Those who exceed such time-limits for completion of respective task, should be suitably punished.
11. Above all, if the Chief Secretariat of Tamilnadu is geared up ensuring more speed and efficiency, its impact will percolate upto bottom most level of administration for positive results.
12. All training programmes meant for various levels is of officials should be streamlined and upto-dated. Periodical orientation should be imparted to all officials for motivation and sensitization.
13. It is undeniable fact that without the consent or bending of officials, no politician can indulge in any corruptive activity. This fact holds good particularly to all India Service Officers—I.A.S. Officers in particular. Hence any complaint of political interference is nothing but a farce. So if these All India Officials act boldly with complete integrity and honesty, 90% of corruption can easily be weeded out.
14. A Central law should be enacted to regulate and discipline all registered and recognized political parties wherein the political parties should be mandated to submit every year (1) their audited annual accounts (2) their list of members (3) Details of donations received during the year of report to their respective legislative bodies, the Controller and Auditor General of India and National Election Commission.
15. Bringing in Police reform and Judicial reform.

By bringing in above reforms, we can definitely ensure clean and good governance with transparency, efficiency, accountability and speed with maximum people's participation thereby honouring human rights and strengthening our democratic credentials.

Corruption and Good Governance

M. Sarumathy
NIRD, Hyderabd

CONSTRUCTION AND PERSPECTIVE

Corruption is anti-public and opposed to democracy. Corruption is never an end itself. Wealth, power, influence and control are other means of corruption. Crime is the other form of violence closely allied to serious matter of corruption. Both together cause turbulence, impinge on the economy, destroy the culture and tremble the socio-economic political system. Weak or absence of important leadership positions often play influencing role mitigating corruption. Absence of positive and sever measures, environment conducive to corrupt behavior, lack of education and poverty are some of the factors contributed to severe disease of corruption. Corruption is counter to culture and erodes cultural integrity and moral systems of societies and thus has a deep and long lasting impact on the continuous evolution of human society

The problem of corruption is a serious source of disorganization or pathology. Herbert Blumer (1971) asserts that 'social problems are fundamentally products of a process of collective definition instead of existing as a set of objective social arrangements with an intrinsic makeup'. Blumer points out that sociological recognition of a social problem is usually preceded by it designation as a problem by the public[1] Chibnall and Saunders (1977), which is of direct relevance to my approach. It adopts a social construction of reality perspective in regarding corruption as a 'negotiated classification of behavior' rather than as an inherent quality of behavior.[2] Accusations of corruption usually originate from such 'modernizing elites'. In the developing countries, these elites often see corruption as an integral part of the political culture[3]. As Etzioni-Halevy (1985) pointed out, elites are the ones who safeguard democracy, but they are also

---

[1] Vinod Parvarala, Interpteting Corruption Elite Perspective in India (New Delhi: Sage Publication, 1996), 21
[2] Ibid.
[3] Ibid, 26.

the ones who, under certain circumstances, augment their power by corrupting the rules and procedures of democracy[4]. Nye' (1967:417) defined corruption as the behavior which deviates from the normal duties of a public role.[5] Behavior such as bribery, nepotism and misappropriation are viewed as phenomenon from the public office prospective. Van Klaveren conceived maximizing unit primarily a market centered public office as corruption. Etzioni (1984) attempted a definition to corruption, which is delegitimate financing of political activity. Roebuck and Barker, 1974). Heidenheimer *et al.* (1989: 156–157) categorize corrupt behavior into 'petty corruption', 'routine corruption' (including acceptance of gifts by public officials, nepotism, and graft) and 'aggravated corruption' (including kickbacks and organized crime). V.O. Key (1936) discusses 'auto-corruption', referring to such things as embezzlement, awarding of contracts to oneself, and so on.[6]

Fluidity, Ambiguity and Equivocation

Corruption is basically deviation from a code of conduct laid down in any walk of life.
- Corruption is something which you are legally not entitled to get-whether it is post facto or not is irrelevant.
- Corruption is a many—faceted concept, not necessarily to do with money changing hands. It may be abuse of position, nepotism.

Historically, all societies are engaged to some extent in what Duster (1970) calls 'the legislation of morality' and India is no exception. In India the most significant law concerning corruption, one that legally draws the boundaries between corrupt and non-corrupt acts, is the Prevention of Corruption Act, 1947 (amended in 1988). Some of the more ambiguous types offered include 'intellectual corruption', corruption of the soul', and 'moral corruption'. Doing anything against your conscience for a consideration is corruption, whatever be the consideration. Corruption implies anything that is not straight forward. In nature there are corrupted things from which arises a corrupted mentality. Corruption has been an integral part of India's economic, political, and social life.

Corruption and Social Science Perspectives

What are the causes…of this curse of corruption? Why do these immoral dealings go on…while everyone pays lip sympathy to the affected but no one takes the bull by its horn? Undoubtedly, the basic reason is that moral and ethical values of 'service before self' has been given a go-by and the 'end justifies the means' has taken over.[7]

---

[4] Ibid, 26.
[5] Ibid, 61.
[6] See Vinod Parvarala, 62.
[7] See Vinod Parvarala, 79.

Social science has paid comparatively less attention to the effects of corruption. Generally, scholars of corruption constitute argument with the set of causes and consequences. Vinod's opinion is there are only few exceptions, many of these studies focus on the phenomenon rather than the dynamics of the process.[8] A set of methodology is generally analytical, baring few on course of action. Corruption may increase the allocation of resources away from consumption and into investment, it may render the rational-legal bureaucratic system more humane in traditional societies, and may improve the quality of public servants.

ETIOLOGIES OF CORRUPTION

Along with transparency and management comes the need for corporate social responsibility which ranges from following labor laws and human rights issues to protecting the environment and contributing to the social and economic development of the regions. The society cannot ignore every year at the beginning of academic schooling, the incident of Kumbakonam. Eighty three school children aged between 8–10 years were charred to death, 20 of them beyond recognition in Sri Krishna School, Kumbakonam, 2004. The fire is believed to have started from the kitchen, where the noon meal for nursery children was being prepared, and soon spread to a row of thatched roof classrooms where students from class one to class five were present, police and eyewitnesses said. According to norms, such thatched roofs are not permissible, especially when there is a kitchen at such close quarters where food under the noon meal scheme is cooked. This is an act of criminal negligence to have a thatched roof at such close proximity to the kitchen. It is clear that the management of the school has not adhered to the norms.

Another example the collapse of Satyam Computer Services Limited, India's fourth-largest IT firm, shocked its clients, whose list included 185 of the Fortune 500 companies, and the industry in general. It also challenged the usefulness of two pillars of Indian corporate governance laws. Satyam Computer Services Limited later emerged with more than $1.5 billion, which was illegally transferred from Satyam to Raju's personally owned firms; these included a property firm, Maytas Infra Ltd., as per copyright, that owned a $3 billion contract to build the Hyderabad Metro Rail system.[9]

A number of scams have recently been reported in the press, notably the Harshad Mehta case (rigging of share prices), ITC case (prosecution for foreign exchange regulations), Reliance Industries (official patronage and manipulation of customs duties), MS Shoes scam (manipulation of the stock exchange), CRB scam (securities scam), etc. Such trends

---

[8] Ibid, 22.
[9] RafiqDissani, Satyam (news item) accessed June 7, 2011 http://frost.com

have been associated with the generation of a parallel black economy and loss of a huge amount of revenue to the government.

CORRUPTION IN THE INDIAN CONTEXT

Corruption in India is neither new nor limited in scope. In a recent study by Transparency International on political corruption, India ranks 85th among the 180 countries.[2] The World Bank ranks India in the 25th to 50th percentile on the ability to control corruption.

Economic corruption in India arose due to state controls of production through licenses and quotas. To gain access to licenses, corporations paid bribes. To gain access to goods and services in short supply, the public paid bribes. Thus, in the public mind, corruption, slow growth, inefficiency, and poor quality became inextricably linked.

A second source of corruption was the misuse of state power. The state has misused power in various ways. These include overstaffing public departments with favored voting groups, reallocating property rights to favored business groups, and dispensing privileges in return for campaign contributions. The third source of corruption was inadequate disclosure and enforcement of corporate actions. With a few exceptions, listed companies were run as family firms that viewed their firms as hereditary fiefdoms.

Many of India's streams and rivers are choked by pollution, making them unusable for farming. In one case in southern India earlier this year, researchers studied a river near 90 factories operated by pharmaceutical companies. The river was a cauldron of 21 different medicinal ingredients used to treat hypertension, gonorrhea and chronic liver ailments. Researchers estimated that one company had dumped 45 kilograms of the antibiotic ciprofloxacin into the river in a single day—equivalent to five times the daily consumption of the medication in Sweden.[10]

Speaking at a conference last month, Prime Minister Manmohan Singh said: "Climate change is threatening our ecosystems, water scarcity is becoming a way of life and pollution is a growing threat to our health and habitat[11]. Domination of the ritual sphere' and establish themselves as legitimate ritual specialists who perform a number of life-cycle rituals for pilgrims and residents of the city. As such, it is to be understood not only as a site of ideological struggle, but also as a sphere of economic competition where access to symbolic resources frequently translate into financial gains.[12]

---

[10]Accessed June 7, 2011, http:// Ganges, environment Gits4u.com

[11]Water politics, PM India: Dying Thirst, September 14, 2009.

[12]Assa Doron, Caste, Occupation and politics on the Ganges: Passage of Resistance (Famham and Burlington: Ashgate, 2008), 116.

Several research studies have been conducted on the consequences of environmental exposure to factory waste dumps. As can be seen from TI's example, this sort of corruption at the corporate level and the link between big businesses and governments in actually creating environmental hazards is widespread and there is comparatively very little accountability. Unless there is some form of connection drawn between environmental hazards, corporate social responsibility and the widespread corrupt practices and misuse of natural resources, all attempts or hopes of preventing global warming or protection of the environment will simply remain unsubstantial.

CAUSES OF CORRUPTION

Gopakumar Krishnan, Asia Programme Manager at the Transparency Index (TI)—Secretariat contemplated that public spending on basic services such as drinking water, education, health and law enforcement represents a significant allocation of scarce resources in South Asia. The survey results show that even when public services are meant to be freely available, bribes and delays keep many from receiving them, and it is most often the poorest in society that suffer most."[13] Gopakumar Krishnan further believed that the direct feedback from the public is a powerful tool to ensure public accountability, which has to oversee the activities of public agencies, which across the region are the sole providers of many basic necessities. The findings also indicate that where the law is silent on standards of service, agencies simply provide poorer services. The TI has identified increasing measures to improve transparency, from citizens' charters to the practice of publicly posting official fees, has proven effective in holding public officials to account and reducing corruption.

The educational sector is considered as one of the most corrupt after the police, judiciary and permit services. Voters are mislead by manipulating ratings and project a fabricated image of political parties rather than the reality. Advantage of the public impressionability and manipulate the public for personal gain of politicians. Good governance prevents and checks all forms of corruption in the public. Large businesses have to be based on transparency since they have to remain accountable to stakeholders and customers.

CRITICISM

However, the Corruption Perceptions Index has drawn increasing criticism in the decade since its launch, leading to calls for the index to be abandoned. This criticism has been directed at the quality of the Index itself, and the lack of actionable insights created from a simple country ranking. Because corruption is willfullly hidden, it is

---

[13]International Public Management Review, electronic journal at http://www.lpmr.net vol.10, issue1,2009@iPMN

impossible to measure directly; instead proxies for corruption are used. The CPI uses an eclectic mix of third-party surveys to sample public perceptions of corruption through a variety of questions, ranging from "Do you trust the government?" to "Is corruption a big problem in your country?" the use of third-party survey data is a source of criticism. The data can vary widely in methodology and completeness from country to country.[14]

The lack of standardization and precision in these surveys is cause for concern. The authors of the CPI argue that averaging enough survey data will solve this; others argue that aggregating imprecise data only masks these flaws without addressing them. In one case, a local Transparency International chapter disowned the index results after a change in methodology caused a country's scores to increase-media reported it as an "improvement". Other critics point out that definitional problems with the term "corruption" makes the tool problematic for social science. Critics are quick to concede that the CPI has been instrumental creating awareness and stimulating debate about corruption.[15]

Corruption in India and elsewhere is recognized as a complex phenomenon, as the consequence of more deep seated problems of policy distortion, institutional incentives and governance. It thus cannot be addressed by simple legal acts proscribing corruption. The reason is that, particularly in India, the judiciary, legal enforcement institutions, police and such other legal bodies cannot be relied upon, as the rule of law is often fragile, and thus can be turned in their favour by corrupt interests.[16]

The Indian democracy is preparing itself a strong fight against corruption. Law makers are law breakers in the case of corruption all over world. And India is not an exception. Hurricane of Fighting corruption is the key issue in India in now a days.

Countries with high levels of corruption, like India, have found themselves less able to attract investment and aid in a competitive global market

The post-independence political leadership has risen from the grassroots level in the form of regional, caste, linguistic and other protest movements. They have transformed the nature of politics and administration. Amoral politics, self-aggrandizement, disregard of the constitutional norms in the pursuit of power, political survival at any cost are their rules of the game. They interfere with the administration of justice and have bent bureaucracy to do their bidding

To combat systemic corruption in India is directly related to the extent of participation of the civil society. The underlying idea is that development is not the product

---

[14]Accessed Corruption perception Index-Wikipedia, April 21, 2011.
[15]Ibid.
[16]Ibid.

of set of blueprints given by the political leadership independently of the civil society but is often a joint output of the civil society itself anti-corruption strategies are not simply policies that can be planned in advance and isolation, but often a set of subtler insights that can be developed only in conjunction with citizen but rather it is deeply rooted in the activities of the civil society itself. The Transparency Index Corruption in South Asia survey strongly supports the case for empowering regulatory bodies, such as the office of the Ombudsman.

The Financial Express commented that year: "The wealth amassed by Indian billionaires—estimated at 340.9 billion dollars by the US business magazine Forbes-is nearly 31 percent of the country's total GDP. This gives them nearly three times more weight in the economy than their American counterparts and over ten times of those in China. The GDP share of Indian billionaires' wealth is more than four times of the global average."[17] As discussed earlier poverty leads to ignorance, disease and apathy, thereby the bargaining capacity of majority of the Indians low where fighting against injustice is not vibrant force of action.

The opinion discussed above has been supported by the survey on notion of corruption highlighted the result that are presented in the chart form.

Chart 1: State Affairs of Corruption

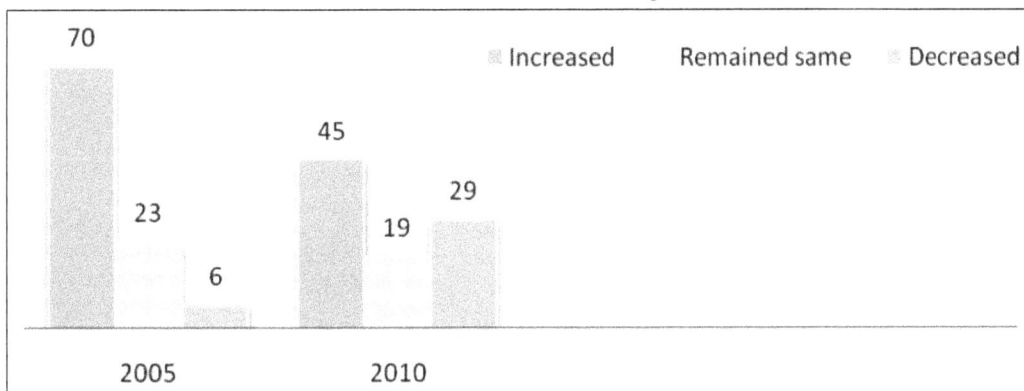

Ranging from Re one to Rs. 950, rural households in the country could have paid a whopping Rs. 471.8 crore last year as bribe to avail basic facilities such as ration, health, education and water supply, says a study.

The 'India Corruption Study: 2010' report prepared by Centre for Media Studies (CMS), a survey of 9,960 households in 12 states, says on an average a rural household could have paid Rs. 164 as bribe for availing these facilities in a year.

---

[17]Arun Kumar, Redifining poverty Line, Frontier, Vol. 24, No. 10, Sept. 19–26, 2010 accessed June 5, 2011. www.frontiervieweekly.com

Chart 2: Average Bribe Amount Paid a Household During a Year

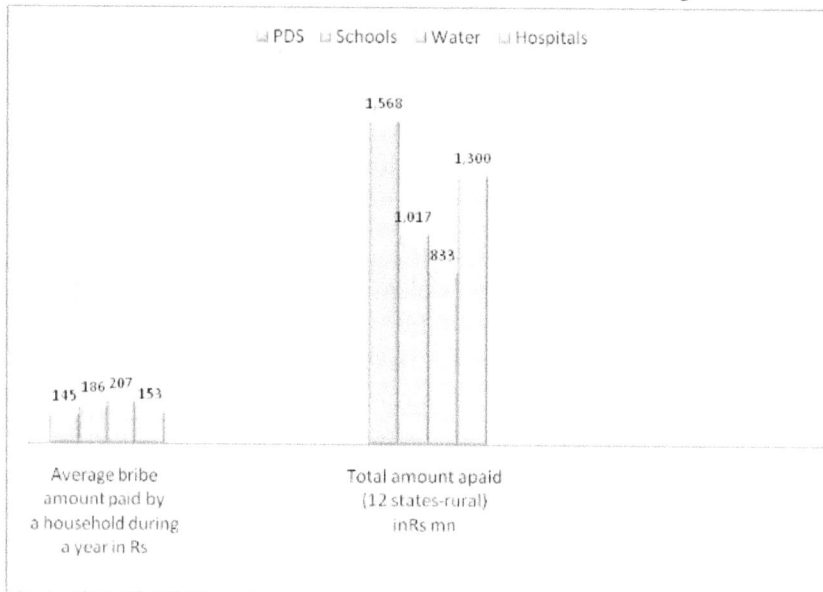

Chart 3: Bribes in the Case Hosptialisation

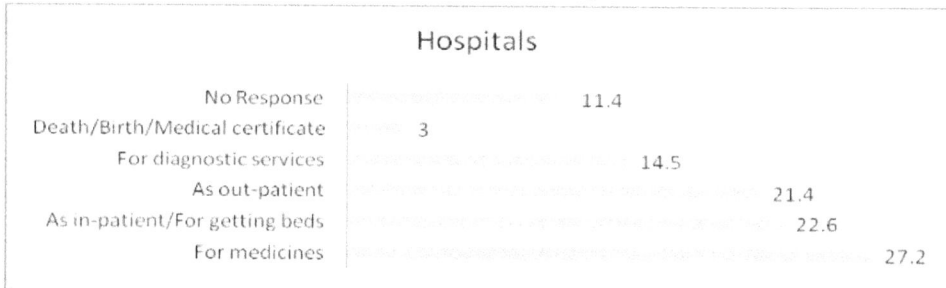

Chart 4: Bribes in the Case of Water

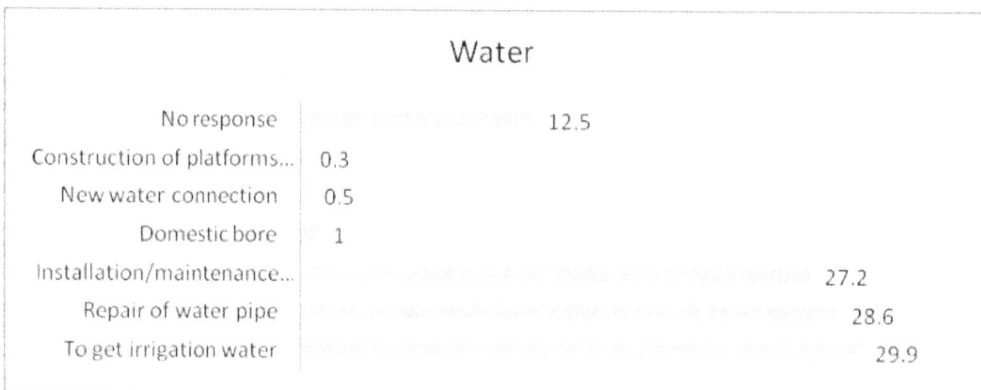

Chart 5: Bribes in the Case of School

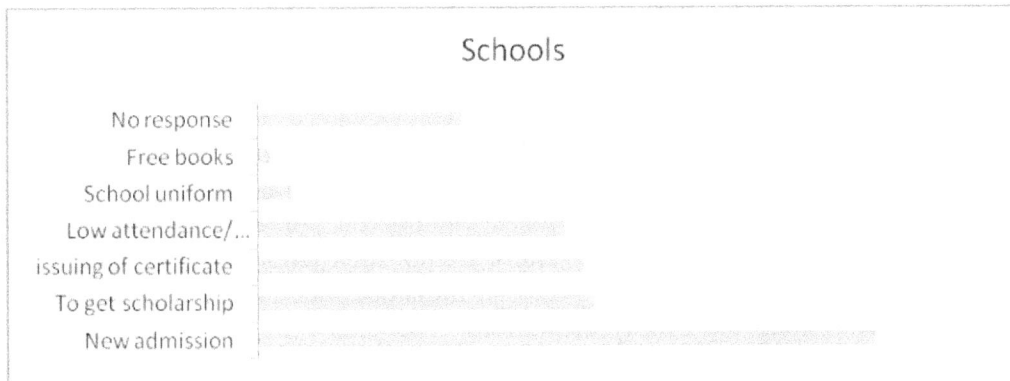

Schools

No response	
Free books	
School uniform	
Low attendance/...	
issuing of certificate	
To get scholarship	
New admission	

Chart 6: Bribes in the Case of Public Distribution System

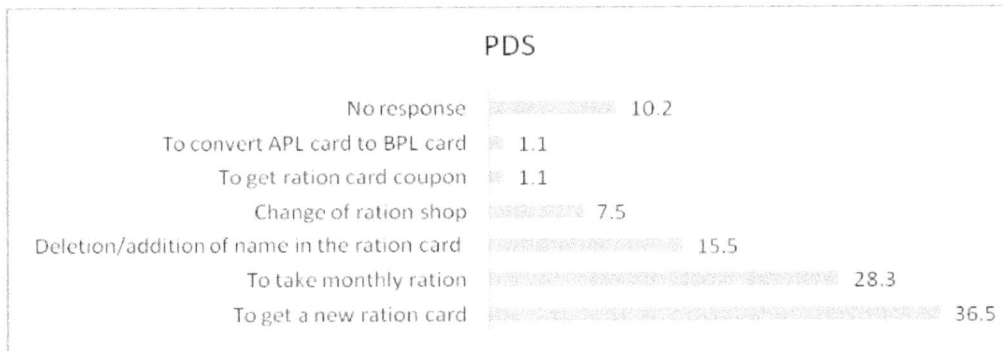

PDS

No response	10.2
To convert APL card to BPL card	1.1
To get ration card coupon	1.1
Change of ration shop	7.5
Deletion/addition of name in the ration card	15.5
To take monthly ration	28.3
To get a new ration card	36.5

The study said the total amount of Rs. 471.8 crore is "equal or less" than the total expenditure made under MNREGA during 2010–11 in states like Assam, Gujarat, Kerala, Himachal Pradesh and Maharashtra. The percentage of rural households that paid bribe during the last year was relatively higher in PDS (11.5 per cent), followed by hospitals (9), schools (5.8), water (4.3)," the study said.

In the foreward for the study, NAC member Aruna Roy said, "The poor fight against corruption and become victims of arbitrary use of power. The bribe paid by these households merely to survive, brings into sharp focus a set of concerns that should engage the interest of the media to fight the system on their behalf."[18]

It has also been termed as royal thievery. Corruption is opposed to democracy and social order, being not only anti-people, but aimed and targeted against them. It is likely to

---

[18] www.financialexpress,jan 10, 2010.

cause turbulence-shaking of the socio-economic-political system in an otherwise healthy, wealthy, effective and vibrating society.

Attitude of the People

The people of the country generally try to get their work done even by bribing the public servant instead of reporting corruption. Even a few of those who have come forward to expose the corrupt have been victimized. The example of Satyendra Dubey of Bihar can be cited here. Transparency International which studied the conditions in the country has concluded that India does not enjoy a respectable place in this regard among the comity of Nations. The then Prime Minister Late Rajiv Gandhi went to the extent of concluding that for every rupee spent on the public, only fifteen paise reached the beneficiary. It has to be remembered that the malaise flourish with the tacit support of the people.

As Santhanam committee emphasized, corruption cannot be eliminated or even reduced considerably unless preventive measures are planned and implemented in a sustained and effective manner. The Union Government acted on a direction from the Hon'ble Supreme court in 2004 and passed the Public Interest Disclosure Resolution which is popularly known as Whistle Blower's resolution. This is a big step in combating the menace of corruption in the central services. This was incidentally the result of the sacrifice of life by Satyendra Dubey, a bright young engineer in the Golden Quadrilateral Road Project in Bihar. The most important feature of the Whistle Blowers" resolution is that the identity of the complainant should not be revealed. This naturally prevents the victimization of the complainant and helps in fighting corruption. The one aspect which might be influencing the bane of corruption in the country is the lack of moral education in the country after independence. Perhaps because of a perverted understanding of the meaning of secularism, basic human values are being forgotten and this one step to reconsider the situation appears urgent in order to raise moral standards and fight the greed to acquire unreasonable wealth.

LOKPAL BILL

The first Lokpal Bill was passed in the 4th Lok Sabha in 1969 but could not get through in Rajya Sabha. Subsequently, Lokpal bills were introduced in 1971, 1977, 1985, 1989, 1996, 1998, 2001, 2005 and in 2008, yet they were never passed and its pending. The Administrative Reforms Commission (ARC) while recommending the constitution of Lokpal was convinced that such an institution was justified not only for removing the sense of injustice from the minds[19] of adversely affected citizens but also necessary to instill public confidence in the efficiency of administrative machinery. Following this, the

---

[19]www.Lokpal-wikipeidia.org accessed 18 April 2011.

Lokpal Bill was for the first time presented during the fourth Lok Sabha in 1968, and was passed there in 1969. Each time, after the bill was introduced to the house, it was referred to some committee for improvements—a joint committee of parliament, or a departmental standing committee of the Home Ministry—and before the government could take a final stand on the issue the house was dissolved.

CRITICISM

The Lokpal bill is intended to provide the common man with direct powers to censure his/her elected representative. However, every complainant has to pay a fees and take full responsibility for leveling charges. In case the complaint is found to be baseless, punitive action extending to two years in jail and monetary fine of up to Rs. 50,000 many be imposed on the complainant. Charges of corruption in the Indian legal system are not necessarily covered only under the Prevention of Corruption Act, 1988 but also under many other Acts, but the Lokpal restricts its ambit to the cases under this Act.

Differences between Draft Lokpal Bill 2010 and Jan Lokpal Bill

Draft Lokpal Bill (2010)	*Jan Lokpal Bill (Citizen's Ombudsman Bill)*
No power to initiate suo moto action or receive complaints of corruption from the general public. It can only probe complaints forwarded by Lok Sabha Speaker or Raja Sabha Chairman.	Have powers to initiate suo moto action or receive complaints of corruption from the general public.
Advisory Body with limitation to forwarding its report to the "Competent Authority".	Much more than an Advisory Body. It should be granted powers to initiate prosecution against anyone found guilty.
Do not have any police powers. It can not register FIRs or proceed with criminal investigations.	Have police powers. To say that it will be able to register FIRs.
CBI and Lokpal will have no connection with each other.	Lokpal and anti corruption wing of CBI will be one Independent body.
Punishment for corruption will be minimum 6 months and maximum up-to 7 years.	The punishment should be minimum 5 years and maximum up-to life imprisonment.
	Lokpal will not be a monopoly for particular area.

Corruption was seen as a sign of incomplete institutionalization, poverty, and an underdeveloped polity. The history of the Ombudsman institution dates back to eighteenth century Sweden when the King appointed an officer to investigate complaints against royal officials. In 1809, the Swedish Parliament appointed a parliamentary ombudsman or Justifier ombudsman to handle complaints against administrative and judicial action (Caiden, 1983a). The idea soon spread to countries like Denmark, Norway, Finland, and eventually, undergoing diverse mutations, to the rest of the world (Stacey, 1978; Weeks, 1978; Caiden, 1983b; Rowat, 1985).

In India, eminent people in different walks of life started broaching the idea of an ombudsman authority In the 1960s to control corruption in government. The Santhanam Committee in 1964 had recommended some kind of permanent government body to deal with the problem. A Parliamentary committee studied the idea in 1965, and in 1966 a high-powered Administrative Reforms Commission recommended the establishment of a Lok Pal at the central level and Lok Ayuktas at the state level (Maheshwari, 1972).[20]

AIMS TO RESOLVE

Corruption was a failure of citizenship. The administrative procedures and practices which are cumbersome are another major cause of corruption in India. India's legal and administrative system was designed in the middle of the nineteenth century to serve the interests of colonial administration. System based on distrust of the 'natives' and a firm belief in their inability to govern themselves. It has in built provisions for delays, prolonged litigation and evasion. Its provisions are ideally suited to the promotion of corruption at all levels, as graft provides the quickest immunity from delays and punitive action. Another factor to the growth of corruption in India is that the cases relating to corruption are often handled in a casual and clumsy manner. Public administration is a sub-system of the social system. Therefore the societal culture or societal environment has powerful impact on public administration. The impact of corruption on the quality of public infrastructure is all too clearly visible in the towns and cities of India. The film industry, a substantial par of the construction industry and a large number of small industries are run on the basis of black money" (Vittal 1999).

Morals and ethics can percolate only through proper education and thus education remains the strongest tool to prevent corruption. Education spreads awareness against corruption and thus helps in strengthening the moral or ethical values of society. Raising general levels of awareness in the population is essential as this establishes citizens' demands for accountability, and education creates a culture of accountability by emphasizing ethical practice and by creating the need for such practice. Developing responsible citizens through education and promoting values and ethics within the educational system and by developing a sense of awareness in people so there is a greater demand of accountability and transparency. Ethics is thus created by and within the educational system. Corruption ranges from exorbitant illegitimate fees and bribes

---

[20]by vinod pavarala, Opcit., 88.

and donations that deprive the less economically privileged and also leads to poor quality.

Therefore, sheer discussion on the serious issue will not yield any result unless the academic forum addresses knowledge intervention, by which the community emerges as the vibrant society with knowledge to manage from resources of the nation. Subsequently, protect them from such a false way of life. The community should together surface as counterfeit for achieving four important purposes:

Purpose 1: To establish an entitlement

Purpose 2: To establish standards

Purpose 3: To promote continuity and coherence

Purpose 4: To promote public understanding.

A Study on the Print Media Coverage of the 2G Spectrum Scam with Respect to the Times of India and Dinamani

Sunitha Kuppuswamy

Department of Media Sciences, Anna University, Chennai

INTRODUCTION

Political activity in many countries is conspicuously and frequently interrupted by allegations of corruption, sleaze and scandals, and India is no exception. The plethora of scandals in the year 2010 has focussed much of media and public attention. The country is simply shaken by scam fever. Media has attempted to let its people know about the undesirable closeness that existed between large financial contributors and leadership of political parties which has lead to subversion of democratic processes and more simply straight forward bribery. The concern stems from a personal proximity to the epicentre of earthquake rocking politics, business and the media— all pillars of the Indian establishment. The issue of 2G; short for Second Generation, Spectrum Scam has got wide dimensions. A basic understanding of the issue can be achieved by getting to know about the controversies adjoining the allocation of spectrum, the Comptroller and Auditor General of India report, the Radia Tapes and how the news broke out in the news media.

THE ISSUE OF THE 2G SCAM

Allocation of the Spectrum

The Ministry of Telecommunications is in charge for Spectrum Allocation that offers mobile phone services in the country. Ex-telecom minister Mr. A. Raja allotted second generation spectrum for GSM (Global System for Mobile communication) service providers amidst a lot of controversies in 2008 itself. The minister rejected the allegations against him, and says whatever procedure as followed in 2001 has been adopted by him as well. Back in 2001, the government was nurturing the mobile services market, because there were mere 50 lakh subscribers. Spectrum was not auctioned then. Government was in such a position that it had to motivate and attract private players in. The market then grew by leaps and bounds. There were 37.5 crore mobile phone users by the first quarter of 2008. At that time, both domestic as well as multi national players considered investing in telecommunications as they found it extremely profitable. The government fixed the same price following the same procedure as in 2001, which was too small a price for the 2G Spectrum. The allocation of the 2G Spectrum was undertaken in an arbitrary, unfair and inequitable manner. Department of Telecom broke its own guidelines on eligibility and procedures, giving advantage to certain companies.

TRAI (Telecom Regulatory Authority of India) a statutory body found by the Government of India in 1995 to avoid excessive government interference in pricing and policy, has been advising the Telecom Ministry on auctioning the spectrum. Mr. A. Raja had completely neglected TRAI's recommendations and allotted the spectrum on a first come first served basis. The telecom ministry had ignored all the crucial recommendations of TRAI and considered a few points for name sake. The ministry issued 2G licenses to Datacom Solutions, Yestel, Shyam Telelink, Loop Telecom, Spice, Idea Cellular, Tata Teleservice, Swan and Unitech. Of these companies, Swan and Unitech do not have any prior experience in the business of mobile phone, broadband and related services. Swan Telecom has obtained spectrum license to operate in 14 circles for an amount of 1537.01 crore. Unitech has obtained license to operate in 22 circles by paying 1651 crore. Within a matter of six months these two companies have sold majority of their stake to foreign companies. Swan telecom had sold 45% of its shares for a whopping amount of 4500 crore to ETISALAT based out of United Arab Emirates. Due to which valuation of Swan Telecom had increased to 9990.56 crore. Unitech sold 60% of its shares to a Norway based company called Telenor for 6200 crore. Due to which the valuation of Unitech had increased to a monstrous amount of 10,731 crore. Just by leveraging their ability to acquire spectrum license, Swan and Unitech had made a massive 700% return on their investment within a matter of six months. Mr. A. Raja's ministry made 10,72.65 crore by selling 2G license to nine companies. Whereas, Swan and Unitech just by selling half of their stake had proved the fact that their license is worth more than 20,000 crore. This way our country incurred a loss of over 60,000 crore rupees. The ministry of telecom allotted licenses by favouring ineligible companies at lower rates on a first cum first served basis with an arbitrary cut-off date.

The Comptroller and Auditor General (CAG) report

There are a number of organisations subject to the audit of the Comptroller and Auditor General of India. Department of telecommunications is one among them.

CAG does regulatory audit to have a check on the compliance and does performance audit to see whether the government has achieved the desired objectives and given the intended benefits. The CAG report on the allotment of 2G Spectrum licences held former Telecom Minister Mr. A Raja responsible on many fronts for violating guidelines, indulging in favouritism and costing the government Rs. 1.76 lakh crore by mishandling the allocation of the 2G spectrum in 2008. The report, bits of which had become known in the days before it was tabled, has the Opposition parties up in arms and demanding a joint parliamentary committee inquiry. Parliament has not functioned for a single day in the winter session with the Opposition forcing adjournments. The CAG report makes several damning conclusions about what Mr. A. Raja did incorrectly. Some of the points made by the CAG Report:

- 85 firms suppressed facts, and gave fictitious papers to the Department of Telecom
- Department of Telecom kept spectrum pricing issue out of Group of Ministers' purview
- A Raja ignored Prime Minister's, Finance Minister's and Law Ministry's advice
- Spectrum was rare national asset and it should have been auctioned
- 2G spectrum allocated to new players at throwaway prices
- Undue advantage given to Swan Telecom in allocation of spectrum
- Email ID of Swan Telecom shown as that of a Reliance ADA group official
- Spectrum allocated beyond contracted quantity to 9 firms including Bharti, Vodafone, Idea, BSNL, Reliance, Aircel
- Idea and Spice not given spectrum on grounds of proposed merger—this was against the rules
- Allocation of 2G spectrum led to loss of Rs. 1.76 lakh crore
- DoT did not follow its own practise of first-come-first-serve in letter and spirit
- Calculation of loss based on 3G auction earlier this year
- Cut-off date for license letters advanced arbitrarily by a week
- This went against time-tested procedures of government functioning
- Entire process lacked transparency
- Undertaken in arbitrary and inequitable manner.

Media Manifestation of the Scandal/Scam Unearthed by the Media

The Scam was out in the media as a result of an investigative stunt. The investigative team of *The Pioneer* a medium-sized English language newspaper published from seven locations across India sensed a scam Swan and Unitech started offloading shares at whopping prices of 4,500 crore and 6,200 crore in September 2008. Mr. J. Gopikrishnan of the same newspaper broke the story. His dogged persistence uncovered Mr. A. Raja's hidden links to firms that profiteered from the spectrum sale. It was his series totalling over 100 reports beginning on December 11, 2008 that precisely detailed names of Mr. A. Raja's kith and kin in a firm that got money from Swan Telecom, a beneficiary of the discounted spectrum sale. He also unveiled Genex Exim, another little known firm formed with a paid-up capital of just Rs. 1 lakh, and how it was allotted Swan's shares worth Rs. 380 crore. He then connected the dots to reveal Genex's link to a Dubai-based real estate conglomerate ETA Ascon Star Group, which is currently involved in many infrastructure projects in Dravidar Munnetra Kazhagam (DMK) ruled Tamil Nadu. It was he again who uncovered the evidence of conversations between Mr. A. Raja and lobbyist Ms. Niira Radia. The team luckily got a whistle blower who knew the ins and outs of the Telecom Ministry and narrated the entire range of corruption in the Ministry.

On November 2010, two magazines "Open" and "Outlook" carried stories which reported the transcripts of some telephone conversations of corporate lobbyist Ms. Niira Radia with senior journalists, politicians and corporate houses many of whom have denied the allegations. Ms. Radia's conversations show hoe even cabinet berths can be decided by this select oligarchy. The tapes also paint a dismal picture of how everything from cabinet berths to natural resources is now available for the right price. The now controversial 2G allocation was just one of the many manipulations orchestrated by players in high places.

NEED FOR THE STUDY

Corruption has always been an obstacle for the much needed progress of the country. In the Indian Context, it is not just involving the politicians but also bureaucrats, power brokers and other industrialists, it is affecting the common man. The Study will throw light on the web of connections that exist among the worlds of business, politics and journalism. The primary responsibility of media is to keep the common man informed by putting the information in the public domain. But then how the common man was informed about the biggest scam ever in the history of Indian politics is the question. The common man is found to be a passive spectator to the blame game. The power entrusted on the elected representatives has been abused of private gain. The former telecom minister enjoyed enormous discretionary powers, and the departmental autonomy that flowed out of coalition politics stemmed out the scam. Popular faces of media have involved themselves. The boundary between legitimate news gathering, lobbying and influence peddling was transgressed. Media here has to publicise the political sins without taking stands, thereby promote good governance and control corruption. But a pluralistic media that provides flow of information can upset the public opinion over wrong doers and can even vote them out of the race to elevate government institutional performance. Only if the elected representatives perform well, they will be provided with political support. If they are found to perform poorly, voters would surely disapprove of their performance and withdraw support. Indeed the perceived seriousness of the problem will be figured out. The scam became sensational just months before the Tamilnadu State Elections 2011, the intensity of the impact the scam reportage is to be studied.

AIM

The aim of the research is to study the discourse of the 2G Spectrum Scam in the print media of Tamilnadu with special reference to newspapers The Times of India and Dinamani. And also estimate the impact of the media coverage with a view on the forthcoming Tamilnadu State Elections, 2011.

OBJECTIVES

- To examine the reportage of 2G Spectrum Scam in the print media of Tamilnadu.
- To do a comparative study of the media coverage of the scam with respect to a English daily The Times of India and a Tamil daily Dinamani.
- To find out the impact of this media coverage on people with special reference to The Tamilnadu State Elections 2011.

METHODOLOGY

For this study the researcher had followed Content Analysis and Survey methodologies.

A Quantitative analysis of the content of articles on the 2G Spectrum Scam, published by The Times of India and Dinamani was conducted from November 2010 to February 2011. The newspapers were analysed for their content of messages and articles on the issue. There were various units of measurements that were considered for analysis. They were:

- *Length of the News Story:* The length of the stories was taken as a unit of measurement. Stories were classified into two categories; stories exceeding 500 words and stories that were less than 500 words.
- *Type of the News:* Type of news item is the next unit of measurement. News items were articles or editorials or graphics. Some news items had exclusive full as well as half page coverage.
- *Source of News:* This unit basically distinguishes the news items based on their sources. News Stories were either reported through the reporters and special correspondents or through secondary sources such as press releases.
- *Base of the News:* Stories were based either on interviews or on research. Interview based stories added weightage to the news story.
- *Tone of the News Story:* The tone of the news stories were also taken into consideration. Stories were factual, anti-governmental, pro-governmental, neutral and even election oriented.

- *Placement of the News Story:* Major news items are those appearing in the front page and Minor news items are those that appear in columns in the inside pages
- *Key Words Used in Headlines Concerning the Scam:* The various key words that were used in the headlines and sub headings of the news stories concerning the scam were taken for analysis.
- *Size of the Photographs:* Major photos measure 2 to 8 columns in width running up to 4″ to 8″ in height and Minor photos measure 1 to 1½ columns in width running up to 1″ to 2″ in height.
- *Graphics:* Graphics were in the form of Cartoons, Polls, Box items and Bullet point boxes.
- *Content Analysis of Photographs:* Photographs were analysed on the following categories: Internal political relations, Scandalised politician in focus, Relationship between politicians and other key players and others.
- *Data Analysis:* Salience, Attributes, Image, Scope, Linkage and Participants of the issue were taken for data analysis.

A questionnaire was framed for testing the attitude of the general public towards the government as a result of the 2G Spectrum Scam reportage. The questionnaire contains a total number of 34 questions, of which the first four obtain the demographic characteristics of the respondents, the rest of the questions were subjective. The questionnaire was designed with the intention of eliciting the perception of the scam among the people and the impact of that perception with respect to the party preference in the forthcoming Tamilnadu State Elections, 2011. The questionnaire is a kind of Pre-election Survey. A 5 point Likert Scale was used in the questionnaire giving the respondents a chance to specify their level of agreement to the role of Central Bureau of Investigation in investigating the Spectrum Scam. Questionnaire examines the relationship between a voter's perception of the extent to which the former telecom minister and his affiliated party was involved in the scam and the subsequent change in the behaviour and attitude during the Tamilnadu State Elections 2011. Questionnaire was circulated online and about 200 samples were got.

SELECTION OF SAMPLES

The respondents for the study were selected using simple random sampling method and they were between the age group of 18 to 70 years. It was made sure that the majority of the samples were regular readers of Tamilnadu's Dailies keeping a track on the headlines and politics. Age was used as a control for two reasons:

- Because, the sample had been purposely drawn to disproportionately include young voters.
- Other studies have show age to be an important variable in political analyses.

ANALYSIS AND INTERPRETATION

Content Analysis

Coverage of the 2G Spectrum Scam in the Times of India and Dinamani

Different Keywords and abbreviations used in the headlines of the two newspapers:

Table 1: Keywords Found in the Headlines of The Times of India and Dinamani

The Times of India	*Dinamani*
2G [Second Generation]	2G [Second Generation]
IT [Income Tax]	CBI [Central Bureau of Investigation]
IB [Intelligence Bureau]	CAG [Comptroller and Auditor General of India]
SC [Supreme Court]	CVC [Central Vigilance Commission]
ED [Enforcement Directorate]	PAC [Public Accounts Committee]
LS [Lok Sabha]	TAPES
CAG [Comptroller & Auditor General of India]	SPECTRUM
DoT [Department of Telecom]	
IFS [Indian Forest Service]	
BCI [Bar Council of India]	
JPC [Joint Probe Commission]	
FDI [Foreign Direct Investment]	
PUCL [People's Union for Civil Liberties]	
CBDT [Central Board of Direct Taxes]	
PMLA [Prevention of Money Laundering Act]	
FEMA [Foreign Exchange Management Act]	
LOGJAM	

From the Table 1 it is found that more number of keywords were used in The Times of India when compared to Dinamani. Certain keywords used in the headlines did not have an explanation inside the news story. This created a complexity in understanding among the readers.

Following is the Percentage of the News Stories on the Scam Reported in the Front Page of The Time of India and Dinamani.

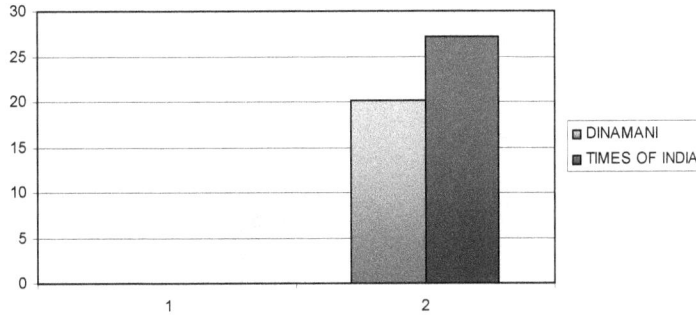

Fig. 1: Percentage of News Stories Actually Reported in the Front Page

From the Figure 1, we can find that The Times of India reported more number of stories in the front page when compared to Dinamani. Issue gained more prominence in The Times of India. Percentage of the news stories on the scam in Dinamani is 20.18% and in The Times of India it is 27.21%.

Following is the Percentage of Major and Minor News Items in The Times of India and Dinamani

- *Major News Item:* News items that appears in the front page
- *Minor News Item:* News items that appear in columns in the inside pages.

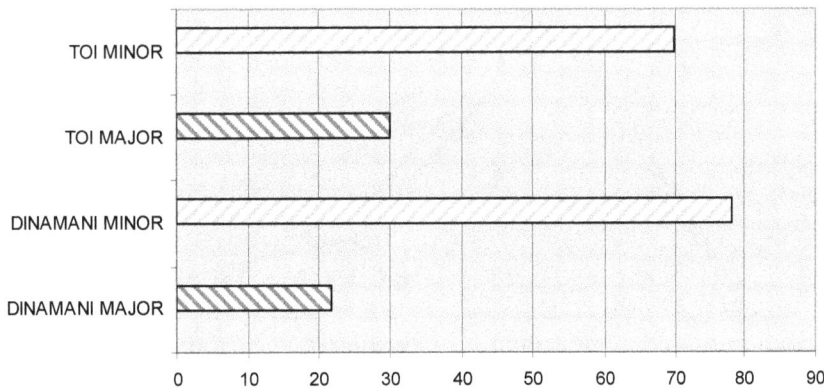

Fig. 2: Percentage of Minor and Major News Stories

From the Figure 2 we understand that The Times of India had carried more number of major stories and Dinamani had carried more number of minor stories. Percentage of the minor and major news stories on the scam in Dinamani is 78.23%, 21.77% and The Times of India 69.96%, 30.04% is respectively.

Following is the Percentage that Reflects the Different Tones of the News Stories in The Times of India and Dinamani.

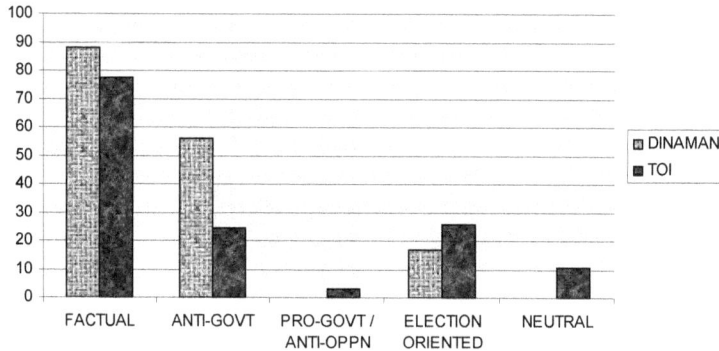

Fig. 3: Tone of the News Stories

From the Figure 3, we understand that most of the reportage on the 2G Spectrum Scam was factual. Dinamani was explicitly taking the anti-government stand. The Times of India carried stories on a neutral tone to a minor extent. But in a few stories it was supporting the ruling government.

Following Represents the Month Wise Coverage of the Scam in
The Times of India and Dinamani

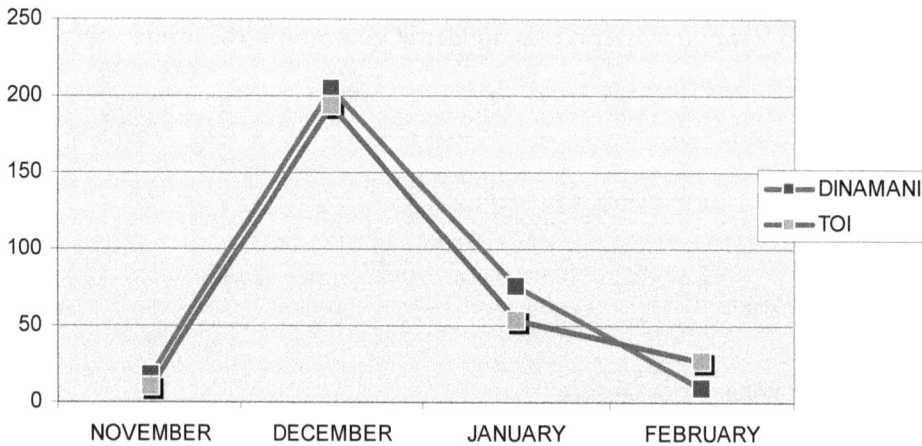

Fig. 4: Coverage of the Scam from November 29, 2010 to February 3, 2011

From the Figure 4 it is known that Issue was covered at the peak in December both in The Times of India and Dinamani. Scam coverage started to be sensational in November, attained its peak in December, and started to decline in January ending with the arrest of the former telecom minister in February. Election oriented stories popped up in December in both the newspapers.

Following is the Percentage of the News Stories that were based on the Interviews in The Times of India and Dinamani.

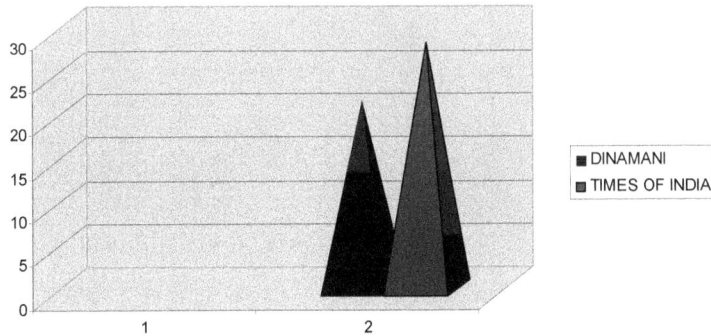

Fig. 5: Percentage of News Stories Based on Interviews

From the Figure 5, it is found that Interview based news stories was more in The Times of India compared to Dinamani. The number of blind interviews was also more in The Times of India. They are interviews where the source is not mentioned. Percentage was 21.77 in Dinamani and 28.27 in The Times of India.

Following is the Comparison of Exclusivity Coverage in
The Times of India and Dinamani

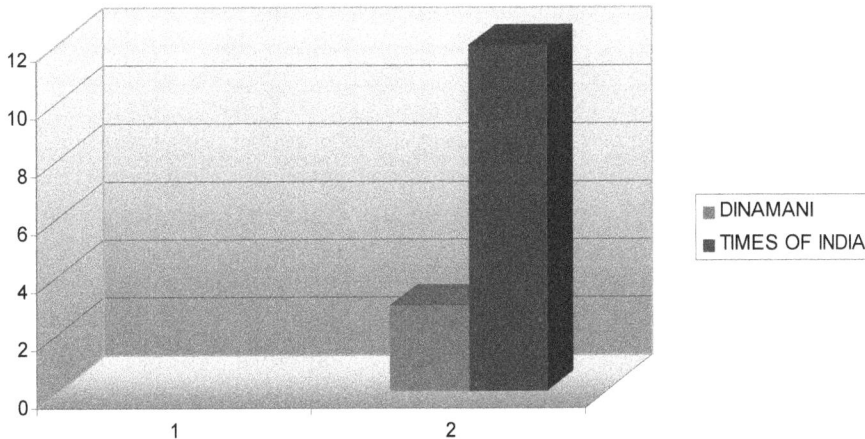

Fig. 6: No. of Days of Exclusive News Coverage

From the Figure 6 we understand that, The Times of India had devoted more exclusivity in the coverage of the scam. But a point to be noted here is that number of editorials was more in Dinamani. There was a total of three days exclusive coverage in Dinamani and 12 days in The Times of India.

Following is the Number of Stories Categorised as per the Length of the News Stories

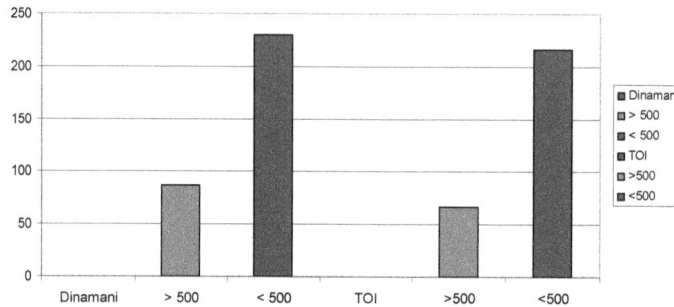

Fig. 7: Number of Stories Greater and Lesser than 500 Words

From the Figure 7, it is known that majority of stories in both the newspapers was less than 500 words in length. But, the number of stories that were greater than 500 words in length was more in Dinamani.

Source of the Reports

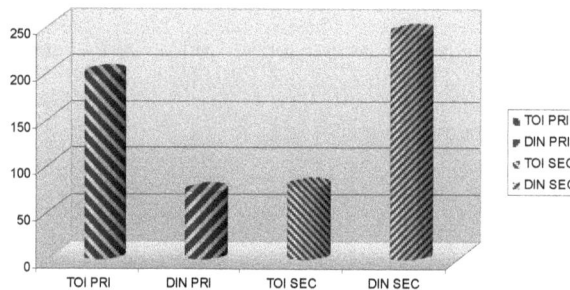

Fig. 8: Reports by the Newspapers through Primary and Secondary Sources

From the Figure 8, it is known that The Times of India being a national newspaper carried a lot of stories with primary source of information. News stories on Dinamani were mostly based on press releases and it had more number of follow up stories, whereas The Times of India came up with newer stories with varied dimensions.

Content Analysis of Visuals

Following is the percentage of the major and minor Photos in The Times of India and Dinamani

- *Major photo:* 2 to 8 columns in width running up to 4″ to 8″ in height
- *Minor photo:* 1 to 1½ columns in width running up to 1″ to 2″ in height.

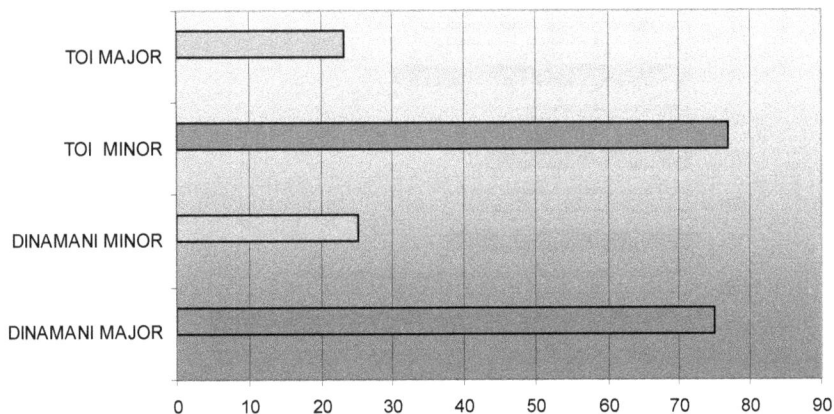

Fig. 9: Percentage of Minor and Major Photos

From the Figure 9, we understand that the percentage of major and minor photos in both the newspapers were almost the same. Percentage of minor photos is higher compared to the major photos. Percentage of minor and major photos in Dinamani and The Times of India are 74.88 & 25.12 and 76.85 & 23.15 respectively.

Table 2: Percentage of the Various Graphics Used in The Times of India and Dinamani Graphics Usage in the Newspapers

Newspaper	Cartoon (%)	Poll (%)	Box Item (%)	Bullet Box (%)
Dinamani	34.85	28.79	22.73	–
Times of India	48.48	9.09	57.58	34.85

From the Table 2, it is known that Cartoon usage was more in The Times of India and Poll usage was more in Dinamani. Overall usage of graphics in the news items was more in The Times of India.

Content Analysis of Photographs

The photographs were analysed by classifying into the following four categories:
- Internal political relations
- Scandalized politician in focus
- Relationship between politicians and other key players
- Others.

From the Figure 10, we understand the stand of the opposition was given much importance in the photographs as well. The former telecom minister was more in focus in the case of The Times of India.

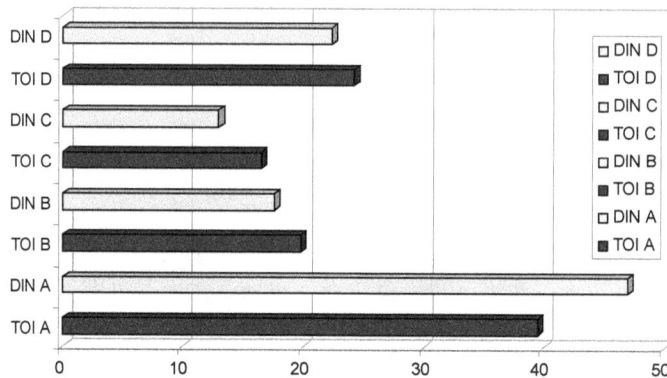

Fig. 10: Percentage of the Various Picture Categories in The Times of India and Dinamani

Internal Political Relations

This picture category covers photographs of politicians belonging to the opposition parties commenting on the evolving 2G Spectrum Scandal. The leaders of the opposition parties in the central as well as the state government stood out as major political actors by being in focus on relatively many of the photographs. The visuals are dull, mainly consisting of conventional facial portraits. This was the major picture category.

The Scandalized Politician in Focus

The pictures in this category represent the protagonist A. Raja [former telecom minister] alone. The portraits vary from small identity type pictures, half figure shots to full length photographs. In some of these portraits, the minister is captured with vivid facial expressions. The scandalized politician faces media without evading and is found to be confident prior to the investigation of the Central Bureau of Investigation (CBI).

Relationship between Politicians and Other Key Players of the Scam

This picture category consists of images that foreground the relationship between the politicians and other key players involved in the scandal such as lobbyists, bureaucrats and policy makers. The presence of this picture category to news items (those appearing in the first page) involving both parties mentioned above.

Others

All other pictures that do not fall under the above mentioned categories come under this picture classification. Reactions of the supporters of the scandalized politician, their protests, members of the Central Bureau of Investigation, Central Vigilance Commission and other minor political figures are a part of this picture category.

Data Analysis

Issue Salience

Prominence of the scandal was more in Dinamani. It carried more number of stories than The Times of India.

- Number of stories in Dinamani: 317
- Number of stories in The Times of India: 283

Issue Attributes

Issue can be framed in many different ways, different attribute dimensions which can significantly affect the agenda setting process and lead to different policy outcomes.

The anti-government stand was evident from the news items, editorials, cartoonscape and polls of Dinamani. Impact of the scam on the political relations was emphasized. It did not stop there and was extended to how it would impact political allies for the Tamilnadu State Elections, 2011. The reactions of the opposition parties to the scam were predominant. Intensity from The Times of India and Dinamani on projecting the scam started to dip by January. Number of stories began to reduce drastically. Graph goes upward in February with the news on the arrest of A. Raja.

There is a lack of professionalism in Dinamani in terms of placement. Stories on the political relations were placed under the world news section. Dedicated exclusivity was found in The Times of India by way of full page coverage and half page coverage by special correspondents. Content simplicity was prevalent in Dinamani as not many keywords or jargons were used. Some news items in The Times of India did not bother to explain the keywords or jargons inside the story.

Issue Image

The issue was indeed sensational in terms of projection as it was the mother of all scams involving very huge money. Readers were sure to be awed by the reportage. Public understanding of the issue is that the government is highly corrupt and the country is simply scam driven.

Issue Scope

It refers to the geographical or jurisdictional area affected by the issue. The entire nation was shaken by the issue. Regionally speaking, Tamilnadu suffered a set back because of the affiliation of the scandalized politician. The level of authority, the central government dealing the issue is also affected with demand for a Joint Probe Commission. Logjam happened for an entire parliament session as the opposition was not satisfied with the ruling government dealing with the scam.

Issue Linkage

Issue is greatly linked to the Tamilnadu State Elections, 2011. Reportage has the potential to alter the public opinion and might even have a devastating effect. The family ruling the Tamilnadu state has a high possibility to experience that. The issue is much spoken about in the election campaigns.

Issue Participants

The issue involves the conflict between the ruling and the opposition. Both are playing the blame game. The issue has state as well as central participants. Apart from those politicians, lobbyists, bureaucrats and other policy makers constitute a part of the issue participants. In short, we can say 2G led to CAG [Comptroller and Auditor General of India] which in turn led CBI [Central Bureau of Investigation] to the DoT [Department of Telecom]. A lot more participants like IT [Income Tax], SC [Supreme Court], PUCL [People's Union for Civil Liberties] are also becoming a part of the scam. Day by day, the circle of issue participants is only broadening.

SURVEY

The survey conducted was online based, and the sample size being two hundred. The survey aimed to find out the impact of media's report on the 2G Spectrum Scam.

From the survey, 90% of the respondents feel media plays a critical role in curbing corruption. Majority of the respondents believe that Public accountability should be made compulsory, as shown in Figure 11. 53% of the respondents see the media to be biased; and 91% of the respondents feel that media serves to improve citizen's access to information.

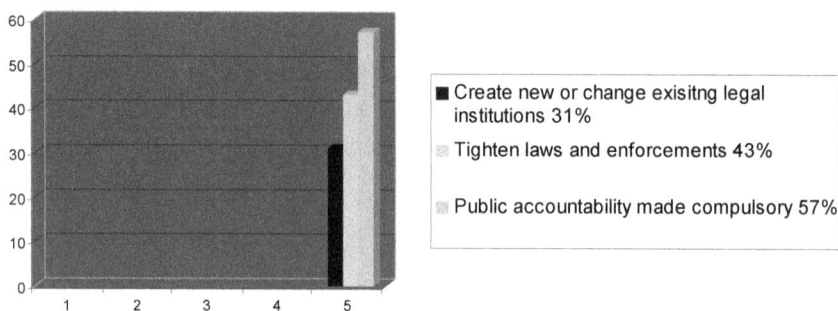

Fig. 11: Reforms Necessary in Order to Reduce Corruption

For 79% of the respondents, development of visual technologies plays a major role in altering the nature of political portrayal. Meagre number of respondents has reacted against corruption at a higher political level. 92% of the respondents feel the government lacks transparency and 67 % of the respondents feel media's report is likely to impact the state elections 2011. 73% of the respondents feel newer laws are required to deal with wealth acquired through illegal means; 62% of the respondents see a change in the report by media after the arrest of the former telecom minister; and 64% of the respondents feel the new government is not going to take any step to put a full stop to these kinds of scandals. Also, 77% of the respondents state that the media is making news. Majority of the respondents (57%) feel the levels of corruption will stay about the same as shown in Figure 12.

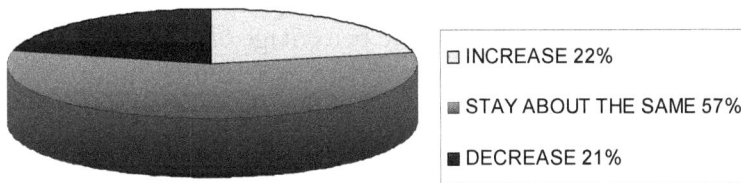

□ INCREASE 22%

■ STAY ABOUT THE SAME 57%

■ DECREASE 21%

Fig. 12

51% of the respondents feel the government is not at all committed in handling the issue of 2G Spectrum; majority of the respondents have rated the role of CBI in investigating the scam as 2 as shown in the Figure 13; and 82% of the respondents feel media's report on the 2G scam stands as an eye opener to the forthcoming state elections.

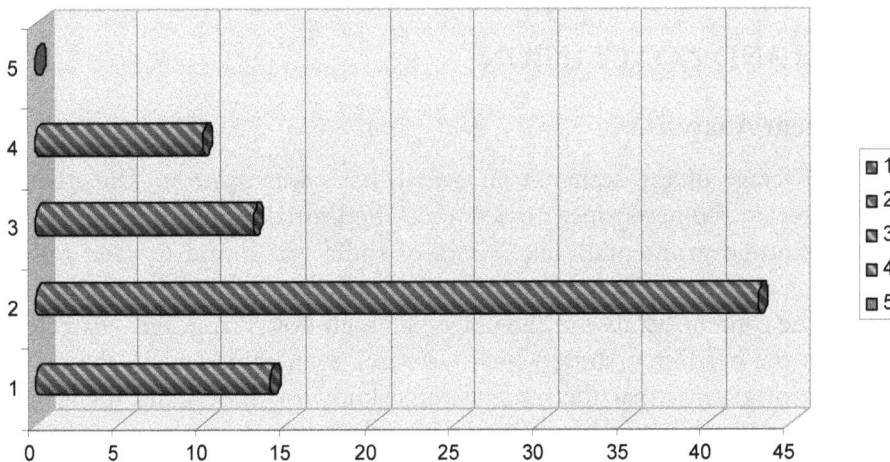

Fig. 13: Rate the Role of CBI Investigation of the 2G Spectrum Scam with a Five Point Rating Scale [1 least, 5 best]

INTERPRETATION OF THE RESULTS

From the Survey

People believe that media plays a very critical role in combating corruption in a country like India. Majority of the respondents feel media is taking stands on the issue reportage. It is the media which is found to be the most important source of information to the common man. Developments in the field of visual technology have altered the way politicians are projected in the media. It seems to have an overwhelming effect. Every other respondent accepts the fact that corruption is one of the serious problems the country is facing but only a negligible percentage of them have raised the issue at a higher level of authority. The country has to resolutely push systemic changes promoting greater transparency and accountability. Elected representatives are indeed accountable to the taxpayer. People in the power are found to misuse the same and hence newer laws are required to have checks on wealth acquired through illegal means. Media has sensationalized the issue. But it was media's investigative stunt that brought the news out. Reportage lacked consistency and media was more bothered about the patronage of the news. It was less fervent. Substantiate claim, intensity and thirst came down post the arrest of the telecom minister. Public trust is lost in the political parties. Newspapers have given more space to the scandal; overall coverage more with the newspaper having a broader circulation base.Media's reportage on the 2G Spectrum Scam is likely to have a considerable impact in the forthcoming Tamilnadu State Elections, 2011.

FINDINGS AND CONCLUSION

From Content Analysis

The news coverage of the scam on an overall basis was more in Dinamani. Apart from news stories, the newspaper carried a lot of editorials and cartoonscape, most of which were anti-governmental. The Times of India was found to cater only to the elite audience and not to the common man. Intricacies were involved in trying to understand the content because of the usage of a high flown language. Many keywords were used in the headlines, some which were not even explained in the news story. It was taken for granted that the readers would know or understand them. Extensive use of graphics and other visuals were viewed as effective tools to appeal to the audience with a comparatively low level of education. This was evident in the case of Dinamani. Prominence for the scam was given in terms of placement in The Times of India. Front page coverage was allotted to most of the scam reports. The scam was covered from various dimensions in The Times of India. The size of the photographs accompanying the news stories was almost the same in both the newspapers taken for analysis.

Detailed stories were more in The Times of India. Shorter versions were more in Dinamani. The Times of India being a national newspaper was able to designate Special correspondents and reporters solely for reporting on the issue of 2G Spectrum. Issue was reported at its peak in December. That is when stories on the scam had a link to the political allies for the elections. A number of stories were reported in both Dinamani and The Times of India. Dinamani was continuously attaching much importance to the stand of the opposition parties on the scandal. It was giving more space in covering their activities such as staging protests for: demand for Joint Probe Commission, arrest of the former telecom minister, prime minister to be summoned for the Public accounts committee. The Times of India had a mix of views regarding the political orientation and avoided taking stands.

From Survey

People believe that the exposure of the scam in the media was a political stunt. The regular intriguing reports on the issue made it sensational. Media sensationalized the issue, with a view to increase the viewership and readership. It did not bother to state how the common layman will be affected because of the scam. The scandalized politician is highly affiliated with the state of Tamilnadu, yet it was not the media from Tamilnadu that exposed the scam. The scam is nothing sort of a corporate-political nexus. Government has discharged itself from all moral and ethical responsibilities and that is the reason it does not find itself under any obligation to answer the questions raised by the public and the media. Intensity of the news has gone down post the arrest of the former telecom minister.

Before the arrest, there was much speculation on media but after the arrest it cut them loose. Indians seem to have lost faith not just in its political class and bureaucrats, but in just about every major institution. Corrupt politicians have achieved the purpose of being elected. People expect the Communist and Marxist Parties to bring about institutional changes that will put a full stop to corruption and enhance governmental performance. Media along with the nation will forget the scam, soon it will move on to the next sensational news available. Government is scam-driven and is always hungry, no matter how much money is tossed to their appetite for their quarry remains undiminished.

SUGGESTIONS

The country has to resolutely push systemic changes promoting greater transparency and accountability. The situation has to be rectified and a modicum of faith to be restored in the people. Allowing things to drift along as they have is clearly a luxury we can no longer afford. Elected representatives should be indeed made accountable to the taxpayer. The newspapers should focus on the needs of the common man and should not be interested in the growing gray areas in the ethics of journalism because of an atmosphere of increased competition. Qualitative, independent media reporting is the need of the hour that will pressurize the government to act in public interest. Being a watch dog, media should play a key role in processes of establishing and maintaining well functioning government institutions. Apart from all these, the country is in need of sincere, well-intentioned honest individuals who will restrain the country from a near total collapse of governance in almost all spheres creating a proliferation of scam and corruption.

REFERENCES

[1] Kothari, C.R. (2004). "Research Methodology"—New Age International (P) Ltd. Publishers, New Delhi.

[2] Gregg, B. Johnson and Bayer, A. Schwindt (2009), Vol. 1, Issue 3, 33–56.

[3] Journal of Politics in Latin America.
http://web.missouri.edu/~schwindtbayerl/docs/johnson_schwindtbayer2009_JPLA.pdf

[4] Rothstein, B. (2007). Vol. 3, Issue 7, 27–33. Anti Corruption—A Big Bang Theory. The Quality of Government Institute, Department of Political Science, Göteborg University. http://www.qog.pol.gu.se/working_papers/2007_3_Rothstein.pdf

[5] Oscarsson Henrik (2008). Vol. 2, Issue 12, 12–43. Media and Quality of Government: A Research Overview. The Quality of Government Institute, Department of Political Science, Göteborg University.
http://www.qog.pol.gu.se/working_papers/2008_12_Oscarsson.pdf

[6] Adsera Alicia, Payne Mark and Boix Carles (2003). Vol. 19, Issue 2, 445–490. Are you being served? Political Accountability and Quality of Government. Journal of Law, Economics and Organisation.
http://www.international.ucla.edu/cms/files/areyoubeingserved.pdf

[7] Zamora, C. Kevin, Walecki Marcin and Carlson Jeffrey, Vol. 13, Issue 3, 291–326. Political Integrity and Corruption—An International Perspective.
http://www.ifes.org/~/media/Files/Publications/Money%20and%20Politics/Research%20and%20Publications/Reports%20and%20Papers/English/Political_Integrity_Introduction_English.pdf

[8] Tumber Howard, Waisbord R. Silvio (2006). Vol. 47, Issue 8, 110–134. Political Scandals and Media Across Democracies. Sage Publications.
http://www.deepdyve.com/lp/sage/introduction-political-scandals-and-media-across-democracies-volume-i-ESJ0fgbssa

[9] Nogara, M. (2009). DESA Working Paper Series No. 72. Role of Media in Curbing Corruption: the Case of Uganda Under President Yoweri K. Museveni during the "No-Party" System. http://papers.ssrn.com/sol3/papers.cfm?abstract_id=1338167

[10] Prusa Igor (2010). Scandals and Their Mediations Theorizing the Case of Japan.

http://www.japanesestudies.org.uk/discussionpapers/2010/Prusa.html

[11] Frederick, M. (2007). Vol. 4, Issue 4, 30–35. Time to Harvest? Media, Corruption and Elections in Kenya. Ethical Space: The Journal of Communication Ethics. http://www.communicationethics.net/journal/v4n4/v4n4_feat2.pdf

[12] Dobratz, A. Betty and Whitfield Stephanie (2011). Vol. 27, Issue 2. Does Scandal Influence Voters" Party Preference? The Case of Greece during the Papandreou Era. Journal of European Social Review. http://esr.oxfordjournals.org/content/8/2/167.full.pdf

[13] Basu K. Parikshit (2006). 59–68. Corruption: A Theoretical Perspective and Relevance for Economic Growth. Vol. 10, Issue 4. International Review of Business Research Papers. http://www.bizresearchpapers.com/Paper%20Six.pdf

[14] Papadopoulos Andén Kari, Widestedt Kristina. The Mediated Visibility of Political Scandal: How a crayfish party turned a Swedish minister into a poodle? Paper presented at the International Communication Association Conference in Dresden 2006. http://www.oru.se/PageFiles/24081/Paper%20Mediated%20visibility%20nr%2014.pdf

[15] Ekström Mats, Johansson Bengt. Talk scandals. Submitted to ICA'S Annual Conference in San Fransisco May 24–28, 2006. http://www.oru.se/PageFiles/24075/Talk%20scandals%20ICA%20nr%2016.pdf

[16] Erickson, M. Moana, Hills, M. Roderick. Research on Corruption and Its Control: The State of the Art. From a Workshop Sponsored by The Zicklin Center for Business Ethics at the Wharton School of Business, The CSIS-Hills Program on Governance, The World Bank Institute. http://www.improvinggovernance.be/upload/documents/wharton_proceedings_nocrop.pdf

[17] Andvig Jens, Fjeldstad, O. Helge, Inge Amundsen, Tone Sissener, Tina Søreide. Research on corruption: A Political Oriented Survey. Commissioned by NORAD Final Report, December 2000 Chr. Michelsen Institute (CMI) & Norwegian Institute of International Affairs (NUPI). http://www.icgg.org/downloads/contribution07_andvig.pdf

[18] Papadopoulos Yannis. Political Accountability in Network and Multi-Level Governance. Department of Political Science, Institut d'Etudes Politiques et Internationales, University of Lausanne. http://www.mzes.unimannheim.de/projekte/typo3/site/fileadmin/research%20groups/6/reader/Papadopoulos_Connex_Paris.pdf

[19] Puglisi Riccard, Snyder. M. James. Newspaper Coverage of Political Scandals Departments of Political Science and Economics, Massachusetts Institute of Technology, December 5, 2010. http://scholar.harvard.edu/jsnyder/files/political_scandals_22_complete_0.pdf

[20] Snyder, M. James, David Strömberg. Media Markets' Impact on Politics. September, 2004. http://polisci.osu.edu/intranet/cppe/snyder_paper.pdf

[21] Capelo Tereza, Walter Annemarie. Measuring the Blame Game: The Coverage of Political Scandals and Accounts in The Netherlands. http://www.essex.ac.uk/ecpr/events/generalconference/pisa/papers/PP1881.pdf

[22] Pacoy, P. Emilia. Vol. 3, Issue 1, Tracking Anti-Corruption Initiatives: Perceptions and Experiences in the Philippines.
http://joaag.com/uploads/6_Pacoy-Final.pdf

[23] Bennett W. Lance (2006). 103–127, Vol. 40, Issue 2. Toward a Theory of Press-State Relations in the United States. Journal of Communication.
http://onlinelibrary.wiley.com/doi/10.1111/j.1460-2466.1990.tb02265.x/abstract

[24] Josh, L. Prem (2005). Political Governance System and Corruption in India. University of Bahrain. http://www.iri.org.in/articles/political_corruption.pdf

[25] Indiantelevision.com Team. Media creating negative impressions in reportage: PM.
http://www.indiantelevision.com/headlines/y2k11/feb/feb142.php

[26] Accessed on: February 16, 2011
NDTV Correspondent. What is 2G Spectrum Scam? Accessed on January 29, 2011.
http://www.ndtv.com/article/india/what-is-2g-spectrum-scam-66418

[27] Sunetra Choudhury. 2G Scam: Dotted line leading to DMK's First Family. Accessed on March 3, 2011.
http://www.ndtv.com/article/india/what-is-2g-spectrum-scam-66418

[28] Chandhan Mitra. The Man Who Felled a King. Accessed on January 5, 2011.
http://www.ndtv.com/article/india/what-is-2g-spectrum-scam-66418

[29] Arinndam Mukherjee. Those Missing Zeroes: What Punishment Awaits the Guilty? And can the Loss be Recouped? Accessed on April 21, 2011.
http://www.outlookindia.com/article.aspx?268078

[30] Debarshi Dasgupta. There Was a Swan, It Had a Tale: Media Grandstanding Aside, it was the Pioneer that Broke Open the 2G Scam.
http://www.outlookindia.com/article.aspx?268077

[31] Auditor of Comptroller and Auditor General of India. Accessed on March 24, 2011.
http://www.cag.gov.in/html/unionaudit.html

[32] NDTV Correspondent. 2G Spectrum Scam: Some Highlights of the CAG Report. Accessed on December 21, 2010. http://www.ndtv.com/article/india/2g-spectrum-scam-some-highlights-of-cag-report-66669

[33] Willams, R. (2000). "Aspects of Party Finance and Political Corruption". MacMillan Press in Association with the University of Durham, United Kingdom.
https://www.palgrave.com/pdfs/0333739868.pdf

[34] Tiffen Rodney (1999). "Scandals: Media, Politics and Corruption in Contemporary Australia". UNSW Press, Australia. http://books.google.co.in/books?hl=en&lr=&id=pu FtfcjU3TQC&oi=fnd&pg=PR7&dq=corruption+and+media+coverage&ots=xRL_JKGo cI&sig=Vj_5EHZdUYs4yszThOQmyai29ws#v=onepage&q=corruption%20and%20me dia%20coverage&f=false

[35] Ferlie, Iwan and Bovens, M. (2005). "The Oxford Handbook of Public Management". Oxofrd Publications Pvt. Ltd., USA. http://igiturarchive.library.uu.nl/USBO/2006120 1222846/Bovens_05_Publicaccountability08Ferlie.pdf

"Good Governance" and "Human Rights"— Utopia or Reality

Andrew S. Philominraj, Juan A. Rock and Maria J. Valenzuela
University of Talca, Chile

ABSTRACT

Following the "Washington Consensus", in the eighties, a model of "good governance" which seeks greater economic efficiency of the system is created. Its functions include the following: offer guarantee to the exercise of political rights and the civil liberties, also governmental administrative efficiency in order to enable the market to develop freely. This model aims to free the state from the responsibility to ensure the minimum conditions of social, economic and cultural dignity to its citizens. It is in the field of human rights where the model turns out to be questionable, particularly in the field of economic, social and cultural rights, which involves the state with direct obligations concerning economic, social and cultural development, thus making the model of good governance to be incompatible with the human rights project.

Evidently, during the recent decades, the World Bank, and to a lesser extent, The International Monetary Fund (IMF), have tried to incorporate a dimension of human rights in their programs. However, the reality indicates that things were done "very little and very late", above all, their recent efforts are seen in prospective or in opposition with the negative effects of the politics in turn and the austerity that has been imposed.

The developing countries seek to compete in attracting foreign investment from world powers; this had led to lower tax payments, or to ignore the supervision of working and health conditions. Both strategies have a direct impact on the State's obligation regarding human rights.

This research aims to collect information about how countries of Latin America guide their economic strategy by the model of "good governance" and harmonize these policies with human and civil rights ensuring security for the civilian population. The analysis of this research strikes an important note as it is being performed under the gaze of an Indian researcher, in a context, such as Latin America, particularly Chile, which in many ways contradictory to his country of origin. Thus, there is also an intent to know of how developed global organizations in order to boost global economic growth become compatible with the fulfillment of human rights.

Keywords: Good Governance, Human Rights, Economy, Politics.

INTRODUCTION

The model of good governance can be defined as rules, processes and behaviors in terms of which interests are articulated, resources are managed and power is exercised in society, that is to say, the way how public functions are made, public resources are managed and regulatory powers are exercised. It can also be described as a basic measure of stability and performance of countries.[1]

Good governance assumes all the characteristics of a new method of government, given the fact that it does legitimize the application of a beam of indexes able to discern a good government to bad government, and, more importantly, global institutions can apply the actual code of conduct to designate those who are admitted into the international order.

Major international organizations, led by the International Monetary Fund (IMF) and World Bank lavish recommendations for "good governance" among its member countries, but both their definitions and their contents vary from one organization to another, preventing from setting forth the exact legal boundaries in order to achieve the concept of good governance that could be global and corporate.[2]

Characteristics that are commonly found to identify good governance that could represent an ideal that only few countries achieve are: Responsibility, fair legal framework, transparency, responsiveness, consensus oriented, equity and inclusiveness, and effectiveness.[3] Failure to make advancement on these principles turns out to be very critical barrier to progress in the effort against endemic poverty. We must recognize that there are significant differences in the quality of governance across countries.[4]

---

[1]United Nations Economic and Social commission for Asia and the Pacific, Human Settlement, "What is Good Governance?" www.unescap.org. 2006.

[2]Herrera, R (2004). ¿Buena gobernanza contra buen gobierno? Revista Venezolana de análisis de coyuntura, Jan –June; year/vol.X, number 001.

[3]UNESCAP (2009). What is Good Governance? Retrieved Oct 2009, from http://www.unescap.org

[4]Declaration of the Millenium, 2000. www.un.org

One of the most frequently cited barriers to achieving effective governance is corruption. In the lowest income countries of the South, very often the career growth inside the government, offers a quickest route to personal wealth or richness. In addition to high-level corruption, petty corruption makes daily life miserable. This corruption is the result of extensive deterioration of integrity due to unpaid salaries, political patronage, lack of supervision, few penalties for poor performance, and few incentives for good performance.[5]

WHAT IS THE RELATIONSHIP BETWEEN HUMAN RIGHTS AND GOOD GOVERNANCE?

Good governance and human rights reinforce bilaterally, as both are based on principles of participation, accountability, transparency and accountability of the state.

Human rights need a supportive and enabling environment, based on rules, institutions and appropriate procedures that define the State's actions. Human rights provide a set of performance norms that makes the government and others to be accountable. On the other hand, the policies of good governance must give individuals the opportunity to live in dignity and freedom. Although human rights empower people effectively but they cannot be respected and protected in a sustainable way if there isn't good governance. In addition to relevant laws, processes and political institutions, of management and administration that respond to the rights and needs of the population are required.

There isn't a single model of good governance as the institutions and processes evolve over time. Human rights strengthen the frameworks of good governance and demand to go beyond the ratification of human rights treaties, in order, to effectively integrate human rights in legislation and policy and practice of the State; to establish the promotion of justice as the objective rule of law; to understand that the credibility of democracy depends on the effectiveness of its response to political, social and economic demands of the population; to promote systems of checks and balances between the institutions of formal and informal governance; to make the necessary social changes, particularly in regard to gender equality and cultural diversity; to generate political will and participation along with public awareness, and also respond to key challenges in human rights and good governance, such as corruption and violent conflicts.[6]

Accountability is a key element for both human rights and good governance. Applied to the context of human rights, accountability rests primarily on the duty of states to protect, enforce or promote the rights that have been internationally ratified.[7]

---

[5]Campaign, 2010, p. 76. http://endpoverty2015.org

[6]United Nations, 2006. Frequently asked questions on the focus of human rights in the cooperation for development.

[7]Thede, N. (2005). Gobierno local y los derechos humanos: brindando buenos servicios.

Several authors have sought to find a statistical correlation between direct foreign investment and progress in human rights. However, the fact is, it hasn't been possible to find a causal relationship between foreign investment and human rights situation.[8]

As it is well known, international human rights organizations have raised specific proposals, putting pressure on major powers to take moral responsibility in human rights. In short, the model of "good governance" in the globalized world is particularly hostile to human rights project. The search for alternatives is always a possibility. However, we must recognize that the choices and room to maneuver that developing countries face and their decision makers are extremely limited.[9]

GOOD GOVERNANCE IN LATIN AMERICA

The Latin American experience shows that institutional reform destroyed the existing structures without contributing to a more democratic, effective and stable solutions. The disintegration of the old welfare state carried along with it the social protection functions. The previous redistributive model should be replaced by a social intervention directly targeted towards vulnerable groups. But when these most vulnerable groups— such as in Brazil—constitute the majority of the population, the budget constraints of the model imply a waiver of fact to the role of social protection. Calls for the reform of the state, on the other hand, persist in a time when the living conditions of the population have vanished.[10] In the nineties, the crisis, the austerity programs and endemic debt produce increased poverty, unemployment, growing middle class, deeper social fragmentation, child labor, decline of the schooling amidst the most vulnerable, soaring crime, rising corruption and drug mafia. Good governance would suppose not only more political participation, but local economic recovery and protection of disadvantaged groups, but over time such objectives are to meet the immediate goals of macroeconomic stability that private investors and creditors put before any other consideration. Often the state reform and the low public sector wages have not done more but to erode the moral of the population and exacerbate the uncertainty and apprehension. In such circumstances, governments experiment increasing difficulties to meet their basic administrative functions, all of which enhances the legitimacy deficit. On the other hand, the marked tendency to direct foreign aid to NGOs, bypassing the state provides these organizations with local "civil society" means to secure services that the state does not provide. It is true that this favors the participation of the population and even improvements in quality of service care are

---

[8]Freeman, M. (2002) Human Rights; an interdisciplinary approach.

[9]Anaya, A. (2004). El modelo de "buena gobernanza" y el proyecto de derechos humanos en http://www.choike.org/esp

[10]Petiteville, Franck (1998) Trois Figures mythiques de L'Etat dans la theorie du développment. Revue Internationale de Sciences Politique. Paris, UNESCO n° 155.

verified. But these actions rest on fragile foundations due to the fact these aid programs are not unlimited and therefore do not constitute long term solution. And above all these things, acting in this way helps to weaken the public sector institutions. To remedy this situation, a governance guided by the following criteria has been suggested some years ago; (i) abandon the unique scheme of governance applicable to any case by appealing to the creativity of people in concrete social situations, (ii) a proposal to replace technocratic institutional reform to an open dialogue on necessary and possible changes, (iii) avoid drawing false boundary between state and civil society in order to strengthen the public sector and make it rewarding at the same time with the help of the contributions deriving from the non state institutions; (iv) avoid separate analysis of institutional reform and macroeconomic policy by recognizing the necessary relationship between the two; (v) abandon the artificial distinction between national and international levels of governance. Taking the good governance by hand, the World Bank put forward the claims of "modernization" of the old states, now suspected of protectionism, waste and corruption. Simultaneously with this political – institutional offensive circulates the controversy regarding the new world order emerged from a pseudo equilibrium in effect for more than four decades.[11]

CONCLUSIONS

Good governance is recognized as an essential ingredient in the development and the eradication of poverty. However, the constructive discussions in the international arena between the high and the low income countries, on the issues of good governance are often difficult and fruitless, precisely because the nations prioritize economic development leaving aside the basics of human rights. The quality and accountability of governance is fundamental to achieving the goal of holistic growth of a country.

Gathering information about the current status of these concepts in Latin American countries, always with a vision of an observer of an eastern culture such as India, objectively, we could conclude that while economic indicators in countries of Latin America have gone up, however, public policies and bilateral agreements do not provide a transparent and accountable governance to the society and vulnerable groups, instead governments base themselves on market growth and economic level position in the world. The developing countries seeking to compete in attracting foreign investment from world powers, has managed to lower taxes, or left un touch the monitoring of working and health conditions. Both strategies continue having direct impact on the State's obligations regarding human rights and give us evidence that the implementation of "good governance" even in societies where development is not reached continues to be a dream.

---

[11]Graña, F. (2005). Diálogo Social y Gobernanza en la era del "Estado Mínimo".

Observations and Recommendations

This seminar has discussed extensively the impact of corruption on human rights. There is a consensus that corruption undermines the principles of non-discrimination through discretion, favoritisms and nepotism, and it undermines the rule of law when judges are bribed to issue judgments in favor of the highest bidders.

This national seminar is well attended by scholars, practitioners and members of NGOs from different parts of the nation. There are 200 participants for the two-day seminar involved in various deliberation having both academic and practical values. The seminar work was started in the month of April 12, 2011 asking for abstract from those who are specialized in human rights issues and by August 25, 2011 we had received 102 abstracts and 40 full papers. This indicated the great success and the public spirit of the participants. There are 6 major panels divided on the basis of sub-themes of the seminar's major theme. They are as follows:

- Corruption and Human Rights Linkage
- Corruption and Political Rights
- Police Corruption and Right to Life and Liberty
- Securing and Protecting Different Kinds of Rights
- Corruption and Economic Rights
- Corruption and Specific Rights Issues.

Every panel was scheduled in the right time and paper presenters were given the opportunities to register their views followed by debate and deliberations. The Chairmen of the panels are as follows:

- Prof. Joseph Benjamin
- Prof. A. Vijayarajan
- Dr. M. Sakthivel
- Dr. M. Sarumathy
- Dr. P.S. Vivek
- Dr. C. Ramanujam

There has been an active participation by the following NGOs:

- Anti-Corruption Movement
- Fifth Pillar
- We the People of India and
- Transparency International-Chennai local branch
- Institute for Human Rights, Chennai.

Besides NGO the seminar is also supported by registered society such as Indian Institute of Public Administration, Puducherry Local Branch along with its training Institute faculty members.

There are 60 papers were presented. Each day the programme started by 10.00 am and ended with 6.30 pm continuing with discussions. The panels are also supported by Co-Chairpersons and Rapporteurs. Based on the presentations and deliberations the following resolutions, recommendations and observations are made.

The seminar main focus is to link human rights with anti-corruption measures for more effective way to check corrupt practices. If corruption is shown to violate human rights, this will influence public attitudes. When people become more aware of the damage corruption does to public and individual interests, and the harm that even minor corruption can cause, they are more likely to support campaigns and programmes to prevent it.

This report refers to human rights that have been recognized in widely ratified international human rights treaties, such as the International Covenant on Civil and Political Rights (ICCPR), the International Covenant on Economic, Social and Cultural Rights (ICESCR), and the Convention on the Rights of the Child (CRC), each of which imposes binding obligations on state parties.

Scholars have argued for recognition of a right to live in a corruption free world. They do so on the grounds that endemic corruption destroys the fundamental values of human dignity and political equality, making it impossible to guarantee the rights to life, personal dignity and equality, and many other rights. The impact of corruption on the economy has also been discussed at this seminar.

This seminar focuses on the human rights recognized in major international treaties. These rights are legally binding on states that have ratified them (state parties). The report builds a case for saying that, where rights are guaranteed and implemented, corruption will drastically reduce.

The seminar examines more closely the ways in which corrupt practices may violate specific human rights and the protection of human rights of anti-corruption advocates.

It explores the possibilities of collaboration between human rights and anti-corruption organizations (Anti-Corruption Movement, Chennai and 5th Pillar, Chennai), and where such collaboration will create opportunities and obstacles. It provides some recommendations for human rights organizations that wish to work on corruption.

OBSERVATIONS

Corruption plagues a nation's economic, social and political development. It can divert public resources for private gains. According to Kofi Anan, the former UN General Secretary "corruption has a wide range of corrosive effects on societies. It undermines democracy and the rule of law, leads to violations of human rights, distorts markets, erodes the quality of life and allows organized crime, terrorism and other threats to human security to flourish"

Further, corruption hurts human development, diverting public resources to private gain and reducing access to public services. Integrity is essential to democracy and meeting the Millennium Development Goals (MDGs). State institutions must be capable of managing resources to benefit all.

The most fundamental question the seminar pose is: how can the Government operationalise the right to corruption-free governance with a view to protecting and promoting human rights in general? In the Indian context, Section 2(d) of the Protection of Human Rights Act, 1993, has defined "human rights" to mean, "the rights relating to life, liberty, equality and dignity of the individual guaranteed by the Constitution or embodied in the International Covenants and enforceable by courts in India."

Corruption impacts men and women differently and reinforces and perpetuates existing gender inequalities. Corrupt practices harm three other rights that are particularly relevant to children: a child's right to be protected during adoption procedures; the right to protection from trafficking and sexual exploitation; and the right to be protected from child labour.

Where political rights are not effectively protected, opportunities for corruption increase. Low political participation creates conditions for impunity and corruption.

Corruption in the health sector often violates the right to equality and nondiscrimination.

Corruption in police administration shall lower the morale of the officials and creates law and order situations.

RECOMMENDATIONS

1. Anti-corruption measures must necessarily include human rights elements drawn from international and national instruments so as to make anti-corruption movement a mass based movement.

2. There is need for close link between Human Rights and Anti-Corruption organizations for an effective way to fight against corruption.
3. There is an urgent need to create awareness on the part of vulnerable people about the negative impact of corruption.
4. Value based education must be greatly emphasized for the young mind so that they can grow with corruption free-mind.
5. Rights to education, free access to best health facilities and right to development should be protected from the greedy public officials who stand as an obstacle for its enjoyment by weaker sections.
6. Human Rights education must be made compulsory for all courses.
7. It is only recently anti-corruption jurisprudence is unfolding and seminars like this one help in this effort to combat corruption.
8. Economic corruption particularly by the corporate World will create wider economic inequalities in developing countries.
9. Promoting transparency in government and providing access to information.
10. People centric administration and need for enhancing a healthy democratic practices.
11. The good governance agenda includes protection and promotion of human rights and rule of law. Both these functions will not be fully accomplished if corruption is rampant in government
12. The Government of India must bring out the most acceptable Lok Pal Act to curb the rampant corruption among legislators, judicial members, executives non-governmental organizations and media persons.

HIGHLIGHTS OF THE SEMINAR AND IMPORTANT QUOTES

"Power corrupts and absolute power corrupts absolutely."

"The nexus among politicians, civil servants and mafia will further accelerate corrupt practices and violation of human rights."

"The bondage between Good Governance and human rights are natural and much needed."

"A poor human rights record breads corruption."

"The net effect of corruption is that, on a large scale, money that is meant for social services is diverted into private pockets. Money meant for roads, schools, clinics, infrastructural development and education is diverted into private hands."

"Often times, champions of the fight against corruption are also key human rights defenders; often times, they are the same people."

"The mentality that if you get to the government, it is to make money, needs to be done away with."

"If anti-corruption is supposed to address the issue of dignity, the only framework that defines dignity is human rights."

"Disregard for human rights in fighting corruption is a moral and strategic mistake."

"The more respect for human rights, the less opportunity to engage in acts of corruption."

"Both human rights and anti-corruption are supported or undermined by the same system: rule of law."

"Protecting human rights are the hall mark of Good Governance."

www.ingramcontent.com/pod-product-compliance
Lightning Source LLC
Chambersburg PA
CBHW080610270326
41928CB00016B/2991